Marlene Evans ~ A Biography

by
Jane Grafton

CHRISTIAN WOMANHOOD • CROWN POINT, INDIANA

*Mrs. Evans with her
successor, Cindy Schaap,
at Spectacular 2000*

Dedication

This book is dedicated to my pastor's wife and my boss, Mrs. Cindy Schaap. One of the first statements she told her staff when she became the editor of Christian Womanhood after Mrs. Evans' Homegoing was that she believed each of us had the potential to do things we didn't know we could do. She wanted to help us reach that potential. She has done that for each of us, and I am grateful. Cindy Schaap is the epitome of the "different woman" Mrs. Evans attempted to influence and inspire by her speaking, her teaching, her writing, and her life.

Cindy Schaap

Acknowledgments

Publisher
Christian Womanhood

Project Director
Mr. Dan Wolfe

Page Design and Layout
Mrs. Linda Stubblefield

Proofreading
Mrs. Rena Fish

Consultants
Mrs. Leslie Beaman
Mr. Jimmy DeYoung
Mrs. Kathryn Emery
Mr. David Evans
Dr. Wendell Evans
Miss Gina Eyer
Mrs. Belinda Gaona
Mrs. Kris Grafton
Miss Annie Ruth McGuire
Mr. Judson Mitchell
Mrs. Vicki Mitchell
Mrs. JoJo Moffitt
Mrs. Joy Ryder
Mrs. Doris Smith
Mrs. Linda Stubblefield
Mrs. Carol Tudor
Mrs. Loretta Walker
Mr. Dan Wolfe

© 2004
CHRISTIAN WOMANHOOD
8400 Burr Street
Crown Point, Indiana 46307
(219) 365-3202

ISBN: 0-9745195-2-9

All Scriptures used in this volume are taken
from the King James Bible.

Printed and Bound in the United States
Dickinson Press, Inc., Grand Rapids, Michigan

Table of Contents

Acknowledgments

Credits

Miss Gina Eyer
Miss Kina Fink
Miss Carissa Grafton
Mr. and Mrs. Tony Merced
Miss Yashinca Pontillas
Mrs. Doris Smith
Miss Kathy Wilkie
Mrs. Janice Wolfe
Mrs. Rachel Wolfe

Photo Credits

Dr. Robert Auclair
Mr. and Mrs. Skip Buskol
Mr. David Evans
Mr. Mel Graves
Mrs. Pat Hays Hehn
Mrs. Linda Meister
Mrs. Sara Rivera
Mrs. Doris Smith
Mrs. Linda Stubblefield
Mr. Larry Titak
Miss Lois Tomlin
Mrs. Carol Tudor

Dust Jacket Photos

Professional photographs by
Larry Titak Photography,
Schererville, Indiana

Marlene Evans
A Biography

Preface

This project began as an idea several years ago. The timing wasn't right to begin it as Marlene Evans had just died. But before she was gone from us too long and before memories failed, we felt this book should be done.

The year 2004 seemed to be the right time. The idea came, then the date, and then the authorization. The next logical step was to consult Wendell Evans, her widower. This our managing editor, Dan Wolfe, did, and Dr. Evans was thrilled with the prospect, consented to many interviews, and read the manuscript as it was written. In fact, all of Mrs. Evans' immediate family members were happy and grateful that a book was being written about her life.

The next task was to enlist a skilled writer. Jane Grafton, an author of five books, a monthly columnist in the *Christian Womanhood* paper, and an experienced editor, was asked. Conveniently enough, she's also a lady in our employment; a lady who worked with, traveled with, and who intimately knew Marlene Evans for 26 years.

This biography wasn't her idea. Jane was apprehensive about taking on this monumental task, but we are thankful she consented to write Mrs. Evans' biography. We are very pleased with her work. Jane loved Marlene Evans, and as Joy Evans Ryder, Mrs. Evans' daughter, stated, "You got her life…you understood her."

This book is not meant to be an exhaustive history of the life of Marlene Evans, rather an overview of her life. We rather doubt if it will be the only book ever written about her. But it is the first, and we are pleased to publish it.

– Christian Womanhood Publications

A Word from the Author

Jane Grafton

When Brother Dan Wolfe and Mrs. Cindy Schaap asked me to write Marlene Evans' biography, I was overwhelmed. Having known Mrs. Evans and having worked quite closely with her for nearly a quarter of a century, I just didn't see how I could adequately portray her on the written page. However, I believed that I ought to write this book because leadership had asked me to do so.

My heart has been touched, my life has been influenced, and my desire to be used of God has increased as I have worked and reworked this manuscript. I labored closely with Mrs. Evans, but as I interviewed those who knew her best—especially her husband—I realized there was so much I did not know. I learned more about her than I was able to include, and my admiration and respect for her has grown to a new level.

I ask for your mercy as you read these pages. I have tried to be thorough in my research and careful in my writing, but you may remember situations or anecdotes differently than you find them written. I understand your feeling "that's not how it was!" because sometimes three different people had three different "versions" of how an event transpired. I also realize that you may feel there were important stories that should have been included in this manuscript but, due to space, couldn't be. To you, apologies also. I simply pray that your life will be touched and influenced as much as mine has been!

Foreword

I have not seen Marlene Evans' legal last will and testament. But I can testify to the "things" which she left to those whom she loved—her 17 books, her 316 issues of the Christian Womanhood paper, her over 100 speaking tapes, and her hundreds of teachings, such as the five sins of Christian women, spiritual reproduction, and time-released teaching. The "things" she left will be used and spent but never exhausted for she left truths, philosophies, and a zest for life that will only continue to enrich those whom she loved.

One generally leaves things to those whom they love, to those who hold a special place in one's heart. Whom did she love? She loved everyone from the mentally disabled to the college professor, from the homeless person to the millionaire. Everyone was special to Marlene Evans. So I guess she left all this to all of us.

There is an old saying, "Give a man a fish, and he will eat for a day. Teach a man to fish, and he will eat for a lifetime." Marlene Evans had that wonderful ability to light up a room when she entered it and bring laughter, joy, and life to it. She also taught others how to enjoy life so they were not dependent on her or anyone else to brighten their day.

Marlene Evans' greatness came in her transparency. She was able to reveal enough of herself to make her relate to the common man but then use those events to teach uncommon wisdom.

I am thankful for this book because it will give each of its readers a chance to gaze into the window of Marlene Evans' life and see who she was, where she came from, and what things impacted her life so.

– Dan Wolfe

Dan Wolfe
Managing Editor,
Christian Womanhood

Introduction

*I*t was almost as if God wanted to announce to the world that a most unusual child was arriving when He chose the circumstances surrounding the birth of Marlene June Zugmier. She was a "double-digit" baby in nearly every sense of the word, born at the Mennonite Hospital on 11/11/33 at 1110 North 10th Street in Beatrice, Nebraska. It is also interesting to note that the Mennonite Hospital first opened its doors in July of 1911. (She would go on to get married at the age of 22 in 1955!)

There is nothing spooky or prophetical about all of those elevens or double digits, but it does seem to reflect the fact that this was no ordinary baby being born in the midst of some of America's most difficult days, The Great Depression. Marlene seemed to bring a special spark to her family during this dark period of our nation's history, just as she would do for Christian women years later when America was experiencing traumatic change and upheaval during The Sexual Revolution of the 1960s and '70s.

It seems God chose to use this unusual woman to give America's Christian women Biblical purpose, definition, and leadership at a time when these women were tempted to listen to the radical, unscriptural teachings of N.O.W. (National Organization of Women) who led the so-called "Women's Lib Movement." God used Marlene Zugmier Evans to help Christian women understand that in Christ they are already liberated and that listening to and putting into practice the teachings of those in the women's movement would actually lead to bondage.

Her story is one of grass roots—hard work…integrity…struggles…family…love…church…diligence…and patriotism. And yet, with all those "common" factors in her life, she was no "common" woman. Anyone who talked with her soon realized that this woman was different.

Marlene Zugmier, 8 months

*Marlene Evans*
A Biography

Above: Marlene Zugmier
c. 1937

Page 11 Photos (clockwise):
Marlene, c. 1937;
Invitations "sent" by Marlene
for her third birthday;
Four-year-old Marlene swinging

Though her life experiences were common and ordinary, the way she handled these experiences, and then used them to help others, was anything but common and ordinary; and that is what made Marlene Evans so extraordinary.

Dr. Don Boyd, principal of Hammond Baptist High School, made the statement, "It mattered that Marlene Evans lived." In all likelihood, the greatest reason it mattered that Marlene Evans lived is that it mattered to her that others lived. As you will see in the pages of this manuscript, it really did matter that she lived. Marlene Evans was, in a most unusual way, a woman greatly used of God.

Part One

Grandma & Grandpa
Zimmer.

Blue Springs,
Nebr.
Nov. 10, '36.

Dear Grandma & Grandpa:
  Your presence is
requested at my birthday
dinner tomorrow Nov. 11
at 12:30 at my home.
  Hope you can
be there.
    From
      Marlene June.

The Early Years

John Zugmier, a door-to-door salesman for KKK Medicine Co.

Alvin Zugmier

Marlene Evans
A Biography

Born August 28, 1912, in O'Dell, Nebraska, Alvin Dale Zugmier was the fourth of eight children. The family later moved to Blue Springs, Nebraska, where Alvin grew up. The Zugmiers were staunch German pioneer people who displayed few expressions of love or affection. Alvin's dad changed jobs frequently, doing every type of work from his employ in the flour mill to being a door-to-door salesman selling medicine for the KKK Medicine Company (this company had no connections with the Ku Klux Klan!) from the back of his black truck. Alvin's father, and his father before him, were very gruff, brusque, harsh men who were verbally abusive. However, details were never known beyond the family because it was something never talked about by Alvin or any of his siblings. It seems that "what happened at home stayed at home."

Alvin's hurt and feelings of rejection extended beyond his home. School was also a difficult struggle for this young man. Quite possibly the tumultuous relationship with his teachers stemmed from the fact that he did not learn effective human relationship skills at home. But from a story he periodically told as an adult, it seems his teachers were somewhat at fault as they did not always use wisdom in dealing with their young student.

Each time Alvin would tell one particular story, he seemed to relive the hurt and rejection he had experienced so many years previously at school. "I was doing my push/pulls in penmanship [an old-time penmanship drill where the student does an up-stroke and then retraces it]. The teacher came by and didn't like my work. She took my paper, wadded it up, and threw it away." Being so graphically mistreated by a teacher would, of course, be a very devastating experience for a student. And so, not feeling he could achieve and feeling discouraged by his stormy relationship with teachers, Alvin quit school when he was in ninth grade. He immediately went to work at the Black Bros. Flour Mill in Wymore, Nebraska, where his strong work ethic coupled with his leadership abilities soon promoted him to the position of mill foreman.

Alvin's parents were people of integrity and character, but they were divided on spiritual matters. His mother was a religious woman, and probably a saved woman, though his dad was uninterested in spiritual things until his older years. He did, however, allow the family to attend the Christian church in Odell regularly. It was Alvin's godly mother who, years later as a grandmother, would take all of the little children upstairs to teach them the real Christmas story and the real Easter story while aunts and uncles were preparing the downstairs for egg hunts or candy bags.

From a completely different type of background than Alvin Zugmier, Mary Helen Fauver (who went by her middle name Helen) also grew up in Blue Springs, Nebraska. Born March 20, 1903, she was the fourth of six children. In 1906 when she contracted polio at the age of three, there was no vaccine or cure available, and she never completely recovered from this dreaded disease. Helen's entire left side from the waist down was affected, so she did not grow properly; her left leg was considerably shorter than her right leg, which caused her to walk with a limp the rest of her life. When Helen graduated from high school, she enrolled in business college. After completing her training, she took a job in Blue Springs as a secretary.

Helen Fauver and Alvin Zugmier lived across the street from each other in Blue Springs. The two homes in which they grew up were as different as night and day. While the Zugmier home was clouded by hurt and verbal outbursts from Alvin's dad, the Fauver home was a loving, happy, fun-filled place where people loved to gather. Helen's mother, Dolly Fauver, was especially known for being a fun, upbeat type of person. In referring to the difference between the two families, Marlene Evans once said, "The Fauvers were more *genteel* than the Zugmiers."

Probably this tremendous difference in their home lives and in their families attracted Alvin to Helen, who was nine years his senior. Alvin and Helen were also opposites in their personalities—Alvin was gruff, bold, and the leader type, while Helen was sensitive, cute, and fun. Though a hurting young man, Alvin had a very colorful personality that people enjoyed. Helen had a group of girls she ran with when she and Alvin were dating. He teasingly referred to them as the "Sixteen Dizzy Dames." After dating for a short time, 19-year-old Alvin and 28-year-old

Above: Helen Fauver
Below: Alvin Zugmier and Helen Fauver pause beside a road grading machine.

Helen married on October 25, 1931, at the farm home of Helen's sister.

Helen and Alvin desperately wanted to be parents and were discouraged about being unable to have a child. When they shared their concerns with a trusted friend, the person said, "Just wait; there's one in the cabbage patch." He was right…there **was** a little "cabbage" in the patch! The Zugmiers had been married just two years and seventeen days when they were blessed with a baby daughter. How excited they were to have this bundle of joy. Marlene June Zugmier was the firstborn child of this union on November 11, 1933.

Marlene's first memory was an incident that occurred when she was just three years of age. Alvin was working late one night at the flour mill as he did so often during harvest time. This sometimes made the evenings seem long for his family. In order to provide some excitement for her daughter, Helen popped a dishpan full of popcorn, carefully covered it with a clean dish towel, cleaned Marlene up (who once said, "I was always dirty after playing!"), and walked to her Grandpa Fauver's house to talk and eat popcorn. When Helen discovered that her parents were not home, she and Marlene took the popcorn and surprised their neighbors. This whole ordeal was no small undertaking, considering the fact that for the physically-challenged Helen, walking two blocks with a very active three-year-old was as difficult as walking two miles would be for most people. This was one of those situations that helped shape Marlene's attitudes about fun. While people often let something as small as "forgetting the salt" ruin a picnic, Marlene always seemed to find another way to make fun happen if her original plans were foiled.

She was an energetic and exciting child from the beginning, but when Marlene was almost four years old, she was the cause of real excitement at the Zugmier household. One day, rather than putting her ball in the toy box as she had been directed, she placed the rubber ball in her mother's oven.

After deciding to bake a cake, Helen had turned on the oven and left the room. She returned to find black smoke in every nook and cranny of the kitchen and immediately ran out into the yard yelling, "I'm so excited I don't know my name! I'm so excited I don't know my name!"

A retired minister walking by the Zugmier house yelled back, "My name is Grenfeld, Ma'am, Grenfeld."

"No, no! I said I'm so excited I don't know **my** name. My stove's on fire!" Helen shouted, wringing her hands in despair.

"We'll go in and put it out," Mr. Grenfeld said calmly.

So a fragile little lady with a limp and an elderly man who had difficulty hearing ran back into the house to extinguish the fire. They tried to jerk the stove away from the wall, but when this failed, Helen called the Blue Springs Volunteer Fire Department. When the firemen arrived a few minutes later, they charged into the house ready for action...until they opened the oven door and, of course, discovered Marlene's rubber ball.

After this eventful episode was over, Alvin's admonition to his four-year-old daughter was a firm, "You should've gotten all the way to the toy box." Perhaps it was this incident that gave Marlene an intense drive to be thorough and finish the job, no matter how big or small.

As hard as she tried, Marlene just could not seem to conquer her "thumb-sucking habit." When she was about four, her parents helped her along by offering her a shiny red tricycle. With this enticing incentive, it wasn't long before the childish habit was conquered, and Marlene was speeding along the sidewalks of Blue Springs on her prized, beautiful red tricycle.

Alvin Zugmier was the assistant fire chief of the Blue Springs, Nebraska, Volunteer Fire Department. Because Helen was afraid to be left alone at night, Alvin felt there was nothing to do but take his family with him if a fire occurred in the middle of the night. When he heard the siren blow, Alvin would jump out of bed, grab a quilt, wrap Marlene up in it (P.J.'s and all), get Helen into the car, and then hand Marlene to her. Off the family would speed to the Blue Springs City Hall where they would fall in behind the fire truck and follow it to the site of the fire. After the fire, Marlene would go to sleep in her mother's arms. She enjoyed the cozy feeling when she was awakened only enough to know her dad was putting the quilt around her and carrying her into her bed. She felt so safe and protected. With memories such as these, it is no wonder that the adult Marlene would sometimes declare, "I don't want bad things to happen, and I am saddened when there is any type of accident or fire...but if it's going to happen, I want to be there!"

Around the age of four, Marlene fell in love with the "vrroomm... vrroomm...vrroomm..." of a motorcycle. Alvin had a big Harley-

Above: Alvin with baby Marlene
Below: Marlene on her third birthday

Above: A helpful Marlene on the back porch in Blue Springs
Below: Marlene at 17 months and 3 weeks

Davidson which provided his transportation each day from Blue Springs to the Black Bros. Flour Mill in Wymore. If Marlene wanted a ride around the block when Alvin came home from work, she had to be out at the front of the yard, looking down the road waiting for him. Occasionally she would get so busy playing that she'd forget and not be ready with her gunny sack when she heard the "vrroomm…vrroomm…vrroomm…." She'd go into hysteria, trying to find the gunny sack (burlap bag) that her dad required to place over the gas tank on which she would be perched in front of him.

When Marlene and her husband Wendell Evans worked for Dr. Lee Roberson at Tennessee Temple College in Chattanooga, Tennessee, they would sometimes ride motorcycles through the Smoky Mountains. Their good friend, Paul Perry, owned a small motorcycle and would sometimes loan it to Wendell and Marlene for a few weeks at a time. They would often go to breakfast, and if they took the motorcycle, one of them would ride the motorcycle and one of them would drive their car. One particular day when they went out to breakfast, the weather was cool and Marlene was wearing a cape. When she got on the motorcycle and drove away, her cape was flying straight out behind her! Dr. Cliff Robinson, the dean of students at Tennessee Temple, happened to see this whole scene and later chuckled as he said to Wendell, "Your wife did *not* go unnoticed this morning!"

In a *Grandmother Remembers* book after a line that says, "Everyone thought I shouldn't, but I was glad I…" she wrote to her oldest grandson Jordan Ryder, "…did ride a motorcycle a little bit. Knowing that many people get hurt for life on them, I stayed away from them most of the time." But she never lost her love for motorcycles and the excitement they provide. Her eyes would light up as she would notice a "ruby Gold Wing" or some other top brand of bike. For just a minute she seemed to go back in her mind to the days when, as a four-year-old girl, she rode securely on the gas tank of her dad's Harley-Davidson.

A very big lesson was learned when Marlene went with her mother to Dr. Gafford's auction. Just before she became interested in the proceedings of the sale, Helen told her young daughter to stay right by her side. Instead, Marlene started to look around at things and wandered off. She had no idea how long she was away; she just knew there was big trouble

Marlene Evans
A Biography

when she returned to her mother's side.

Mrs. Zugmier was in the middle of a heated and intense discussion with some concerned adults and excited children. As they saw Marlene coming, they pointed to her. Helen said sternly, "Come on. You're going to the doctor's office." To which Marlene replied, "But I'm not even sick!"

As they walked toward the office, Marlene heard the strangest tale she'd ever been told. Dr. Gafford stored old medicine in a barn behind his house, and a girl had accused Marlene of throwing some of that medicine into a boy's eyes. Marlene cried that she did not do it, but the girl insisted that she had.

Mrs. Zugmier did not know what to think; all she did know was that Marlene had been missing. Fortunately for everyone involved, the boy's eyes were washed out and were fine. When the Zugmiers got home, it was decided that Marlene would not be punished until they learned more facts. All her life Marlene declared that she had never even seen the barn, but her parents said it would have been no problem if she had simply stayed where she was supposed to have been.

Though there were not any strong, soul-winning churches in their area of southeastern Nebraska during Marlene's growing up years, her parents tried their best to find ways to meet the spiritual needs of their family. One of the opportunities they took advantage of was a preaching service at a conference grounds in Milford, Nebraska. It was a camp-type meeting with sawdust on the floor—which made Marlene cough. There was also a sign on the wall behind the preacher which said, "Follow thou me." Marlene, of course, could not yet read, and so she would nudge Alvin and say, "What does that sign say?"

To which he would respond, "Follow thou me."

Then she would cough and hack from the sawdust; after which she would nudge her mom and say, "What does that sign say?"

Helen would answer, "Follow thou me." This went on throughout the service with Marlene first asking Dad about the sign, waiting a few minutes, coughing, waiting a few minutes, then asking Mom about the sign. Though it was a struggle for her to get through that service, those words seemed to plant spiritual seeds which gave Marlene a hunger and desire to follow God and His will for her life.

Above: Marlene on her red "trike" which she received when she stopped sucking her thumb!
Below: Marlene Zugmier, age five

Clockwise:

October 25, 1931, wedding day (l-r) Pastor Ray Baker, Carl Forsyth, Alvin and Helen Zugmier, and Lela Forsyth; Grandpa John Zugmier with Marlene; Helen and Marlene by the back porch, Wymore, Nebraska; Helen and Marlene; The Alvin Zugmier family

Page 19 photos: *Four-year-old Marlene on her first day of school; Marlene and her dog Ginger*

Marlene Evans
A Biography

Part Two

Elementary School Years

Above: Five-year-old Marlene at her birthday party
Below: Marlene and her doll

Marlene's first day of kindergarten was a never-to-be-forgotten day in the Zugmier household. With her limitations from polio, it was difficult for Helen to keep up with the ever active Marlene, who seemed to run everywhere she went. A very sensitive person, Helen was somewhat of an idealist who had pictured herself sweetly walking hand in hand with her only child to her first day of school. However, in typical style, Marlene was so eager to get to school that she ran ahead of her mother. Of course, this was a great disappointment to Helen whose ideal picture had been shattered. Completely disheartened, she turned and walked home in tears.

Not only did Marlene run everywhere she went, she also exaggerated life's events that she experienced. Just a few months after Marlene entered kindergarten, Helen Zugmier hosted a birthday party for her daughter. Marlene later acknowledged, "I doubt that there were 90 kids in the entire school, but I told people there were 90 kids at our house for my party. The house was tiny; the town was tiny; the school was tiny; and there were *not* 90 kids at my house. There might have been nine, but I had never had nine in my house before, and I really felt there were 90 people there. I know I feel things bigger than they are."

Marlene did feel things big; life was big to her, which was a part of her greatness. For that reason, as an adult, it was a common habit for her to call her dad and check her stories with him. She never trusted her memory as she was afraid of remembering things bigger than they really were. Dr. Wendell Evans made the statement, "I often heard Marlene making these phone calls verifying details." Then he added chuckling, "Her dad, a self-proclaimed realist, often brought her back to reality!"

Marlene walked to and from kindergarten each day. Blue Springs Grade School hired high school seniors as crossing guards for the children. When children came to the corner and had to cross the street, the guard would "shepherd" his charges safely to the other side. Some of the youngsters did not like to wait for the guard and became troublemakers by crossing the street "by their own selves."

Marlene Evans
A Biography

Marlene admitted that she became one of those "little rebels" on the wrong day. It was snowing so profusely that she was blinded by the snow and ran into a slow-moving car. The driver, a lady on her way to a doctor's appointment because of a difficult pregnancy, was very upset. She had heard the "thud" of Marlene hitting the car, so she stopped, jumped out, and then began to scream. Marlene was fine except for a broken collar bone. (She later admitted that she did enjoy being allowed to stay home and be babied for several weeks!) This incident was definitely an early lesson in Marlene's learning to stay with and obey the leader.

When Marlene was in the first grade, Alvin bought a white frame house which had two bedrooms, one bathroom, a living room/dining room combination, a kitchen, a basement, and a front and a back porch. The house was located just two blocks from the flour mill where he worked in Wymore.

This change of residence was not a long-distance move by any stretch of the imagination, since Wymore and Blue Springs are less that one mile from each other, but it did cause a transfer in Marlene's schooling. She entered first grade at the East Ward School in Wymore, a small school in the corner of Furnass Park, located directly across from the Zugmier home.

A highlight of that first-grade school year involved her bulldog Ginger. Because Marlene's house was so close to the school, the entire class went there to see Ginger's new puppies—the epitome of "show-and-tell!" (Mrs. Evans was a great proponent of "show-and-tell" even as an adult and felt everyone of all ages should have regular opportunities to "show-and-tell" what was important to them at the time.)

From second grade through graduation, Marlene attended the "big school," Wymore Public School, about eight blocks from her house. She kept her connections with the East Ward School, however, as the teacher, Miss Craig, would call Marlene to her schoolroom and give her a nickel to take her weekly reports from East Ward School to the "big school." Marlene was a very responsible girl even at this young age.

Alvin Zugmier spent long days at the flour mill, especially during harvest time in late summer and fall. This was a favorite time for Marlene, who loved to go down to the mill and watch her dad supervise the unloading of the trucks of wheat. This whole process was quite an ordeal. A sam-

Above: Marlene with Ginger and her puppies

Below: Miss Anne Craig, Marlene's first grade teacher in 1938

Above: The first day of school was commemorated with a picture
Below: Marlene poses in front of her mother's heavenly morning glories

Marlene Evans
A Biography

ple of the grain would be extracted for testing (to determine its moisture content in figuring its weight). The trucks would then be driven up onto a large scale to be weighed. Unless the truck had its own hydraulic lift on the box which carried the grain, the entire truck would be elevated to about a 45° angle. Once unloaded, the truck would be lowered and then weighed again so the amount of wheat could be determined. Sometimes as many as 16 trucks would be in line to be weighed and unloaded. This was a beautiful and exciting site to young Marlene. She loved all the action involved with this process and fondly remembered it as an adult.

Physical prowess did not come easy for the little Zugmier girl. One of the struggles she encountered was that she had great difficulty in learning to tie her shoes, "sturdy" oxfords which she absolutely disdained. Since her first-grade schoolhouse was just across the street she simply ran home to her mother whenever Marlene needed to have her shoes tied. However, beginning in second grade, school was eight blocks from home, and one day she went off to school having forgotten to have her shoes tied. About one-and-a-half blocks from home she turned and ran to have her mother tie her shoes. The Zugmiers' next door neighbor, Mrs. Shoff, called out and said, "Let me help you so you won't have to go 'plumb' home." Marlene was intrigued by that colloquialism, as she had never before heard the term, and appreciated the help Mrs. Shoff gave her. But this also made her realize that her "secret" was out, and she soon learned to tie her shoes by herself.

Marlene was pleased that Mrs. Shoff wanted to help her. She seemed to know that some people would have said, "You, a great big girl, don't know how to tie your shoes?" or "My girl could tie her shoes when she was four years old." Marlene was still remembering that act of kindness over 50 years later even though the Shoffs moved to California shortly after this tying of her shoestrings happened.

May was an especially exciting time of the year in Wymore because all of the school children exchanged May baskets on the night of May 1. The children would go to their classmates' houses, leave a basket on the doorstep, knock on the door, and yell, "May Basket!" They would then hurry and run away. If they were caught, the recipient was supposed to kiss them.

Mrs. Zugmier spent much time every year making a tray of frilly baskets filled with pink popcorn (her specialty for which she was known), candy, gum, and flowers. She sewed crepe paper skirts and put them on cup cake containers using lots of imagination to create masterpieces for Marlene's friends. One particular year she even used the inside of a roll of toilet tissue to make one of the baskets. She fixed it up beautifully, and it was actually one of the prettiest baskets she made that year.

It was this particular year that Marlene told her mother she was not going to give "Ol' Priggy" a May basket. (As thoughtless children are prone to do, "Ol' Priggy" was the unaffectionate term they had pinned on Gladys Prigga, a girl that, for some unknown reason, no one liked.) Mrs. Zugmier told Marlene that she was going to give everyone in her class a May basket, or she wasn't going to give a basket to anyone. Hatefully, Marlene responded, "Okay then, I'm going to give her the toilet paper one," meaning the one decorated on a toilet paper tube.

On May 2, all of the students were checking to see how many May baskets everybody else had received the night before (cruel monsters that they were!). When they got to Gladys Prigga, she turned, looked directly into Marlene's eyes, and said quietly, "One." Marlene had learned a real lesson in loving treatment and acceptance of the underdog, a principle she put into practice the rest of her life.

Third-grader Marlene (age 7) poses in front of the morning glories

A hurtful and disappointing incident occurred when Marlene was in Mrs. Woods' second grade class. She came back into the school to get her jump rope after the children had been sent out to the playground for recess. Four teachers were standing outside the door of her classroom talking about one of her friends and that friend's family. Marlene was crushed! She had gotten through kindergarten, first grade, and part of second grade before she was disillusioned by a teacher's gossipy tongue. Prior to this, she had assumed teachers were planning good things for the students as they stood talking in the hall together. Years later, as a teacher herself, she realized that teachers often gossip in the name of being "interested" in the students. Dr. Evans says that the entire time he knew Marlene, she hated gossip. Quite possibly this was the beginning of that attitude as she saw how hurtful and damaging gossip really is.

During Marlene's childhood days, one could receive two cents for an empty beer bottle. As Marlene walked past Scoggins' Drive-In every day to and from school, she observed all of the empty bottles on their lot.

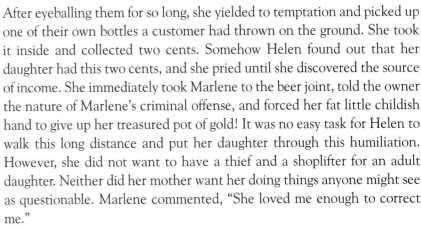

Inset: Marlene

Two photos of Marlene's fourth grade classmates (Arrows point to Marlene)

*Marlene Evans
A Biography*

After eyeballing them for so long, she yielded to temptation and picked up one of their own bottles a customer had thrown on the ground. She took it inside and collected two cents. Somehow Helen found out that her daughter had this two cents, and she pried until she discovered the source of income. She immediately took Marlene to the beer joint, told the owner the nature of Marlene's criminal offense, and forced her fat little childish hand to give up her treasured pot of gold! It was no easy task for Helen to walk this long distance and put her daughter through this humiliation. However, she did not want to have a thief and a shoplifter for an adult daughter. Neither did her mother want her doing things anyone might see as questionable. Marlene commented, "She loved me enough to correct me."

Because of the crippling effects of polio and other health problems, Helen was not always able to nurture the children the way most moms do. And so, Alvin took on some of the nurturing in the Zugmier home that is usually left to the mother. Though Alvin had a loud, booming voice, Marlene contended that he was as "gentle as a nursemaid when we were hurting."

One of those times Alvin nurtured Marlene was when, as a six year old, she was accidentally burned with liniment. (In those days people sometimes warmed the liniment before applying it.) Alvin would rock her to sleep, only to have to get up each time her fitful sleep became disturbed. By the time Marlene finally settled down to peaceful, uninterrupted sleep, it was time for Alvin to go to work at the flour mill. He never gave a word of complaint and seemed happy to be able to comfort his hurting daughter. A similar night occurred when Marlene had chickenpox. When Alvin heard Marlene whimpering in the bathroom, he got up, drew a baking soda bath for her, and settled her once again just in time for him to go to work.

Alvin often got up in the middle of the night to feed the girls their bottles. He also did the washing and the ironing during lunch hours and late in the evenings while he was working long hours six days a week at the flour mill. All of this nurturing on the part of her dad caused Marlene and her sisters to adore their father with an intense desire to want to please him in everything they did. They lived in an era when the words, "I love you," were said mostly by boyfriends and girlfriends, and the Zugmier girls did not hear those words from their parents. But they always felt very accepted and cared for and never doubted for a moment that they were very loved. Though he never really got over the hurt and rejection he had suffered himself as a child, Alvin Zugmier had a special relationship with his daughters and seemed extra careful in dealing with them on matters of discipline.

Coming from a family that did not show a lot of affection, he was not big with praise, but the "girls" (Marlene, Doris, and Kathryn) all agreed as adults that their dad did something that made them want to please him very badly. When he was disappointed, he would be very quiet; but when he was pleased, he would smile. Doris says, "You could tell in his attitude he was happy with what you had done." Occasionally he would give some little reward, such as candy, that would show his approval, but the most meaningful response he gave was that smile and look of approval that seemed to come from deep within his heart and was expressed with great tenderness in his eyes.

To the obvious delight of her dad, Marlene is leading the fun at the Zugmier family reunion she organized and hosted.

With Alvin taking on so many home responsibilities, Marlene worried about his working too hard, so she devised a plan to help him get more rest. She would go into her parents' bedroom and reset the alarm for a later time; this act of thoughtfulness was not at all appreciated by Alvin!

From her earliest days, Marlene had a very outgoing personality. She moved quickly, talked loudly, and decreed exciting ideas to anyone within hearing distance. Often, for that reason, her behavior did not meet with approval at family gatherings. Recalling one particularly hurtful time at a family reunion, Marlene told how she was sent by her dad to the car when there was a problem between her and her cousins. She was brokenhearted because no one seemed to understand her. She could not fathom what she had done wrong to be sent away when others weren't, but probably the greatest drawback to those who did not understand her was that she was not trying to be bad; she was just being herself. It would be many years before she was appreciated for who she was—big personality and all. In fact, she would eventually spearhead a big, wonderful family reunion for these same people who did not seem to understand her as a child.

Marlene's parents bring home baby Doris Marie Zugmier

Marlene Evans
A Biography

Marlene had been alone for a while (an especially stinging reprimand given the fact that she was such a "people person") when her dad came out to the car. He opened the door, leaned inside, and without saying a word, gave Marlene a pack of gum—a precious and rare commodity in those Depression days. That said it all and led her to say as an adult, "He believed in me." How much better can it get for a child when Dad believes in you though no one else seems to?

Marlene's Answered Prayer!

At a very young age Marlene began praying for a sister. She prayed and prayed and prayed. Finally news came that Helen was expecting a baby. Marlene was really, really excited and talked about this coming baby incessantly. This was a time when pregnant women went into public only for funerals and weddings of very special people in their lives; otherwise, they stayed at home, especially the last few months of their "confinement." Marlene quite embarrassed her Victorian-bred mother by talking about her pretty, new navy blue satin maternity slip before her uncle. At the time, such conversation was considered loose and inappropriate, a great concept for Marlene to learn since she would eventually be teaching Christian women Bible propriety in an era of "anything goes."

Marlene was almost seven when her prayers were answered for a baby sister. On August 29, 1940, a second daughter, Doris Marie Zugmier, was born to Alvin and Helen. Marlene absolutely adored this new addition to the family, and these feelings of adoration remained for a lifetime. She was always very protective, loving, and kind to Doris who says of Marlene, "She was like a second mother to me. I could do no wrong…even as an adult."

When the baby finally came, Marlene was beside herself with joy, and it was just about all she talked about. She was so in tune with anything to do with babies that one day, while she was playing with some other children, she thought she heard someone mention a hospital. She knew her baby sister was in a hospital, so right away she started talking about Doris.

Well, she had misunderstood and was crushed when a boy turned to her and said, "That's all you talk about. We're sick of hearing it." She was devastated, but Marlene had learned the importance of staying by people through their "rantings" about their victories and good times. She learned that part of being a true friend is rejoicing with others in their joys.

John Zugmier, Marlene's grandfather, was a colorful character whose personality seemed to be mostly rough strength and very little beauty. He could never seem to express his love in words and would say, "Yeah, I know," if someone told him, "I love you." He had an accident in a flour mill in the 1920s. At that time amputations weren't always successful, and he suffered terribly for years. Seeing how he suffered and said, "It's nothin'; it's all right," came rushing back to Marlene years later when she was in pain with degenerative disc disease.

Marlene would watch her one-legged grandpa tuck two crutches under one arm and dig potatoes. He'd knock off the dirt with one crutch. Then he'd drive up to one of his children's homes, hand them a bag of potatoes, and say gruffly, "I've been over to Velva's" or "I've been down to Dean's" (both siblings of Alvin's). Even driving was a feat for this one-legged man as this was in the days before cars had automatic transmissions.

Marlene would watch John standing with both crutches under one arm to support him as he stood butchering a hog for those same children who received potatoes from him. Alvin would observe, "He has three able-bodied sons, and he can get around with that one leg on that hog butchering better than all three of us put together." He was a man who found ways to help his children with their food budgets during the Depression.

John kept active doing things such as climbing up into trees to knock down dead branches and painting his house. It was a puzzle to Marlene how he could climb up a ladder as he carried paint for a two-story house.

On a softer side, though he seemed to have such a rough exterior, he would go to hospitals and sit long hours with a daughter-in-law or son-in-law (not just sons and daughters).

Helen Zugmier, of course, experienced a lot of pain because walking with a limp threw her back out of place. She also had severe sinus headaches. Throughout Marlene's growing up years, her mother was hospitalized several times, including when she had a hysterectomy after the birth of their third daughter, Kathryn. During one of these times, Alvin told Marlene that if there were something she really needed, she could go

Grandpa John Zugmier with wife Anna

Marlene loved baby sister Doris (1940)

Top: *Marlene reads to her mom
and sister Doris*
Lower: *Doris and Marlene*

to the local drugstore where he had an account and charge it.

Now, this thoughtfulness on the part of Alvin became an unintended carte blanche "license" for Marlene to take all of her "friends" (which seemed to mysteriously multiply during this time!) by the drugstore several times a day to purchase "necessary" items such as ice cream cones, candy bars, and gum. She even purchased a gift box of candy for someone.

One can only imagine the shock Alvin Zugmier experienced when he received his monthly bill filled with Marlene's "emergency" items! However, he did not yell at Marlene or threaten her. Rather, in addition to taking all privileges away from her, he insisted that she find a way to work and earn money to pay for every one of those "emergency" charges. Helen and Marlene sat down and looked over the *Grit* newspaper advertisements. They ordered a big case of all-occasion greeting cards, and for a number of weeks Marlene went door to door in Wymore selling sympathy, get-well, and baby cards, and made weekly payments to the drug store until the outstanding bill was paid in full.

Marlene learned how to face the wrong she had done and learned to find positive solutions to right the wrongs she had committed. She also realized that because her dad had put up with her "antics" as a child, as an adult she felt obligated to put up with others' "antics."

In the Evangelical United Brethren Church at Blue Springs, the young people had Children's Day pieces to speak. Alvin would say, "Marlene, if you're going to speak a piece, get up there and talk so they can hear you or don't get up." He didn't know that he was preparing her to speak to thousands of ladies in a day when people would be used to having their attention demanded by sheer volume. Neither did she expect to teach college speech where she would inspire her students to plan their speeches using the motto, "Stand up, speak up, shut up, and sit down."

Marlene kept very busy as a junior-age girl. She was the type of person who just never got bored. She found things to be interesting and entertaining that most people didn't even realize were available to them. One time she listed all of the fun things she found to do in her little hometown of Wymore:

- She played on the ledge and stairs of the Methodist church.
- She went to the rodeo every summer.
- She watched Doc Hinman (the town dentist) fix people's teeth.

- She checked out what new items came into Newman's Department Store each day.
- She took note of each of the cars at the local dealership.
- She stopped by the greenhouse to look at the flowers and plants.
- She crawled through tunnels in the ditch.
- She crawled on top of the clothesline post and watched the Silver Zephyr Burlington train go by a half a block behind her house.
- She picked strawberries, cherries, peaches, and crab apples from trees in her yard.
- She watched goldfish in their outdoor pool.
- She picked flowers at the side of the garage.
- She spent hours at the Wymore Public Library.
- She took piano lessons from Mrs. Lasher for 50¢ a lesson.
- She was a Girl Scout.

Aunt Lela Forsyth was her Girl Scout leader and often hosted meetings and parties in her home for the girls. Marlene remembered her days as a Girl Scout: "Once we dropped wax candle grease into her piano keys; another time we ate all her home-canned pickles right straight out of the jars with our fingers. One time we had a slumber party on her screened-in front porch and yelled out at the people going by during the night." But Aunt Lela was patient with the girls and made them feel loved and accepted.

Top: Marlene and Doris
Lower: Marlene, Dad, and Doris

The adult Marlene Evans that people knew, loved, admired (...and, yes, sometimes over whom they scratched their heads!) also amazed and confounded people many times during her formative years. She loved to celebrate, and she loved to find reasons to celebrate. Everything was big to Marlene, and if she was going to do something, it was going to be big! One of the most amazing stories of her love for celebrations is the anniversary party Marlene planned for her parents. She was just a primary-age girl (almost eight) and decided that her mom and dad deserved a big "bash" for their tenth anniversary.

Without Alvin and Helen knowing anything about this celebration, Marlene invited guests to the Zugmier home (numbers of family and friends from Wymore), planned the menu (guests were asked to bring the food), secured gifts (guests were asked to bring gifts for the couple along with the food!), and planned a program. It seemed no detail was over-

Marlene and some of her organized war "commandos"

looked, including the use of her mother's good china and silver. Needless to say, Marlene's parents were quite surprised at the party their young daughter hosted for them. It was a big success and truly a foreshadow of things (parties!) to come. It seemed Marlene spent much of her adult life making things happen for people—honoring those who deserved honor, having parties for those who needed fun, and creating a happening as the need arose!

The War Years

America had gone through The Great Depression in the 1930s, but an even greater disaster was looming on the horizon as Adolph Hitler made plans for the German armies to conquer the world. Japan's Imperial army had also become a threat to the world, and when the infamous attack on Pearl Harbor occurred on December 7, 1941, thousands of young American boys were called to active duty. However, they were not serving alone. They had a young patriot—a true zealot—in Wymore, Nebraska, who was ready to do her part in the war effort…and help others do theirs!

Marlene Zugmier immediately began service to her country by collecting scrap metal. Her school had encouraged the students to collect scrap metal, waste paper, and used grease and had promised an award to the class who collected the highest pile of steel. Marlene took the whole project completely to heart and immediately began filling her little red wagon with scrap metal. She worked feverishly at it until she was physically ill…and until she was advised by the police of Wymore, Nebraska, that it was not wise to pick up scrap iron within the gates of Shorty's Junkyard! She also conducted newspaper drives and collected waste grease for the war effort. Collecting the waste grease was her toughest assignment as it was such a disgusting, globby, sticky mess!

Probably her most memorable war "effort" was training "commandos." For some reason Marlene felt it was important that she and her friends be prepared to jump from trees and crawl through tunnels in case of enemy attack on American soil. Therefore, she organized a Commando Club in which she conducted regular "tree jumping" drills. However, Marlene was not ready for "resistance" when, during drills, one of her commandos got

Marlene Evans
A Biography

faint-hearted and refused to jump. Convinced that winning the war depended on her, Marlene simply pushed her out of the tree! To her dismay, her friend could not walk; she had broken her ankle! Marlene's dad decided the only just thing to do was for Marlene to pull her friend around in her little red wagon everywhere she wanted during the weeks ahead until her foot was healed!

Marlene had concerns for her dad at this time also. Though she was convinced that she was a vital part of the war effort and desperately wanted Hitler's armies defeated and wanted complete victory over Japan, she did not want Alvin to have to go to war. She did not realize that he had been deferred because he was the foreman at the flour mill. Marlene knew that draft notices came in the mail, so she began going through the mail and hiding anything that looked like it could be a draft notice. The problem was, she was hiding the Zugmiers' bills! Imagine Alvin's shock as past due notices began arriving; when he found the reason for the unpaid bills, he was not happy with his daughter's plan to keep him from going to war and put an immediate stop to her devices.

Marlene even got the idea to have a "circus." She asked some of the other children in Wymore to help her conduct this circus at Furnass Park across the street from her house. The proceeds were to go toward the purchase of savings stamps. It was a funny kind of circus; there were no elephants, lions, tigers, or even a pony or a dog with tricks. There were some bottles of Kool-Aid which looked like pop and sold for three cents.

The main attraction was leftover junk that would not sell in the Wymore drug stores, dime stores, and other sundry businesses. As Marlene made her rounds to all the local merchants to ask for things which they could sell, she assured them, "Me and my friends are having a circus to benefit the war effort. All the profit we make will go into stamps to apply toward a war bond. If you'll give us things you don't want, we'll make a lot of money."

As Marlene would later recall, they were "heavy on old, dirty pillow slips and doilies which were printed for embroidering." It wasn't easy to sell embroidery pieces and the like, but they did a fair job. However, when the circus was over, a girl Alvin had predicted would mess up the circus did just that.

After dividing the profits, each worker had a little over a dollar.

Above: Marlene enjoyed biking;
Doris enjoyed watching her big sister.
Center: Baby Kathryn
Lower: Marlene holding Kathryn

Marlene's plan was that they would each get on their bikes and go to the post office to buy savings stamps as she had promised the good merchants of Wymore. The girl about whom Alvin had warned Marlene got on her bike saying, "I'm not going to any old post office. I'll do what I want with my money." There was nothing to do. Marlene's reputation was at stake! She had to get on her bicycle, head her front wheel into that "Benedict Arnold's" bike, run her off the road, and take the money from her. This girl was wrong! Marlene was right! There was no question about it! Any court of law would have upheld her position! She later confessed, "The only trouble was, I did right in the wrong way. Therefore I was wrong— dead wrong! If I had listened to Dad, I wouldn't have been involved with that traitor in the first place!"

It is evident from all of these stories that Marlene was a girl with a cause. The fact was, she *always* had a cause. Her sister Doris says, "Having a cause seems to have been her life story!"

During World War II, sugar was a precious product which was rationed very carefully. This rationing created havoc for those who canned hundreds of quarts of fruit every summer. Marlene's mother found a way around the dilemma by learning to use white syrup as a sweetener. One summer day in the midst of canning, Mrs. Zugmier ran out of syrup. She sent Marlene to the store on her bicycle to get more syrup. On the way back home, Marlene got distracted as she rode by Kohlmeyer Hatchery where some newly hatched fluffy little yellow baby chicks were being sported in the front window She stopped, leaned her bike against the window, and partially blocked the doorway. She sat on her bicycle seat and watched the baby chicks. All went well until she suddenly jerked the handle bars and dropped the syrup. The jar broke, and the sticky, gooey, runny syrup mixed with tiny pieces of glass were right in the customers' path. Mr. Meindt, one of the store owners, asked Marlene to go home and said he would clean up the mess himself. As she rode away, she turned to see the store employees using buckets, brushes, and water to clean up the mess she had made. When she got home, her mother told Marlene she should have stuck to the job of getting the syrup rather than getting distracted.

Marlene was a Girl Scout by the time victory came to America in 1944. She immediately put on her uniform and went to town to see a

*Marlene Evans
A Biography*

newsboy yelling, "Extra! Extra! Read all about it!" This was her first time to see such a sight, and she was terribly impressed. Besides the ending of the war, there was more good news in 1944 for Marlene.

A New Arrival!

Three months after Marlene's tenth birthday, a third daughter, Kathryn Ann, was born to the Zugmiers on February 6, 1944. This darling baby completed the Zugmier family. Once again Marlene was thrilled over the birth of a little sister whom she could nurture and "mother." Marlene felt motherly and very protective of her "little" sisters for a lifetime.

One year Marlene had worked to save money to buy a new pair of ice skates. It was near Christmastime, and no ice skates were to be found in her little town of Wymore. Her mother's brother, Uncle Jean Fauver, was at the Zugmier house one day and heard of Marlene's plight. He immediately promised to take her to Beatrice, the county seat, which was 13 miles away. This was a big deal, as in those days people did not just jump in the car and take a 13-mile trip. Marlene felt so important.

Above: Alvin with Kathryn
Below: Marlene at Christmas

When Marlene and Uncle Jean got to Beatrice, they soon found out it wasn't going to be easy to find ice skates—even in that "metropolis." After the first ten stores, Marlene just knew that Uncle Jean would say, "Well, we've tried. I'm sorry, but we'd better go home."

Instead, he actively invited each clerk to tell him of other places to try. They went to drug stores, hardware stores, sports stores, department stores, toy stores, and any other place which vaguely smacked of skates. They walked and walked and walked.

Uncle Jean pushed open door after door until they finally found one pair of boys' skates. They were white—not the heavy smooth leather Marlene liked, but grainy, thin leather. However, that was good enough to satisfy her yearning heart. She'd had a goal, and it seemed as if Uncle Jean shared that goal for an afternoon. She felt so important as they drove back to Wymore with her treasured skates!

While there were many things Marlene did "big," there were some things she could not do. Every woman remembers young ladies in school who seemed to have it all together. Most do not remember being that girl, but rather, remember wishing they could, at least a little bit, be like that girl. Such was the case with Marlene. She recalled a time in her life when she tried to emulate these types of girls:

ONE year in grade school, I determined I was going to have a good year, and I planned how to have that good year. At the beginning of the school year, I stocked up on safety pins, cough drops, handkerchiefs, and everything else imaginable! My desk contained the sum total of anything I could possibly want or need!

However, my ability to be sidetracked caused my handkerchief to be wadded into a ball with a big piece of hard Christmas candy at its center just when I desperately needed to blow my nose. There's no feeling more helpless than the one you have when you have a cold, know you're going to sneeze, and frantically reach into your school desk to find a sticky piece of "board" which used to be a handkerchief!

Really, I wanted to be good and do right. I envied the nice little girls who quietly slipped out to the restroom with their ever-ready safety pin when something broke. I even thought well of the dainty child who, upon emitting the softest cough, would reach into her little purse for her emergency medical supply of Smith Brothers cough drops. My cough drop supply, if existent, was usually melted together in such a way that I had to choose between continued coughing and breaking my teeth off at the roots.

Though a discouraging frustration to her at the time, these kinds of life experiences would become an integral part of Marlene Evans' appeal as a leader of women as she so masterfully identified with the common woman. Whereas most women relate to a "board" hankie or melted-together cough drops, she would find that they related even more when she made comments on issues such as an unbalanced washer walking up the steps. Women delighted in hearing her make statements like, "Do you know the dryer eats my husband's socks!?!" because most of those ladies had socks missing their mates at home.

The many unfortunate and sometimes hurtful incidents in her young life helped prepare her to be the Marlene Evans who influenced thousands. Numbers of similar situations were to come during her teenage and young adult years, and all of these were foundational in forming her character, her personality, and her attitudes for a lifetime.

"Do you know the dryer eats my husband's socks!?!"

Photos on page 35:
Center: Marlene Zugmier, age 14
January 5, 1948;
Right top and below: Junior higher
Marlene Zugmier

34 | *Marlene Evans*
A Biography

Part Three

Junior High School Years

Above: Uncle Carl, the rural mail carrier, and Aunt Lela (below)

| *Marlene Evans*
A Biography

By seventh grade Marlene had completed her growing. She was as tall and as large boned as she would be as an adult. This, of course, meant that she was taller and larger boned than most of her classmates, and it made her very self conscious. She was not at all fat or overweight, but she *felt* she was humongous. This was a source of taunting and ridicule by her peers.

She did, however, find solace in her beloved Aunt Lela and Uncle Carl. Lela and Carl Forsyth, friends of Helen and Alvin Zugmier, were referred to by the Zugmier girls as "aunt" and "uncle." Marlene and her sisters felt extremely loved and accepted by them. As an adult she once referred to them as her "second closest parenting people" (second only to her own mom and dad). Lela and Carl had stood up with Helen and Alvin in their wedding. Because the Forsyths had no children of their own, they "adopted" the Zugmier girls and loved them as their own. Often, when introducing Alvin and Helen to someone, Carl would say, "These are the parents of our three daughters."

Because Uncle Carl was a rural mail carrier, he was often off work by noon. He sometimes used his leisure time in a very "un-leisurely" way as he took Marlene and her friends to parks, ball games, and shopping trips. Marlene later commented, "He couldn't have had much fun listening to our endless chatter and putting up with our adolescent ways. Perhaps he was looking 'way on yonder' to a finished product, as he was used during this time to influence me subtly with words I scarcely noticed at the time."

Marlene spent many hours at the Forsyth home, which was a refuge, a safe haven, for this awkward junior high girl. It was so safe, in fact, that she shared the hurt of her taunting peers with Aunt Lela. The accepting response and empathy she received was one of those "hallmark" times in her life when Aunt Lela said, "Marlene, when you're with Aunt Lela and Uncle Carl, you're with big people." Aunt Lela made it okay to be big and helped her accept herself as God had made her. Not only had she experienced the difficult taunts and rejection of her peers, she had also experienced the unconditional love and acceptance so needed at that time. What an impact this made on Marlene, and how greatly this incident influenced her to be a very loving adult who seemed to accept all people unconditionally.

There were a number of situations during Marlene's younger years where she was reminded that her personality was not always appreciated, especially by family. One such reminder was the fact that each week her Aunt Gertie and Uncle Robin invited Doris to their farm; they did not invite Marlene. Though Marlene adored her little sister Doris and was not jealous of her, there was a tinge of hurt each time she saw her beloved sister drive away with her aunt and uncle, knowing she was never to be invited.

Uncle Carl and Aunt Lela's home, Marlene's "safe haven"

It seemed that God used situations, such as her size and her not being invited while her younger sister was, to help Marlene understand as an adult that people shy away from kids who are different. This is probably why she was such a "safe" person to whom those who were "different" could run. She understood how they felt and did all she could do to protect them and to make them feel they were okay. It was her unconditional love and acceptance that caused people to go to her when they felt no one else would accept them for who they were or what they had done. As an adult, she was constantly surrounded by all types of people from every level of society and hence, had the opportunity to influence and help these people.

Marlene never talked down about or made sarcastic remarks about these people who were labeled as "different." In fact, she was insulted when anyone made those types of comments to her. Rather than focusing on what caused these people to be considered different or sometimes even weird, she focused on helping to pull them toward "normal." When one of her employees commented, "—— sure is different," Mrs. Evans responded, "I wouldn't have noticed if you hadn't pointed it out to me." She never seemed to forget that she herself was "different" and had experienced being considered such many times. She knew the hurt and disappointment, and therefore, kept her energies focused on helping and accepting those people.

Marlene was a bright young student. In her seventh grade year, she won third place in the Gage County spelling contest in Beatrice,

*Marlene's seventh and eighth grade
teacher, Mrs. Thoman
1946-1947*

Nebraska. She was so enthralled with the distinguished honor that she felt she should not have to take any more spelling tests the rest of the year in school. She made the mistake of going home and telling her mother that she no longer had to take spelling tests each week.

Not knowing any differently, Mrs. Zugmier happened to mention to the teacher, Mrs. Thoman, how nice it was Marlene didn't have to take the spelling tests. Though she said nothing to Helen, a few days later Mrs. Thoman leaned over Marlene's desk at school and quietly said, "Marlene, why don't you go ahead and take those tests the rest of the year just to firm up the spelling of those words in your mind?" Marlene knew that Mrs. Thoman knew what had happened, but this gracious teacher had kindly "saved face" for her young charge. This style of correction served Marlene well as she taught school herself, and especially during her tenure as dean of women at Hyles-Anderson College. While she did not let the young ladies whom she served get by the rules or go against administrative policies, she did "save face" for many a young person in working out roommate situations and other problems the girls faced.

When Marlene was about 12, she got her first salaried job picking tomatoes, strawberries, cucumbers, and other seasonal goodies from the truck garden of "Boo" Boughen. Her salary was 25 cents for a 5-gallon bucket. Alvin got her up before he left for the mill so she could get on her bicycle about 4:00 a.m. and ride out to the truck garden. One day when there was no more produce to pick, Mr. Boughen asked Marlene to go into the house to help his wife who'd had a stroke. It seemed he realized that she would be good to and for his wife. Mrs. Boughen was left with very bad speech problems and could only say, "Anybody goes, anybody goes, anybody goes," or a few other meaningless words. Whatever she wanted Marlene to do, she had to know by the inflection of how she said those particular words.

One day Mrs. Boughen said, "Anybody goes, anybody goes, anybody goes, anybody goes." Marlene thought it meant that Mrs. Boughen wanted her to go downtown to get some ice cream, but she was embarrassed to suggest it as it would seem like she was just wanting to go get some for herself (though that did sound awfully good to her!). Marlene mentioned everything she could think of until she finally asked, "Do you want me to go get some ice cream?" Mrs. Boughen let out a great big sigh of relief and

*Marlene Evans
A Biography*

had Marlene take money from the sale of produce to purchase some ice cream. They were both happy!

While working for Mr. Boughen, the Zugmier family took a short vacation. Marlene purchased a post card, wrote a brief message, and mailed it to him. When she returned to work, he said, "Marlene, you're a diplomat." She didn't know exactly what it meant at the time, but she knew it must be something good by the way he said it. This was another one of those times when Marlene felt an adult said something really good about her and made an impression for a lifetime.

At age 13 she began to work at the dime store in Wymore. Her parents were somewhat embarrassed about the way she got the job; she went to the manager and told him she needed a job as her folks didn't have the money to take care of her. Her favorite part of working at Ben Franklin was selling Blue Waltz perfume. She loved the scent and purchased it as gifts for her teachers and loved ones. She also helped people fit eyeglasses to themselves as one of her jobs in the store.

Alvin's sister Edna was a special aunt to Marlene. When Edna was in third grade, she fell victim to polio and, consequently, suffered a speech impediment and other damage which in those days were thought to be irreparable. She never did return to school and became backward because of her being different and lacking formal education.

Edna and Marlene liked each other a lot and had many good times together. Even into her college days and married life, Marlene played a game with Edna that would never fail to make her laugh and giggle. She would pull an imaginary dog around on a leash—training it, giving it rest stops, feeding it, and doing anything else that came to her mind. Aunt Edna would wipe the tears from her eyes as she'd cry, "Why, 'Malene,' you 'cazy' thing. There no dog!" Marlene was so glad she could be "cazy" if it helped to provide Aunt Edna with a little fun. Edna's parents loved her and tried to protect her, as everyone with children such as Edna did in those days. Because it seemed as if Edna always sat back away from everyone, Marlene wanted to give her things and do things for her that would help make up for what she was missing. These experiences also gave Marlene a real heart for people like Edna and were instrumental in allowing Marlene to form close friendships with people such as Susie Taylor (who was born with Down Syndrome).

Marlene with her friend,
Susie Taylor

With the passing of the years, some dark clouds began to surround the Zugmier home. Alvin and Helen's marriage had taken some wrong turns, and for a few years the relationship was a very stormy one at best. Possibly because of her age difference in being so much older than Alvin, Helen seemed to "take the reigns" of running things. These are years that all of the girls remember as a "blur," probably wanting to block out this hurtful time. The situation was complicated by the fact that some of the Zugmiers' closest friends often took Helen's side, further undermining Alvin's leadership in the home. Divorce soon became an option and was mentioned each time Alvin and Helen got into one of their verbal conflicts. Rather than being a place of happiness and safety, the Zugmier home soon became a place of strife and hostility.

Marlene was a deciding factor in Alvin and Helen's keeping their marriage intact. Marlene was nearly beside herself realizing that if her parents divorced she would be forced to choose which parent she was to live with. She reacted defiantly to this thought and refused to accept the inevitable. She was not going to allow this just to happen without trying to do something about it, so she faced her mom and dad head on. She began crying uncontrollably as the words spilled from her lips. She sobbed as she begged them to stay together. She cried that it was not fair to make her and her sisters choose which parent they wanted to live with. Her passionate words had a great impact on Helen and Alvin. She had touched a nerve with them because they both loved their children dearly and did not want to make a decision that would hurt them the way Marlene had described that it would.

With Marlene's words weighing heavily on his mind and seeing the problems as they were, Alvin realized that he must put his foot down. With his background he did not know how to change the situation other than to be harsh about it, but he knew he had to be in control of his home. For that reason, he decided to change his line of work and went into the restaurant business.

Another change was made in the Zugmier home when Alvin bought the restaurant. This new business required both of the Zugmier parents to be heavily involved in the running of the restaurant. Hence, the two youngest girls, Doris and Kathryn, were often left in the care of babysitters. Alvin knew this was not an ideal situation, and as soon as was possi-

The house Marlene lived in from 5 years old to 14 years old on Sixth Street in Wymore

Marlene Evans
A Biography

ble, he added an apartment onto the back of the restaurant and the family moved in. This enabled him to be more "hands on" in family matters, and the spirit and attitudes in the home changed for the better. Though they still had their problems and disagreements in years to come, Alvin and Helen stayed together; they had made it through this turbulent time in their marriage.

Marlene *never* discussed her parents' stormy relationship publicly, and almost never privately. More than once she made the statement, "If something hurtful or negative happens in the life of one of my loved ones, I never want anyone to have heard that negative situation from me." She lived that statement and never discussed private family matters publicly or with anyone who was not part of the solution. The years her parents' marriage was in crisis was a most hurtful time for her and her sisters, but she protected her parents and honored her parents in such a way that people never knew of the hardships her family had encountered. Years later Marlene wrote an "anonymous" article thanking her parents for the decision they had made to stay together.

"Thanks for Staying Together"

Now that you're both gone, Mom and Dad, I can tell you what I think about your spending your lives together. I just didn't know whether to say anything before this or not because I didn't even know whether or not you realized that I remembered as much as I did. Also, I wasn't sure that your watchful eyes could discern that I knew as much as I did about your lives after you decided to "make the best of it."

Helen and Alvin Zugmier

Thanks, Mom and Dad, for not asking that question which all kids are scared to death to hear, "Whom do you want to go with, Mom or Dad?"

Thanks, Mom and Dad, for not believing the world when the world said, "It's better for a child to live in a home where there is peace than to live in a home where there are two original parents." Recently I heard a young man say, "The world's worst marriage is better than the world's best divorce."

I'm not sure that is true ten times out of ten, but it surely has to be true nine times out of ten. I know there are those rare, rare cases, but, oh, they should be rare!

Mom and Dad, I'm glad that I got to live with the tension in the home of my Mom and Dad than with the tension that a divorce causes for the rest of a child's life. Thanks for not believing the humanistic world.

Thank you for not believing the likes of the ERA'ers, before the time of the ERA even, who were saying, "You have a right to a chance for happiness with someone with whom you are compatible." You did not seem to think you had that right.

You didn't seem to be in a church or in a community where you could get help or knew how to get help in order to reconcile your differences, but you just sat through the years of quietness. Thanks for living with very little acceptance, affection, approval, attention, or admiration from each other. I hope I have given you some of all five.

Thanks, Mom and Dad, for the fact that my sisters and I never had to decide, "Shall we go to visit with Dad and his wife or with Mom and her husband?" Thanks for becoming at least partners and yes, at times, even friends, to the point that you could keep a home going to which we could always return and find our original Mom and Dad.

Thanks, Mom and Dad, for all you gave up and for all the hurts and all the sacrifices that I, to this day, am not even aware of or realize.

Thanks, Mom and Dad, that when one of you was probably ready to walk out, the other was not. One of you, at least, was strong enough to say, "One man and one woman for life."

Thanks, Mom and Dad, for being at our weddings—seated together!

Mom and Dad, you've done many great things for us; the greatest of these was to give us love—love enough for us to give us our original Mom and Dad under one roof for our whole lifetime.

Because you didn't say, "We'll stay together until the kids are gone," your kids have no excuse for divorcing when their kids are reared.

Whether or not you ever resolved your differences enough to have much satisfaction out of your marriage, you did believe the Bible when it said, *"Wherefore they are no more twain, but one flesh. What therefore God hath joined together, let not man put asunder."* (Matthew 19:6)

Mom and Dad, your marriage was a success!

Photos on page 43:
Marlene Zugmier;
Marlene in front of the Elk Café,
September, 1951

Marlene Evans
A Biography

Part Four

High School Years

Above: Workers at the Elk Café
(l to r) Helen Zugmier, Mrs. Sterling,
Lois Ewald, Alvin Zugmier, Marlene
Zugmier, Larry Criepe
Seated: Doris and Kathryn Zugmier

Alvin Zugmier and his brother Raymond purchased a building located right next to the Kohlmeyer Hatchery where Marlene had dropped the syrup several years earlier. Alvin and Raymond installed bowling lanes and restaurant equipment in the building, and in 1947 they opened the Elk Café and Bowling Lanes which seated about 70 people and featured a four-lane bowling alley. Though Raymond was a partner for less than two years, Alvin continued the business, and his entrepreneurial spirit, principled leadership, and hard work paid off. The Elk was a great success as the workers waited on truck drivers passing through town, local farmers, and townsfolk; passengers from the many trains that stopped in Wymore were also served.

Marlene worked at the busy restaurant for about seven years right alongside of her dad. She worked as a fry cook as well as a waitress and learned the business so well she could have taken over for him if he had needed for her to do so. Her experience in the restaurant and bowling lanes served her well when she was the head of the Activities Department at Hyles-Anderson College. She had no idea when she was learning details about her dad's bowling lanes that in 1978 bowling lanes would be installed at the college and would be under the direction of the Activities Department she headed.

During school, while most students went home for lunch, the Zugmier girls raced quickly home hoping to get their waitress uniforms on before the noon train pulled in. The riders had twenty minutes to get to the restaurant, eat, and get back to the depot. By then it would be time for the townspeople to eat on their lunch hour. Everyone worked furiously for 40 to 55 minutes, gulped down some lunch, and headed back to school. Sometimes Alvin would drive the girls back to school so they would not be late.

Alvin was protective of ladies. He did not drink any form of alcohol, smoke, or use profanity, vulgarity, or dirty talk. He would often say to construction workers, "Watch your language. There are ladies here." Those

Marlene Evans
A Biography

ladies to whom he was referring were his wife and daughters. If any restaurant patrons gave his daughters (or any of the waitresses for that matter) trouble, Alvin suddenly became those patrons' waiter.

As an adult Marlene was known as a "big tipper." She came by that practice, in a large part, from her experience in the restaurant. She knew the hard physical work that waitressing entails. She also knew how many people don't tip or don't tip well; she knew the "wars" that sometimes rage between the waitresses and the cooks; and she knew the mistreatment waitresses sometimes get from unhappy customers. She never forgot her roots, and that included her seven years toting a pen and pad as she served food to hundreds and even thousands of customers day after day. She was also influenced in tipping as she sat in college chapel at Bob Jones University and heard the college dean admonish the students, "You people who don't have enough money to tip don't have enough money to go out to eat at this Howard Johnson's over here on the corner." (At that time, Howard Johnson's was a very nice restaurant, at least in that city, and all the students loved going to such a nice, new, attractive place.)

It was common for Marlene to sit in a booth of the restaurant and do her homework while eating a meal cooked by her dad. She cherished those memories, and she credited her love of going out to eat to do work to those times she did such in her dad's restaurant. This was especially true if she had some undesirable paperwork to do. Going to eat at one of her favorite restaurants seemed to take the unpleasantness out of the task she faced. Dr. Evans says, "I did not grow up in restaurants, but it was a habit I quickly learned from Marlene. Just this month I was dreading the writing of an article for the [Hyles-Anderson College] alumni paper. I went to one of my favorite restaurants alone, August 11, 2004, and the article came easily!"

Alvin Zugmier minded the details of the restaurant to make it a successful business. While many waitresses didn't seem to care whether or not they put a little bit extra into every dip of ice cream, Marlene later realized that her dad probably put her through college by spending man-killing hours "minding" details such as dips of ice cream and the size of butter patties.

He also "minded" the store so well that he knew who was ordering what, even though his back was turned toward the people as he worked

Marlene in front of the bowling lanes.

over the grill. One of the restaurant's busiest times was Saturday nights when the farmers came to town. Everyone would be working "lickety-split" and Marlene would call out, "Four hamburger steaks (2 medium, 1 well, 1 rare), three hamburger plates, one cheeseburger plate, five hamburgers, and one order of French fries," to which he'd inquire, "Who is the extra hamburger plate for?"

Marlene would answer weakly, "Me," and he'd patiently say, "Let's wait to eat; I'll fix you something later. Tend to business." Again, Marlene learned an important principle for life from her dad.

Marlene's sister Doris has said, "Marlene epitomized unconditional love in her love for me." There is only one time of inconvenience that Doris remembers—a Saturday night when she was still quite young. "I had pincurled my hair carefully to produce nice, bouncy curls for Sunday. I was sound asleep when my sister came home early Sunday morning from working in the family restaurant. She also washed her hair and was pincurling it when she ran out of bobby pins. What could she do at that hour but take out the bobby pins from the side of my head on which I was not sleeping. This is one time I was extremely unhappy with her as I awoke to find straight hair on one side of my head and bouncy curls on the other! But for that one time of inconvenience, there are scores of times she unselfishly and very generously stood beside me and my younger sister, Kathryn."

A dream was planted in Marlene's heart as a ninth grade student when her English teacher assigned the class to write a story about a person they admired. It resulted in the teenage Marlene Zugmier beginning a lifelong search for a "different" girl. In her manuscript she told about a girl who never criticized others and one who kept confidences and shared burdens with other girls. She went on to describe in detail a person she had never known. She later confessed, "After the teacher made me read that bit of fiction, I knew I'd had it, for surely people would ask, 'Who is this girl?' " They did.

A group of girls ganged up around her after class, and she once again experienced the terror she had as a child, when she was surrounded by high schoolers who were throwing snowballs at her. She had felt terrorized as a young child, and now, as a teenager facing her peers, she once again felt that same fear. A girl named Lois came to her mind; and even though

Marlene Evans
A Biography

she was one of the most genuine and most real girls of the group, Marlene knew that Lois was really no different than she was. She knew her friends would have said, "Are you kidding? She just talked about you yesterday." Her heart ached, and that traumatic event was marked in her life. She longed to be different and started that day searching for others to share that desire with her.

Carl and Lela Forsyth continued to be a "staple" in Marlene's life through high school. Among the many acts of kindness they did for Marlene, the one that seemed to be the most outstanding of all and was remembered for years to come was actually something they did for someone else. (For a lifetime, one of the great characteristics of Marlene was that she not only "rejoiced with those who rejoiced," she always seemed more thrilled over being able to make something happen for someone else than when something was done for her.) One of Marlene's close friends did not have a formal dress to wear to the junior-senior banquet. Aunt Lela said to Marlene, "Uncle Carl, you, and I will just take her to Lincoln to get her one." Lincoln, the state capital, was about 50 miles away from Wymore, and driving there to go shopping was something very few people ever did. But the Forsyths did take the girls, and Marlene was thrilled that they all had a part in helping to make good memories for this friend!

Through health problems and physical difficulties, Helen Zugmier never seemed to lose her love for fun, especially corny humor and games like charades. Dr. Evans says that as a son-in-law, he especially enjoyed her corny sense of humor and has many great memories of fun times the family had together. Helen's attitude toward parties, special events, games, and jokes taught Marlene Proverbs 15:15b, *"But he that is of a merry heart hath a continual feast."* As a teenager, Marlene sometimes wished in her heart that her mother was a little more "cool" in her fun, but as an adult, she realized that it was, in a large part, due to her mother's influence that she was able to keep her fun through cancer and other difficulties of life. Helen helped Marlene realize that fun is important and that fun is really a medicine—Proverbs 17:22a, *"A merry heart doeth good like a medicine...."*

Fun came in many forms at the Zugmier home, not the least of which was a love for nature. Alvin would often load the family up in their car and drive to a place in the country which Helen referred to as the "Pretty

Place." Alvin spent hours there with his family pointing out different kinds of birds and helping the girls learn their individual songs. Is it any wonder that Marlene Evans was known for her love of God's creation? Could it be that is where the seeds were planted for "A Graduation Prayer" Marlene wrote many years later?

A Graduation Prayer

God, I Want Them to See Things Other People Don't See!

PLEASE let them see finches perched on a feeder when men walk by without even looking.

Please let them take in the texture of the bark of a gorgeous tree even though folks travel by it regularly without knowing it is there.

Please let them always have sense enough to take time to wait for a big turtle to cross the road when others aren't sufficiently aware of their surroundings to realize there is a turtle.

Please remind them that they have time to wait to watch a blue bunting fly away even though golfers on the other side of the road stare at them as though they are crazy.

Help them never lose the thrill of spotting a redbird when so many seem to say, "So? I see them all the time!"

May they never pass a robin shaking his feathers in a mud puddle without a laugh when there are those who never acknowledge the fact that robins do bathe.

Please don't let them become hardened to the sight of a hurt bird, rabbit, or squirrel along the highway just because people joke about folks who care.

Please let them be amazed when they see a different bird they didn't know existed near them. Help them to go to the bird book to learn of the new beauty they've seen although some would laugh at that as they busily watch their soap operas and don't know there is excitement that fulfills and remains.

Help them never to be so foolish as to call a florist's rose a "flower" and a lovely stem of Queen Anne's Lace a "weed" as others do.

The Zugmiers take a break in their apartment behind the restaurant.

Please don't let them get to the point where they say, "I wish the blackbirds and sparrows would stay away from the feeder." Help them to enjoy the sleek brilliance of the fluffy light brown feathers of a sparrow as well as the morning doves, blue jays, and red-winged blackbirds! Let them forget that some folks gripe because they want all redbirds in life.

Please let them realize the variety You give to them. There is no routine, dull life as they learn the different colors of birds as they go through stages of their lives and seasons of the year. Let them pay no attention to those who think, "You've seen one, you've seen them all!"

Please never let them get over the fact that You put on a show for them every month of the year as the flowers, ferns, and trees change for their entertainment. Some folks don't seem to know that exotic tiger lilies and stately cattails disappear only to be replaced by the next month's purple, blue or gold.

Help them be patient to watch the whole show when it is at all possible to catch the sunset. There are some folks who'd drive miles to watch a fireworks display when it can't compare to what You do in the sky every night.

Lord, if You answer all these prayers, please answer one more.

Lord, cause them to be humble and not feel as though they're glad that they're not as those who see so little. I just want them to see things other people don't seem to see, Lord.

Marlene loved to be involved, and she stayed very busy during her non-school hours. In addition to working at the restaurant, 16-year-old Marlene started a junior choir at the Evangelical United Brethren Church in Blue Springs where the Zugmier family attended. Her sister Doris was in that choir and recalls how she loved being a part of this music group. Of course, as much as Marlene adored Doris, the feelings were mutual. Doris says, "I tried so hard to sing. I wanted to please my sister."

Youngest sister Kathryn was also in that choir and also enjoyed being under her big sister's leadership—most of the time. Marlene realized soon after forming the choir that she needed to keep discipline among her young charges. Wanting to teach them to behave without having to sin-

The United Brethren Church

gle any of them out, she decided to make Kathryn the "class example." And so, she corrected Kathryn publicly (though Kathryn stills insists that she had not been misbehaving!). Of course, Marlene soon realized that justice must be done. She learned to keep control of her choir members—no longer doing so at the expense of her younger sisters!

Marlene was as diligent and excited about leading the choir as she had been about any other activity in her life. She made it big. She decided her choir needed to look special, and so she designed outfits just for them. She enlisted the ladies of the church to make maroon choir capes with white collars and big gold bows for each of the nearly 25 children in the choir. This was a first-class choir that even sang at the radio station in Beatrice, the county seat about 13 miles from Blue Springs.

Marlene realized that faithful attendance was important if the choir was going to be first class. So, she promised every choir member a silver dollar if they came so many weeks without missing a practice. She knew her dad had silver dollars in his restaurant safe, but she had neglected to ask him if she could have them. This was not an endeavor he wished to be a part of since it had not been decided upon and settled ahead of time, but he did let her use the silver dollars.

Marlene was also involved in many high school activities. One of her favorite extracurricular activities was the marching band. She started taking clarinet lessons when she was in fifth grade, which got her into the marching band when she was in the seventh grade. She once said:

T HE best thing about my high school years was the high school band. Mr. Russell Cummings was one of those steady, good music teachers that let you have a little fun, but not too much, and saw to it that your organization always got superior ratings whenever you went to a contest. I never remember band practice being cancelled. I never remember having to have wild practices at all hours of the night or in the early morning. We just practiced when we were supposed to practice. We got so good that there were contest managers who asked that we not come to their contests anymore, but go into the "Class A" contests—competitions for schools way above our school population.

As soon as I got my band uniform, I put it all on with its hat, plume, and everything that went with it and went up to the flour mill

The Wymore public school marching band
(Arrow pointing to Marlene)

Marlene Evans
A Biography

where Dad was working at that time and marched around in there to show off to him. It was black, red, and gold. It had a braid, a gold feather plume, tails on the jacket, a nice belt, and everything else that one would want in a band uniform."

Marlene was a member of the Wymore Y-Teen Club (a division of the Y.W.C.A.). She was in the Senior Class Play, "Meet Me in St. Louis," playing the part of Mrs. Waughap, and she was also in singing groups. In the spring of 1951 the City of Wymore and the Wymore Schools hosted the annual Mudecas Contest, Southern Division. Marlene sang in the mixed chorus of Wymore High School which ranked "Superior" in this District Music Contest.

As a teenager, Marlene faced the normal temptations and emotions most young people experience during that stage of life. She wanted to be liked; she wanted to have nice clothes; she wanted to do the things the other kids did; she wanted to be accepted. However, the Zugmiers did not have in mind for Marlene to do things just because "everyone else is doing it."

A common response Helen Zugmier gave her daughter when she wanted to participate in a worldly activity such as attend a school dance was, "Grandma Wilkins always said the church is dancing into the world and the world is dancing into the church until you can't see the difference."

Marlene would walk away pouting as she thought, *Grandma Wilkins Schmilkins...who cares what some old lady said? She's dead anyway! She didn't know anything.* It wasn't many years until Marlene did understand what "Grandma Wilkins Schmilkins" was saying and why, but until then, God gave her parents who protected her from the world.

God also used her lack of physical prowess to protect her from sin and the world. Marlene would see women smoking and thought they always looked so "cool." Finally, she somehow got her hands on some cigarettes and matches and decided to try and emulate the beautiful, "cool" women she saw in the advertisements. It just didn't work. It must have been quite a scene in the back of her dad's restaurant as she clumsily tried striking the matches, coughed and hacked and choked when she breathed in while lighting the cigarette, and bent the cigarette in half as she tried tak-

ing another "drag." She immediately got the picture that she was not meant to be one of those "cool" women smoking a cigarette. Of course, she was later a very grateful woman that God had used her seeming "clumsiness" to protect her. She once said, "I just wasn't coordinated enough to ever be what the world considers a really 'cool' person!"

The Zugmiers attended a church that was rapidly becoming liberal and eventually did not uphold the Bible as the Word of God, did not mention the plan of salvation, and did not believe the doctrine of the blood of Christ, calling it a "slaughterhouse religion." Such "distasteful" songs as "Nothing but the Blood" were being removed from the hymn books. The church wanted to have a more loving "social gospel" which would "meet the needs of modern-day people."

When Marlene was 12 years old, she had some kind of religious experience—whether it was just that or actually her salvation, she never knew: but the minister did take her through a class and let her join the church at that time.

Being concerned for Marlene's spiritual welfare, Alvin and Helen provided the way for her to attend a denominational church camp when she was 15. One night at camp she became so burdened that she and a friend went up to a group of pastors after the service. She didn't know what to ask them, but she later realized that she had been under conviction that night. One of the pastors responded to the girls' pleas with, "You're all right. You're good girls or you wouldn't be here." Within the heart of this young teenager was an insatiable hunger for God and for truth. The counselor's words pacified her temporarily, but in her heart she knew she had not gotten the answers for which she was longing. However, God knew the hunger in her heart and was about to provide some almost miraculous ways of meeting those spiritual needs and satisfying that longing for truth.

A local boy who attended the same church as the Zugmiers ran away from home and became a door-to-door salesman in California. While Leroy Leland was at one customer's house, the lady asked him to go to church with her the next day. He made an excuse to not have to go, but God was dealing with him, and his thoughts drove him to find a Bible. In a drugstore they told him they'd look in the back for one. They found a yellow-paged New Testament which he purchased. Leroy went on his way, walking down the road carrying a sample case in one hand and reading a

Marlene Zugmier and Leroy Leland

New Testament held in front of his face with the other hand. A car went by, slowed down, and backed up. The driver yelled, "Hey there! Are you a Christian? That's a Bible you're reading, isn't it?"

The young man replied, "It is. I'm not," and the driver of the car, who was a preacher, had him get into the car where he led him to the Lord. After a few hours' instruction, the man gave Leroy one copy of *The Sword of the Lord*, a Christian paper whose editor was the great evangelist, Dr. John R. Rice.

Leroy immediately believed God had called him to preach. He began memorizing Scripture and returned home to finish high school, in order to go to Bible college that fall. While he was finishing high school, he jumped into that liberal church full force. He didn't know he wasn't supposed to talk about getting saved and, therefore, started telling others about his salvation and praising the Lord. This forced some rethinking on the part of a lot of people. Marlene's parents, along with other adults, were beginning to see what was happening in that church which had known revivals in earlier years.

Leroy gave Uncle Carol and Aunt Lela his copy of *The Sword of the Lord* the preacher had given him. In that paper they saw an advertisement for a Sword Conference on Revival and Soul Winning in Siloam Springs, Arkansas, to be held August 6–11, 1950. Aunt Lela and Uncle Carl decided to attend this conference and invited Marlene to go with them. This was a remarkable decision for them to make because they were not the type of people to do things like that—take off for parts unknown!

Though as a teenager she did not realize what a blessing it was, Marlene was not in with the most popular students in school. That caused her to learn to work hard and earn the approval of her parents and other adults. She always felt that the hours she would have been running around with friends (whose thinking, no doubt, would have colored hers in a wrong way), she spent working as hard and fast as she could. She really believed that she would not have been interested in attending the Sword conference if she had been in big with her peers. Because she was not popular, she could afford to be impressed and therefore afford to learn, ask questions, and absorb what was going on in the adult world around her.

When the Forsyths and Marlene arrived at the conference, the

Above: Marlene with Uncle Carl and Aunt Lela
Below: Uncle Carl's name badge from the Siloam Springs conference

Sword Conference on
REVIVAL AND SOUL WINNING
Siloam Springs, Arkansas

Mr. Carl Forsyth
Wymore, Nebraska

August 6-11, 1950

teenager found what she had been searching for. She heard preaching as she had never heard it before as she listened to men like Dr. John R. Rice, Dr. Bob Jones, Sr., and Dr. Joe Henry Hankins. She didn't even try to meet any young people; she was just wanting to meet God. She sat alone on the second row soaking in everything. The music and the preaching blessed her beyond anything she had ever heard or ever imagined. These men were the first men of God she ever saw who had both strength and beauty, grace and truth, blue denim and lace. They preached hard but had a heart of love for God and for others.

Marlene was especially captivated by Miss Fairy Shappard when she stood on the platform and, in a light green dress with long chiffon sleeves and black patent heels, sang, "I'm Going Higher Someday." Miss Fairy was a young lady in her twenties who worked for Dr. Rice. She dressed so femininely and classy. She looked like such a lady. Miss Fairy looked like a different woman, the kind of lady of whom Marlene had dreamed when she wrote that English paper in ninth grade. Miss Fairy's voice broke as she sang, and Dr. Rice got up to sing with her. It was beautiful; Marlene had never seen anything like this. Then Dr. Rice had everyone sing, "The Windows of Heaven Are Open" and "We'll Never Say Goodbye in Glory." Marlene's account of this was, "It was so good that my heart just about beat itself to death!"

Miss Fairy Shappard, who captured the heart of Marlene Zugmier

Marlene also had the opportunity to observe Mrs. John R. Rice, a woman with whom she would develop a deep and wonderful friendship in years to come. She saw Mrs. Rice, who was in charge of the book table, be publicly corrected by her husband for keeping the table open after a service had started. She then saw her, with a smile on her face, cover that table with a cloth and graciously accept her husband's authority. What an impression this made on the young teenager from Nebraska!

One of Marlene's favorite speakers at the conference was the fiery evangelist and college founder, Dr. Bob Jones, Sr. He told the conference delegates that he had a college for young people where they could come without having their faith wrecked. Sitting on the second row so captivated and moved by his words, Marlene vowed, "I'm going there."

Marlene had one year of school left, but Leroy was ready at the end of that summer to go to college. Aunt Lela and Uncle Carl told him all about the conference, Dr. Bob, and Bob Jones University. He left that month for

Greenville, South Carolina. His reports of what he experienced at college helped keep Marlene from going back on her words to herself when she decided, "I'm going there."

In Wymore at that time, no one, absolutely no one, knew of Bob Jones University. When Marlene would say she was going to Bob Jones University, people would say, "Is that a golfer's school?" (Bobby Jones was a celebrated amateur golfer of that era who never went pro but retired from golf with 13 major championship titles—a record that stood for more than 40 years.)

When people would ask where Bob Jones University was located, Marlene would always answer, "South Carolina." However, Alvin misunderstood, and what he heard was, "South of Salina," a town in Kansas only a few hours from home (which was considered more than far enough away from home for people in the town of Wymore!). But God was in her decision to attend Bob Jones University over a thousand miles from home. Though it was a long struggle, God seemed to convince her parents that attending this college in South Carolina was a right decision.

Marlene graduated from Wymore High School on May 22, 1951, and the following days and weeks were focused almost entirely on leaving for college in the fall. In addition to working many long, hard hours in the restaurant, paying for Marlene's college tuition was helped along by setting up a fireworks stand at the Nebraska-Kansas state line close to Marysville, Kansas. It was an endeavor which also provided the Zugmier family with a whole lot of fun and good memories. Most importantly, however, Marlene's decision to go to Bob Jones University would take her one step closer to seeing the dream she had written of in her ninth grade English paper being fulfilled.

Sixty-Fourth Annual

Commencement Exercises

of the

Wymore High School

WHS

Tuesday, May 22, 1951

8:00 P. M.

Wymore High School Auditorium

Wymore, Nebraska

Anderson, Barbara Lee
DeRoin, Ruthelma
Eklund, Dixie Dolories
Ewald, Lois Jean
Engel, Betty Jo
Graham, Doris Marie
Hotz, Margaret Ann
Jones, Carolyn June
Keck, Mary Ruth
Lane, Joan Louise
Meints, Imogene Grace
Mullens, Beverly Ann
Smith, Patricia Ann
Sterling, Margaret Irene
Zugmier, Marlene June
Dawson, Dorothy Deane

MOTTO

"Today We Follow—Tomorrow We Lead"

Nebraska High School Activities Association

Date *7-14-51*
Activity *Music*
This is to Certify that
NAME *Zugmier, Marlene*
Is a Member of the *Mixed Chorus*
Of *Wymore* High School
Which ranked *Superior* in the
District Music Contest.
Signed *[signature]*
O. L. WEBB, Secretary

Mudecas

Music Contest

(Southern Division)

—★—

March 27, 1951

Wymore :-: *Nebraska*

—★—

Competing Schools

BARNESTON   CORTLAND   STERLING
BLUE SPRINGS   FILLEY   TABLE ROCK
BROCK   JOHNSON   VIRGINIA
BURCHARD   LEWISTON   WYMORE
COOK   HOLMESVILLE

Morning   Afternoon   Evening

JUDGES
LESLIE MARKS
Director of Instrumental Music, Nebraska Wesleyan University
LEONARD PAULSON
Vocal Music Dept., Nebraska Wesleyan University

ADMISSION PRICES EACH SESSION
Adults 30c — Students 20c
(includes federal tax)

4:00—4:45
iger, Cortland
Colgrove
rings
uensing, Holmesville
iddings, Filley
elberg, Cortland
ehlenbeck, Cook
insenmeyer, Holmes-

jors, Brock
illman, Cook

EDIUM VOICE—

ll 4:45—4:50
tre, Wymore

W VOICE—CLASS D
ll 4:50—5:20
merson, Holmesville
dge, Filley
ufman, Blue Springs
ke, Brock
oltman, Cook
Smith, Holmesville

itorium

EDIUM VOICE—

ium 10:05—11:25
Beinsche, Cook
Betkin, Cook
yn Boesiger, Cortland
ston
lene Bohlmeyer,
ston
ret Christy, Brock
beth Doty, Lewiston
ce Foreman, Filley
Gillman, Blue Springs
Kotalik, Table Rock
a Jean Lidolph, Virginia
yn Maine, Blue Springs
ene McClarnen,
le Rock
Mients, Cortland
a Stoddard, Brock
a Zabel, Johnson
llis Hardy, Holmesville

MEDIUM VOICE—
C
torium 11:25—11:35
1. Ruthelma DeRoin, Wymore
2. Cheryl Everson, Wymore

GIRLS LOW VOICE—CLASS C
Auditorium 11:35—11:45
1. Janet Boettcher, Wymore
2. Marlene Zugmier, Wymore   ↙

10. Virginia Reed,
11. Leona Seeba, Cook
12. Marianne Shuey, Lewiston
13. Barbara Switzer, Holmesville

GIRL'S HIGH VOICE—CLASS C
Auditorium 9:55—10:05
1. Edna Free, Wymore
2. June Ellen Rutan, Wymore

Clockwise: Memoirs from Marlene's
high school years
Commencement Exercises Program
High School Activities Association Card
Music Contest Program

Photographs on page 57:
College graduation portraits
Marlene during her first year at college

Marlene Evans
A Biography

Part Five

College Days

Marlene during her first year at Bob Jones University

Oh, how Marlene had looked forward to college; it was a dream come true. However, at the last minute she got "cold feet." It seemed that no one except Aunt Lela and Uncle Carl wholeheartedly supported her decision to go to Bob Jones University. The Wymore Christian Church that she now attended even offered to start a children's home and let her direct that home if she would go to one of their nearby colleges. She had stood firm for many months knowing that Bob Jones University was God's will. She had fought hard; sheer determination kept her on track, believing she was making a right decision in the midst of so much resistance from those she loved.

In spite of this, when the time came to actually leave for college, Marlene decided she just could not go. Thankfully, as usually happened at just the right times in her life, her dad's greatness came through at this critical moment. Alvin's response to Marlene when she changed her mind about college was short and to the point as he firmly declared, "You're going!" Though he himself was not really in favor of her decision to go so far from home, he had the wisdom to realize that her change of mind was an emotional decision, and he had the integrity and character not to use her temporary weakness to his advantage. She got on the train at the scheduled time and headed for Greenville.

The local newspaper had interviewed and photographed those young people from Wymore who were going away to college. Marlene later confided, "It's a good thing they ran my story, or I would have been back home before I ever had a chance to attend the first class!"

Marlene arrived in Greenville, South Carolina, in the early morning hours. About 5:00 a.m. she heard the lonely, faraway whistle of a passenger train rolling down the tracks—a most familiar sound that took her mind back to Wymore. She suddenly felt that awful, empty loneliness of homesickness and began to ask herself, "Where am I?" "What am I doing here?" "Will I ever belong any place again?" "Is there any way I can ever undo what I've done?" She wanted to leave the very place for which she had prayed and begged and worked.

Attending Bob Jones University changed the whole course of Marlene's life from the very first day she was on campus. She loved telling her salvation experience: "The first evening at Bob Jones University when I was 17 years old, Dr. Bob Jones, Sr., told us to make sure that night whether or not we were going to go to Heaven when we died. I went to the front of the Rodeheaver Auditorium, found someone who could help me, and made sure of my salvation." For the rest of her life, Marlene never doubted her salvation and, though she'd had other "experiences" as a young girl and teenager, she always looked to this first night in college as the time she got assurance of her salvation.

By her own account, Marlene's first days of college were extremely difficult and trying:

Above: Marlene with several of her college roommates
Below: Marlene with roommates (l-r) Lorraine Swartz, Michigan; Jo Jennings, West Virginia; Virginia Patterson, Oregon; Marlene; Betty Meador, Virginia; and Doris Ireland, Tennessee

Wᴴᴱɴ I went to Bob Jones University as a very frightened seventeen-year-old, the school was larger than my whole town back in Nebraska. In my little high school we didn't even register. They just told us what to take and wrote it out for us.

When I found myself in that mile-long registration line with fifty million forms to fill out, I just went to my room to sleep it off and avoid the rush.

Finally, a roommate took me by the hand and led me to the slaughter. They asked me something about matriculation, and I thought "Right here in public?" I was thinking of "regurgitation," and felt like it, but didn't think they meant right there.

They asked me, "What school are you in?" And I said to myself, "This school ain't what it's cracked up to be, I don't guess. They don't even know I'm in Bob Jones University, and I'm standing right here in the middle of it." I was mighty disappointed in them until I found out they meant, "Are you in the School of Fine Arts, Education, Religion or what?"

I pondered on that question for quite a while. I knew I was there to learn religion, but I was also there to get an education. I didn't know what the School of Fine Arts was, but I didn't figure I belonged there. So I said, "School of Education," and that's why I have the name "teacher."

In addition to homesickness and all of the other usual adjustments of college life, Marlene's severe sinus problems the first few months at Bob Jones made the transition time even more difficult. But she loved the practical, fiery preaching she heard in chapel each day, especially that of Dr. Bob Jones, Sr., and she added him to her list of heroes—which included her dad, of course, whom she absolutely adored; and Uncle Carl Forsyth. Marlene's dad was a tease, and because Marlene quoted her college founder so often, Alvin would occasionally say, "If Dr. Bob and I died on the same day, you'd go to his funeral instead of mine!" Of course, that was not true, and he knew it. He actually respected the woman that Marlene was becoming as he saw her grow and mature into a fine, dedicated Christian.

Whatever Dr. Bob taught, preached, or suggested from the pulpit, Marlene tried immediately to put into practice. One piece of advice he gave was, "Try out for everything." He explained by stating, "Try out even if you don't think you'll make it. The experience of trying out is good for you." So Marlene did just that. She became involved in student life at Bob Jones. She remembered that adage for the rest of her life and used it to encourage young people to get involved. Many a time she told a teenage girl, "Go ahead and try out for cheerleading even if you don't think you'll make it. The experience will be good for you."

Besides homesickness and illness during her freshman year at college, an even more difficult time was to come. Marlene was devastated when she got the news in March of 1952 that her mother had breast cancer and was scheduled for surgery. While Helen was in the hospital, Marlene wrote to her dad to tell him how she wished she could be there to help him with her two younger sisters and the restaurant. She also told him she was sorry for all of the worry and trouble she'd ever caused him—remembering the many antics she had committed as a child and teenager. Alvin Zugmier never wrote many letters, but he wrote what Marlene considered to be a masterpiece that she kept for a lifetime. About half way through his correspondence he wrote:

"Going back to your letter, Marlene, that is what parents are for—to

Dr. and Mrs. Bob Jones, Sr.

tell the children and try to guide them in the right way of living. The main thing is the way they turn out in the end. I always expected to be wrong then, but someday [to] have it soak in and [be able to] see the results."

Her dad's profound words gave Marlene a new perspective on investing in people. She began to realize that one doesn't always see immediate results; she learned to look for the finished product and began to understand that the teaching, training, and investments people make in others often "take hold" somewhere down the road. It was her first realization of a truth she embraced and taught years later—that of "time-released teaching."

Marlene learned many valuable lessons through her mother's cancer, including proper attitudes and actions when facing cancer. She did not realize at the age of 18 that 30 years later she would face her own cancer battles including breast cancer and then ovarian cancer—which would eventually take her life. She also learned a lesson as the loved one of a cancer patient. This lesson was extremely helpful to her as dean of women at Hyles-Anderson College. When Marlene received the news of her mother's cancer diagnosis and impending surgery, she was very tempted to

Above left: A portion of Alvin Zugmier's letter
Above: Marlene Zugmier

go home. There were several reasons for these feelings: 1) She did not like being away from her family when there was such devastating news and such uncertainty about the surgery and prognosis. 2) She knew how instrumental her mother was in the daily workings of the restaurant and realized what great demands this would put on her dad. 3) She had such a deep love and concern for her family that the importance of college and the ability to stay focused was greatly diminished.

She was tempted to go home, but she did not. Those (both at home and at college) who loved her most and had her best interests at heart advised her not to leave. She never regretted her decision to stay in college, and her actions during this difficult time helped her relate to and wisely counsel college young people with similar situations in years to come. She had a deep understanding of the emotions and doubts a young person experiences when faced with difficult circumstances, and she also had confidence in her counsel because of the right decisions she herself had made as an 18-year-old college student over 1,000 miles from home.

Marlene went home each summer and worked in her dad's restaurant. She was a very willing worker and loved being a part of the family business. However, the preaching and teaching she heard each day at college helped her begin forming many of her own spiritual convictions. One of these was that she felt the restaurant should not be open on Sundays. And so, one particular Sunday when she was in charge of opening the restaurant, she called the staff and told them not to come to work. Unsure of what her dad's response would be, she then went to Aunt Lela and Uncle Carl's to hide out! When Alvin arrived and found the restaurant closed, he called one of the workers to find out why they weren't there. As one can imagine, Alvin was not at all happy when he heard what his daughter had done. He called each of the employees and had them immediately report for work.

He opened the restaurant that Sunday, and for one or two more weeks (probably to make a statement to Marlene that she was not the decision maker for the Elk Café), and then kept it closed on Sundays from that point on. Alvin did seem to realize that Marlene was not simply trying to get out of work, nor was she trying to be malicious. Keeping a business closed on Sunday was not a new concept for him as many people of that era—especially farmers—had a respect for Sunday and chose not to work

A family photo made while Marlene was home from college

on that day. This was even true for those who were not faithful church attendees.

Marlene later acknowledged that she was completely out of line to take such action, especially considering the fact that she had never even discussed it with her dad. She stated that he was trying to make a living for his family; it was his business that he had built by his own blood, sweat and tears, and she had no right to make such a decision. Though it was the mistake of a zealous young person, this incident did show the depth of her convictions. Once Marlene made a decision regarding any particular conviction, she never changed. She never checked to see which way the wind was blowing; she simply stood for what she believed. What did change in years to come was the manner in which she held on to her convictions. With the passing of time and experiences, she learned to stand strong without overstepping her boundaries outside her sphere of responsibilities.

Besides working at her dad's restaurant during the summer, Marlene also sometimes had opportunities for Christian service. It is understandable why she never talked of these opportunities as it did not take too her long to realize she was going against a biblical principle, but it does show her heart to serve God and help others. The churches in Nebraska were small, and it was often difficult to get a full-time pastor. Though the Wymore Christian Church was quite conservative in its views, many of the Nebraska churches were not. When people in these churches learned of any young person studying for full-time Christian work, they would ask them—both young men and young ladies—to speak to their congregation. And so, more than once Marlene was asked to fill the pulpit on Sunday morning in some of these liberal churches. (Someone remarked that it may well have been the best preaching those people ever received!)

One particular Sunday Marlene was asked to speak at a church about 20 miles from Wymore. She always referred to herself as "directionally challenged," so Alvin drew a very simple map in order for her to be able to drive to the church. What her dad did not realize, however, was that she could not read the directions backward, and therefore, Marlene had a terrible time getting back home that day!

Marlene had a lot of fun and created a close bond with nearly all of her roommates. Most of her roommates adored her and stayed in close contact with her for years. One of her roommates came to college from a difficult situation back home. Near Christmastime the young lady expressed her fear of not being strong enough to stand against the temptations she would face if she went home. Marlene invited her to spend the holidays with her in Nebraska, and this was a turning point in her life. The young lady broke up with her boyfriend back home and eventually married a preacher. She and her husband have been faithful servants of God for many years. Marlene played a major part in that lady's living her life for God.

One of Marlene's college roommates, Lorraine Swartz, believed that God had called her to be a missionary and was preparing for this endeavor. Since it was against her parents' wishes, she was receiving no financial assistance from them. It was difficult for Marlene to comprehend that parents would treat a daughter in this way when she knew that, while her own parents had not really been in favor of her going off to Bob Jones University, they had, nonetheless, supported her both financially and emotionally. (It is noteworthy that as the Zugmiers received letters from Marlene, they realized more and more that she had made a right decision in attending Bob Jones University, but even until that time, they did support her.) She wrote home and explained that her roommate was going to have to leave school in the middle of her junior year because of finances.

Helen's response to Marlene's letter astounded her. She wrote, "One night after reading that letter, I had a dream in which the Lord seemed to tell me to take that beautiful bowl Dad and I got for a wedding gift and have it sold at Mrs. Mann's antique store." Helen, who was not a woman given to dreams and visions (and had none that anyone knew of before or after that time), felt she was supposed to send the money from the bowl to Marlene's roommate.

She took the bowl to Mrs. Thomas Mann who said, "Mrs. Zugmier, this is not an antique, but I'll leave it here in this cupboard and tell why it's here. Maybe someone will buy it." The first person who noticed the bowl was a man, but he didn't want to purchase it; rather, he gave Mrs. Mann $5.00 for the needy college student. That man's money seemed to plant a seed that took root and multiplied. Such interest in Marlene's roommate was created that it led to her receiving about $1,000 from the good people who lived in the Wymore, Nebraska, area. The money not

Another snapshot of Marlene at Bob Jones University

only helped Lorraine be able to finish her junior year, it helped her with her senior year of college, and after she graduated she was able to go to Formosa as a missionary. Before leaving for Formosa, Lorraine went to Wymore and thanked the people of that community for their help.

On Helen's birthday she happily accepted the pretty bowl when it was returned to her with a message taped on bottom: "Back home—mission accomplished." It is easy to understand why Marlene readily "took up" for people and helped raise money for so many throughout her life—from college students who lacked the necessary finances to pay their tuition, to suffering individuals who required medical treatment, to grieving friends and coworkers who did not have the money to attend the funeral of a loved one. She learned the art of helping others in need from her own parents.

Of course, she did not realize at that time that one day she would have a daughter on the mission field as her son-in-law and daughter, Jeff and Joy Ryder, would travel half way around the world to reach tribal people in Papua New Guinea for Christ.

Marlene also received some financial assistance from people back in Wymore. One of these was Mrs. Mary Lane, a sweet Christian widow lady who lived across the park from the Zugmier's. She was a cheery woman who showed special interest in Marlene. She sent her $2.00 a month from her social security check along with a little note stating that she prayed for her. Marlene faithfully visited Mrs. Lane every time she went home in the summer or for Christmas vacation.

Dish Was Beginning Of Answer To Prayer

(The Sun's Own Service)

WYMORE — A fledgling missionary, who is able to go to Formosa because the good people of Wymore and vicinity answered the prayers of her friends, will visit her benefactors for the first time next week.

She is Miss Lorraine Swartz of Detroit, who will speak at the Bethal Presbyterian Church south of Wymore, commonly known as "the Welsh Church," Sunday evening at 8 o'clock, and will spend the week with her friend Miss Marlene Zugmeier in Wymore.

Funds Running Out

Miss Swartz was attending the Bob Jones University in Greensboro, So. Carolina, with Miss Zugmeier, training to become a missionary. She had reached the middle of her junior year, and although she was working, was running out of funds and could not see how she would complete her education.

Marlene and others of Lorraine's friends gathered together and prayed for help. Marlene wrote to her mother, Mrs. Alvin Zugmeier telling of what they had done.

Mrs. Zugmeier, to help a little, took a dish, which had been a wedding gift, to Mrs. Thomas Mann, who runs an antique shop in Wymore, asking Mrs. Mann to sell the dish, intending to send the money to Lorraine. It would not see her through school by a wide one except Lorraine knows what they totaled, but Wymoreans say they would run into several hundred dollars. They not only saw her through her junior year, but helped during her senior. She graduated this spring.

Soon Lorraine will be on her way to Formosa, but on her way she will have a chance to meet those who answered the prayers of her friends, and the people of Wymore will get to know "their" missionary to Formosa.

GIRL MISSIONARY: Miss Lorraine Swartz, Detroit, left, and Miss Marlene Zugmier, Wymore, display the dish that helped Lorraine fulfill her ambition to become a missionary in Formosa. When Marlene's mother, Mrs. Alvin Zugmier, tried to raise money for Lorraine by selling the dish in a Wymore antique shop, it started a chain reaction of contributions that helped the fledgling missionary complete her education at Bob Jones University. Lorraine is now in Wymore visiting the friends who helped her before leaving for Formosa. "Wymore people, all of them, are wonderful!" she said.

*A picture of Marlene (r) and Lorraine and a portion of the article featured in the **Beatrice Daily Sun** c. 1953*

Above: Marlene with her Child Evangelism children
Below: a snapshot of Marlene at Bob Jones

When Mrs. Lane became too ill to be alone, she was taken to the geriatric division of the local hospital to live permanently. Aunt Lela would ask Marlene to be sure and go visit her, but vacation after vacation, she put off doing so by saying, "I want to remember her as I knew her in her home." Marlene wrote later:

"I'M just now realizing how selfish I was. It sounded so noble to me at the time. Now I know I could have remembered her as she was in her home and still could have seen her in the hospital. I was protecting myself from having to realize that someone who had been a part of my life was no longer to be counted on for a little part of my security. I wasn't thinking of the fact that this lady needed a visit from me! I wasn't thinking of the fact that she did for me out of her poverty! I did not make the effort to give out of the abundance of my time! I wish I had! 'I want to remember them as they were' sounds really great, but think about it, will you?"

Though she had grown up as a very outgoing and bubbly person, Marlene went into a shell during her first years of college and was painfully shy except with her own roommates. For those who knew her as an adult, it is difficult to imagine that she would walk all the way around a block just so she wouldn't have to think of what to say to someone who was coming toward her.

However, things changed when Miss Hazel Claire Riley, the dean of women, asked Marlene to be a floor monitor in charge of 160 girls during her junior year in college. This was an esteemed responsibility in which upperclassmen were placed in charge of dormitory floors to check rooms for cleanliness, make sure that everyone was in bed on time, see to it that girls were quiet after lights out, and that type of thing.

This responsibility proved to be very helpful to Marlene as she began to think about some of those girls. It took her mind off of herself as she wrote notes to the young ladies when they were in the infirmary for a few days and checked on them regularly after the death of a grandparent or after some trouble within their own family or church back home. Because she started reaching out to others rather than being so self-conscious about what others thought of her, she began to be singled out and chosen for offices in student groups. With the responsibility of being a monitor, however, also came one liability. Unless a girl already had a steady boyfriend or was engaged, she seldom dated once she accepted that esteemed role. It seemed that young men were fearful of dating someone so close to the administration. For that reason, Marlene chose not to be a monitor her senior year.

Marlene loved her college days, and it was, in fact, her involvement in college life that caused her to meet the young man she would marry— Wendell Lee Evans, a farm boy from Marathon, Iowa. Few students had cars in those days, and so students would ride the city buses for transportation. Shortly after arriving back at college for his junior year, Wendell took the city bus downtown to do some shopping. On the way back only a few people were on the bus. This was in the days of segregation when white people sat in the front of the bus and black people were forced to sit in the back. There were no blacks on the bus this particular day; instead, Wendell noted a group of girls (Marlene and her roommates) who were sitting in the back of the bus. He says, "I was greatly impressed with this group of girls who were having so much fun in such an appropriate way. Of course, it was Marlene who was the ringleader of all that fun in the back of the bus!"

Wendell Evans as a junior at Bob Jones University

Both Wendell and Marlene were active in the mission prayer bands at Bob Jones University. There were about 1000 students who participated in the prayer bands. They were, no doubt, some of the best students on campus. These were young people who took the time from their busy schedules to pray for missionaries each day. When elections for prayer band officers were held in November, both Marlene and Wendell were elected as president of their respective prayer bands—he of the men's mission prayer band and she of the women's mission prayer band.

Though they later realized that they must have been in the same History of Civilization class two years previously, neither ever remembered meeting the other during that time. Wendell's only recollection of Marlene up until they began working together as leaders of the prayer bands was the time on the bus.

A few days after the elections, Marlene ran into Wendell as he was leaving the library. She immediately began talking of ideas she had for the prayer bands, but he did not take the suggestions so well. He says today,

Above: The letter Marlene earned because of her involvement in the Zoe Aletheia Society at Bob Jones. Below: Marlene (r) with her roommate Edie

"I was intimidated as she gave me '1200 ideas at once' and I thought, 'Get this woman out of here!' I had no idea that the very thing which almost caused me to write her off as someone I would never date was one of the things that would help me the most in my ministry....I tell men to marry a smart woman. You get free advice and free ideas! I feel sorry for guys who have to marry someone to whom they feel superior; they'll never reach their potential."

Marlene's ideas were revolutionary. Wendell had felt they would run the prayer bands as they had always been run, but Marlene was not a woman who was content with the status quo. As she had done her entire life, she saw things big and wanted big things to be accomplished when she was involved.

Playing "Cupid"

Wendell and Marlene's roommates needed their help. Marlene's roommate, Edie, and Wendell's roommate, Dick, were dating. However, Edie had done something unwise and was "campused"—meaning she had attained a certain number of demerits and, therefore, could not date or talk with her boyfriend for three weeks. Edie and Dick asked Marlene and Wendell to sit between them at a music program so they could write notes back and forth. Marlene and Wendell politely obliged their friends and did so. However, the two prayer band leaders talked through the entire concert and have no recollection of sending any notes back and forth for Edie and Dick! They so enjoyed each other they have no memories of anything else that happened that night. Looking back on how he had reacted against all of her ideas about the prayer bands, Dr. Evans says, "I am convinced this never would have happened [Wendell and Marlene's dating and marrying] without Edie and Dick having asked us to sit between them."

His sudden attraction to Marlene was bothersome to Wendell. He found that he had really enjoyed the company of this new acquaintance. To ease the turmoil he felt in his heart and mind, he told himself that his dating Marlene was just like the other dates he'd had at college. He was sure he would lose interest quickly, and so, to get beyond his confusion, he asked Marlene for their first official date—to a Bob Jones University

Artist Series program. He thought, "I'll date her one more time, and that'll take care of these feelings." **WRONG!** They both later stated, "We laughed and talked all the way through this Bach concert!" They had talked so easily when they were sitting at a formal event which should have been a rather difficult and uncomfortable time. He was so taken by the way he and Marlene had such an easy time laughing, talking, and joking together.

When asked what attracted them to each other, Wendell immediately answered, "Her fun." Marlene's response was, "He was so balanced. He was interested in missions, he played in a trumpet trio (which toured for and represented Bob Jones University), and he was so well-liked by his peers in Epsilon Zeta Chi, the college society in which he was involved."

The spring Bible Conference at "BJ" (as the students referred to their institution of higher education) was always a big dating time. Wendell and Marlene had been dating throughout each week before the Bible Conference. Marlene had also been dating a young man name Bob on the weekends when Wendell was out in churches with his trumpet trio. Years later Marlene confessed that she really was not interested in Bob. She simply wanted to go steady with Wendell, so she dated Bob on the weekends hoping to make Wendell jealous! (Marlene used this illustration in speaking to ladies on marriage as an example of how women wrongly manipulate men to get what they want.) Her plan worked; Wendell was jealous; he wanted Marlene all to himself. Therefore, even though he felt it might be a little too soon to do so, he asked her to go steady during the spring Bible Conference.

Dating Wendell changed Marlene's plans for the future. She had made the decision to go to nursing school in order to become a missionary nurse when she graduated in May of 1955. However, because she and Wendell were dating so seriously, she decided to return to "BJ" in the fall and begin working on her master's degree in Christian education.

Immediately after graduation, Wendell left for Central America with his trumpet trio, "Christ's Harvesters," a group with whom he traveled on weekends and during the summer for three years. Marlene returned home to Nebraska to work in her Dad's restaurant. The letters flew back and forth between Guatemala (or whichever country Wendell was in at the time) and Nebraska. The miles that separated them could not quench the

Above: Marlene with her sisters, Doris (r) and Kathryn at her graduation
Below: Officers of the graduate class at Bob Jones; Marlene was the secretary; (l-r) Terry Sutfin, Marlene, Russell Dennis, Chuck Fletcher, and Harold Richards

love that was quickly growing between these two fine young people.

Wendell returned to the United States at the end of the summer and immediately went to visit Marlene for a few days. It was a new and interesting experience as he got to know Marlene's family, especially her dad. Alvin was a hard teaser, which Wendell could handle just fine, but he was a little confused over the "shouting matches" that sometimes occurred between Alvin and his brothers. Wendell thought they must really be mad at each other, but after the loud argument ended, the conversation would return to normal, and the brothers would act as if nothing had happened. In actuality, they weren't mad at each other; they just "argued loud!" Wendell, of course, immediately saw that while Alvin was gruff and to the point, he was also a great man of integrity and character and a man whom Wendell grew to love and admire deeply. Wendell soon learned what Marlene had learned—to interpret what her dad said. Marlene once wrote about such interpretations:

"Zugmierese"

I'VE been bilingual since childhood! No, I know not Spanish nor French nor German nor Russian nor any other language of a foreign country. "Then," you ask, "what is your second language?" It is "Zugmierese" which consists of interpreting what my dad, Alvin Zugmier, says.

Sometimes I can't tune in on his dialogue very well, but a lot of the time I read him pretty clearly. When I interpret him out loud to the rest of the family, he grins, remains silent, and doesn't dispute my word; so I'm pretty sure I've got him.

How I learned what I do know about him was to watch his eyes, listen to the inflection of his voice, and remember his past actions. He talks gruffly, and his natural voice is way louder than mine. (My whisper can be heard across a room.) His loudness and gruffness tend to make folks believe he's mad a lot of the time.

When you've spent years watching to see when he's really mad or means what he says, you know he doesn't get really mad very often. When he, his dad, and his brothers used to just visit, some might think they were having a "knock-down-drag-out" just arguing over

Above: Marlene and her dad, Alvin Zugmier
Below: Marlene on Mt. Nebo

Marlene Evans
A Biography

whether or not someone died in 1929 or 1930.

When Dad says upon our return from a Holy Land trip, "You ought to be at the bottom of the ocean," he means, "I've worried every minute you were gone, while I watched the news report on T.V. about the terrorists. I love you so much and was afraid you were at the bottom of the ocean."

When Dad says, "I didn't get any food in for Christmas because I was praying it would snow so you wouldn't be able to come," he means, "I was so afraid something would happen to keep you from getting here that I was not going to get everything in and then be disappointed."

When Dad says, "Aw, you are crazy–every one of you. You're a mess," he means, "I think you are the best kids in the world. You're different from everyone else's children, and I'm proud of you."

This past summer I was in a car with Dad's brother, Uncle Dean, and his daughter, Elaine, and her four children. That day Elaine was driving Uncle Dean back to Wymore from Lincoln where he had just taken the eleventh of about twenty radiation treatments. With the same rough voice as Dad's, Uncle Dean looked at Elaine and said, "I don't know why you want to keep going to London every day, dragging the kids out of bed. I can drive myself. I'd think you'd be tired of it. I sure am." Elaine looked at Uncle Dean so sweetly, smiled, and said nothing. I thought, "She knows Zugmierese!" Uncle Dean was saying, "I'm glad you're going with me, but I'm sorry you have to go through all of this. I appreciate you."

I suspect there are people who speak "Williamsese," "Smithese," and "Jonesese" just as my family speaks "Zugmierese." I hope you learn how to interpret so that you can feel loved by some of the most wonderful people in the world.

Wendell returned to his father's farm in Iowa, and it was then Marlene's turn to visit his family. She was 21 years old and scared to death when she met Wendell's parents, Clarence and Wilma Evans, in the summer of 1955. Although she had been reared in a little Nebraska town, she had not "heard" such stillness in years, especially since her folks owned the Elk Café and Bowling Lanes.

Above: While on a trip to the Holy Land, Marlene kisses a donkey?!!
Below: Marlene rides a camel in Jerusalem

Above: The Zugmier family on a visit to South Carolina
Below: Marlene (r) with Mrs. Clarence Evans

Marlene Evans
A Biography

Marlene's Grandpa Zugmier knew she was planning to visit Wendell's parents and didn't seem really happy about it. He decided to "supervise" the meeting, so he drove her to Iowa. When they arrived in the "greater metropolitan area of Marathon" (as Dr. Evans has always referred to it), they stopped in the middle of town to ask directions to the Clarence Evans farm. They soon reached the farm, and Mr. and Mrs. Evans came right out to the car. Grandpa Zugmier didn't stay but few minutes; after looking his granddaughter in the eyes and firmly stating, "Be a good girl, Marlene," he drove off and returned home to Nebraska. In a few days Marlene and Wendell would take the train from Iowa back to Greenville in time for the opening day of the fall semester.

Those first moments on the farm were a little uncomfortable. The new acquaintances were talking fine, but Marlene got "spooked" by the silence. She would jump every time a rooster crowed or the barn door creaked. Nervousness caused her to mention the quiet so often during the first few minutes of conversation that she felt sure the Evanses must think they had a mental case on their hands!

Soon Wendell took her on a tour of the farm. Her obsession with the word "quiet" was replaced by the words, "neat" and "clean." The farm was kept nicer than some people's living rooms. The buildings were painted and in good repair, and the yard was as clean as a whistle. Necessary junk was placed in one area as inconspicuously as possible, and there were pretty flowers around the house. It was a place people would not go by without a nice comment. It was obvious that the Evans family had a routine to keep things in order.

The visit went well, and a wonderful friendship of many years was started between Marlene and her future in-laws. Marlene and Dad Evans were "two peas in a pod" and would have many great times together in years to come. While Wendell's mother, Wilma, was reserved and proper, Clarence was a tease. He loved to make life happen, he loved to laugh, and he wanted to live life to its fullest. One particular time when his parents came to visit Wendell and Marlene after they had moved to Chattanooga, they drove to a place along the river where snake handlers had once lived and held services. The four adults soon met a lady whose parents had been snake handlers. Marlene and Clarence were immediately quite fascinated with the whole practice and began asking questions.

They wanted to hear details from this woman who had witnessed snake handlers firsthand. Wendell and his mom thought this was a spooky place, and were ready to leave soon after they arrived. However, they had to wait on their partners who were having the time of their life learning about snake handlers! Dr. Evans says of Marlene and his dad, "They were a mess together!"

A December Wedding

On October 6, 1955, in the dating parlor of Bob Jones University, Wendell looked at Marlene and said, "I love you. Will you marry me?"

She did not hesitate for a second and answered, "Yes!" The newly engaged couple immediately went out to the soccer field to watch an Epsilon Zeta Chi game. They later admitted, "Actually, we didn't really go to watch the game. We took advantage of the game to show our friends Marlene's diamond and to tell them of our engagement!"

When Marlene told her parents that Wendell had asked her to marry him they responded, "It's no surprise to us; we've expected it." Though they may have been expecting her engagement, they were not ready for their daughter to get married so quickly. A December wedding was being planned, and Alvin and Helen felt that was too soon. Marlene talked with her pastor who handled the situation so wisely. He asked, "How old are you, Marlene?"

"Almost 22."

"How old is Wendell?" he continued.

"Almost 21."

"Well," he responded, "parents are never really ready for their children to get married, and especially their daughters. It'll be all right."

Her pastor's counsel relieved Marlene, and wedding plans were continued. She had just two months to plan her wedding—which would be held in the Wymore Christian Church over 1,000 miles away. She was also busy with her studies, but she did plan it and did so beautifully. Dr. Evans says, "Dr. Jack Hyles always said it was senseless for a girl to drop out of school to go home for an entire semester to plan her wedding. Marlene was a case in point that great wedding plans can be made while staying in college."

A beautiful December bride!

The newlyweds—
Mr. and Mrs. Wendell Evans

Marlene Evans
A Biography

Wendell and Marlene were married in a simple, but very elegant ceremony at the Wymore Christian Church on Thursday evening, December 22, 1955. The bride wore a traditional white wedding dress. With the wedding so near Christmastime, the colors, of course, were red and green. Her attendants included three college roommates and Marlene's sisters, Doris and Kathryn. Edie Eckhart, the roommate who was responsible for getting Wendell and Marlene together the first time, was her maid of honor.

The wedding was a huge affair, especially for the little town of Wymore. Her sisters thought the wedding was fabulous, but they were especially excited about all the cute boys—"BJ" students—who were there! It was a well attended wedding with over 400 guests. Marlene had been a very popular waitress at her dad's restaurant, and she had also been elected as Miss Wymore. (This had not been a typical "beauty pageant," but was a fund raiser where people paid money to cast their votes.) The people of Wymore knew and loved Marlene, and it showed by their attendance at her wedding.

Wendell had borrowed $300 in order to get married. They did not own a car, and so he borrowed his parents' car to take Marlene to Lincoln, Nebraska, for a brief honeymoon. Since some of the wedding guests—especially Wendell's relatives from Iowa—had driven a long distance to attend the wedding, Wendell and Marlene felt they should stay and visit until most of the guests had left the reception. Therefore, it was quite late when they finally headed for Lincoln. "We didn't even have a motel reservation," says Dr. Evans. "I didn't know I was supposed to; it's a miracle we found a place to stay that night!"

The newlyweds spent two and a half glorious days in Lincoln. They toured the University of Nebraska, visited the sites of Lincoln, and went shopping. Wendell purchased a beautiful ceramic doll from a collection which was quite popular at that time. Marlene treasured that gift for years to come as she realized he had sacrificed to purchase it for her. That doll claimed a prominent place on her bedroom dresser throughout their marriage until she went to Heaven.

Wendell and Marlene returned to Wymore in time to be with family on Christmas day and then drove to Iowa with his parents. (They'd had no way home since Wendell had borrowed their car.) After spending a few days in Iowa with his family they headed back to Greenville. Wendell and Marlene had made previous arrangements by "renting" a college student to take them and all of their wedding gifts to South Carolina.

"Home, Sweet Home"

They drove to a small trailer park they would call home for the next year. They had very little living space in the old World War II era six-foot by twelve-foot camping trailer with one room built onto it. University Student Homes (named such to the dismay of the university administration as the housing had nothing to do with Bob Jones except that its students lived there) could have just as easily been named, "Slums for Students." It was referred to by some as "tarpaper shack town." But the students loved it because it was cheap. They were *not* overcharged, paying less than $30 a month ($15 trailer rent and $13 lot rent). Few of the trailers had bathrooms, so most renters shared a community restroom and shower unit which housed both a men's and a women's facility.

The residents were very close to one another. This fact was true in any way you might wish to think of close. They did have a good spirit of fellowship there, and many families could visit back and forth without even leaving their houses since the trailers were only about six feet apart! The residents often warned visitors not to knock too hard on the doors, which gives some indication as to the fragility of the trailers. Extra rooms were added on to the original trailer as children were born. This was in the days before strict building codes were introduced, and the walls of some of those additional rooms had a dangerously high cardboard content.

It was at this trailer park that Wendell and Marlene met Bob and Charlotte Billings. Charlotte cleaned the unit building, where the restroom facilities were located, in exchange for free rent. It was during this time that Wendell and Marlene walked with Bob to the Rodeheaver Auditorium to hear Dr. Jack Hyles preach at the college Bible Conference. When they arrived, the auditorium was so packed that they had to sit on the platform behind the speakers.

When Dr. Hyles got up to speak the first time, he looked around the huge auditorium and said, "This place sure would hold a lot of hay!"

He was listed last on the program and began reading the list of all the

The happy couple!

speakers' names. All of them except Brother Hyles had "Dr." before their name. He did not have a doctorate at that time and was listed as "Rev. Jack Hyles." He then said, "Oh well, as far as I know, God's not sick. What's He need a doctor for anyway?!" Dr. Bob, Sr., and the students loved it. Wendell later mentioned to the college's dean of religion, "That fellow Hyles is really something, isn't he?" to which the man replied hesitantly, "Yeah…but you never know what he's going to do!"

At that conference he gave his famous "ballpoint pen sermon." The Evanses and the Billings loved what they heard and were impressed with this "Texas Tornado" (as some referred to him and his preaching) but had no idea that they would one day work together for this great man of God. Bob Billings would become the first president of Hyles-Anderson College, Wendell Evans would be the first executive vice president (later to become the second college president), and Marlene Evans was the first dean of women when the college opened in 1972.

One of the biggest changes for Wendell was the way Marlene cooked to please him. He was not used to being catered to in this manner, but he loved it as Marlene regularly asked him, "What do you want for supper tonight?" She had learned well from her own mother as Helen had always cooked to please Alvin and served food that he liked and enjoyed. Marlene had not only learned from Helen to cook to please her husband, she had just plain learned to cook. Helen was well known for the meals she prepared and had taught Marlene well. Though all of Marlene's meals were delicious, her specialties were her fried chicken and her pies.

That first year of marriage Wendell and Marlene spent many evenings together learning all about each other. They talked for hours of their past experiences and even more of their future dreams. It was during this time that Wendell expressed his interest and dream of someday being in on the starting of a college.

Though they were madly in love, Marlene had occasional insecurities about Wendell's former girlfriend. A few times during that first year she would say, "Are you sure you're glad you married me instead of ——?" He was very sure and says today, "She [my former girlfriend] really was a spiritual girl and a very fine Christian. Quite possibly, I would not have ended up serving the Lord with my life if it had not been for her influence. However, I believe I needed a woman like Marlene to help me reach my

The "Texas Tornado"—
Dr. Jack Hyles

Marlene Evans
A Biography

potential." Wendell's ability to take her insecurities seriously and respond with kindness and reassurance soon convinced Marlene that he had no regrets, and the subject was dropped.

Since Wendell had one semester left in order to get his bachelor's degree, it was decided that Marlene would go to work to bring in some needed finances. She would finish studies for her master's degree in Christian education the following year. She was hired by Stones Manufacturing Company in Greenville where she worked on a production line pinning children's play clothes together. She did not receive a paycheck until February, but God took good care of this young, dedicated couple. They received money in the mail totaling $115, which was plenty for them at that time. Wendell also worked as a tour guide in an art gallery to bring in a little extra income.

Wendell continued to be a part of the trumpet trio, which traveled to churches on weekends. Sometimes Marlene would go with him, but when she did not, she attended an independent Baptist church near their home. Marlene helped supplement their income by taking a paid job in the church nursery. She received five dollars per Sunday, which paid half of their weekly grocery budget. She loved caring for the babies, and she looked forward to having good fellowship with the other nursery workers from among the church ladies.

However, she was in for a big surprise! Each lady seemed to reason: "Have opinion…will give!" They filled her in on all the "facts" about the babies and their parents; she heard them reveal that most of the babies had terrible mothers who didn't feed them well, didn't send enough diapers, weren't giving the right vitamins, and didn't spend enough time with them. They also talked about the baby who came to the nursery dirty.

This led Marlene to later write:

I DON'T think the baby's being dirty was as bad as our mouths spewing dirty words about the parents of the dirty baby. "*A naughty person, a wicked man, walketh with a froward mouth. He winketh with his eyes, he speaketh with his feet, he teacheth with his fingers; Frowardness is in his heart, he deviseth mischief continually; he soweth discord.*" (Proverbs 6:12–14) I was very young and didn't have children of my own yet. I really took all this in as the "gospel truth."

In later years, I found out that this self-appointed position of pediatrician, social worker, pastor, judge, and jury is nothing more than holder of the title, "bearer of bad reports." The attitude is one of a critical spirit.

There are a few real exceptions. If there appears to be a case of child abuse, of course, report it to the *one in authority only*. Let them take care of it.

One of the babies who was "not fed well enough" was just a dainty little girl. The pediatrician said she was in perfect health.

The child who "didn't have enough diapers" had a young mother who wasn't careful in her planning, but she surely did show love for her young one.

On and on I could go, but enough said. Nursery workers are to take care of babies while their parents attend church. Period! That's all!

It will relieve you who are nursery workers to know that you are not a teacher who has to give a grade on a report card for every parent of every child in your nursery. *"Walk in wisdom toward them that are without, redeeming the time. Let your speech be alway with grace, seasoned with salt, that ye may know how ye ought to answer every man."* (Colossians 4:5)

If you're truly burdened for some of the parents, open your mouth to God and shut your mouth to people. *"He that is void of wisdom despiseth his neighbour: but a man of understanding holdeth his peace. A talebearer revealeth secrets: but he that is of a faithful spirit concealeth the matter."* (Proverbs 11:12, 13)

Wendell graduated from Bob Jones University in May of 1956. He would begin working on his master's degree that fall, and Marlene would begin working at J. C. Penney company. At the end of September, Wendell and Marlene moved out of University Student Housing and began renting a room from Mrs. McCarter for just $2.00 a week, which also included kitchen privileges. She was a godly widow who lived in an old farm house in the woods. Hassie McCarter was a tall, stately woman and somewhat colorful in her speech. One day she was inspecting her hem length and declared, "Too much Hassie and not enough dress!"

The house had no basement or foundation, and the place was full of mice. Marlene would often sweep the house, which sometimes proved to be somewhat nerve-racking. One day when she picked up the broom, three mice scurried away in all directions, causing her to become quite nervous with "mouse mania."

One night Wendell and Marlene were both cozily asleep in their big feather bed when she heard a "scratch-scratch-scratch" that seemed to be coming from one window protected only by screens. In the pitch dark she could imagine a man climbing in over the window sill ready to club them to death. She sat up and screamed bloody murder. Wendell, a person who does not waken easily, just lay and groaned. When Marlene heard his groaning, she knew someone had gotten him, and she screamed again. They spent quite a few minutes screaming and groaning at each other before they were awake enough to discover a mouse playing with papers in a dresser drawer!

That fall Marlene attended the first meeting of the year of the Student Wives' Fellowship. The ladies were voting for the year's new officers, and Marlene was nominated for vice president. It was the responsibility of the vice president to plan banquets, parties, and other social activities for the organization. She later expressed that she had no idea why she was named as one of the nine nominees.

Her husband was well known on campus because of his being in the trumpet trio, so she didn't know if being Mrs. Wendell Evans got her the vote, or if, when each of the nine nominees was asked to give her name, she did so clearly and loudly—as her dad had directed years before when she was to give her "piece" in the Christian Church on Children's Day. She later said, "I was probably the only one they could hear, so they voted me in because they remembered my name!" In any event, she was more than qualified for the job of planning the activities as she had proven when, as an eight-year-old girl, she planned and hosted her parents' tenth anniversary celebration.

Wendell and Marlene had discovered the beautiful Poinsette Hotel (currently named the Westin Poinsette) in downtown Greenville, which offered an 85¢ dinner special. This was a great price since regular dinner meals were much more expensive—$3.25 and up. They enjoyed all of the amenities of the Poinsette—the organ music, the server who moved from table to table with spoon bread and corn relish for the guests, and the lavish atmosphere of the hotel—while paying a small price for the meal. Marlene enjoyed the Poinsette dining experience so much that she wanted the student wives to have this same opportunity. She went to the manager and asked to have a banquet with those 85¢ meals. She was quite surprised that he agreed to do so because hotels don't usually offer banquet rooms for less; they charge more. But the manager said they would.

As she later recalled the incident, Marlene confessed, "I was sooooo thrilled! I came walking into the meeting and I said, 'We're going to get to go to the Poinsette Hotel!' However, those ladies voted not to go there. I felt so rejected and so stupid and so humiliated. I had to go back to the manager of the hotel and tell him we didn't want their 85¢ dinners. Those dumb ladies ended up paying more than 85¢ for the banquet that was planned! Now that I've had time to look back on the situation, I figure that possibly they didn't feel comfortable or didn't want to be limited to one menu, but I had been humiliated. I worked at J.C. Penney at the time, and I went to my manager and arranged to be scheduled to work the night of the banquet. I was going to see to it that if I could not have my way, I was not going to go to that banquet at all!"

Many years later Marlene recognized her behavior in this situation as the "green-eyed monster," and called it as such. She used this incident when teaching on jealousy and competition that can be so prevalent among women, even Christian women. She observed, "We know we are not supposed to be jealous, so we won't even name it, but we can't fight our sins if we won't name them!"

Graduation—Again!

During this school year Marlene completed her classes, and both she and Wendell graduated in May of 1957 with their master's degrees. That fall he enrolled in the doctoral program at "BJ" to get his doctorate in religion. In September when he returned to school, Marlene joined the seventh-grade teaching staff at the Richard Arrington School in Greenville. There were two great influences on her teaching at this school—the principal and the district supervisor, Miss Mims. Both were ladies who helped form and cement many of Marlene's teaching principles and philosophies.

Wendell and Marlene graduating with their master's degrees in 1957

*Marlene Evans
A Biography*

While most of the teachers resented Miss Mims, who traveled to schools throughout the district and gave evaluations as she would unexpectedly visit different classrooms, Marlene made a friend of her. She had learned from Dr. Bob Jones, Sr., to be teachable and applied it to this situation. She realized she could learn a lot from Miss Mims and kept an open spirit each time this supervisor observed her.

It was during this time that Marlene learned one of the most difficult lessons of her life as she watched a younger "educational star" appear on the horizon in the form of a Bob Jones University student teacher. This student teacher organized her first graders, decorated her room, got top grades, and turned in a performance par excellence in every other teaching area.

The next year that same young lady was hired as a full-time teacher. Marlene was jealous and felt threatened by this star teacher; however, she was not happy when she saw the girl return to do nothing as a paid full-time teacher. She felt the girl's behavior was a poor testimony for "BJ" and for the cause of Christ. The "fireball" had become a "tortoise" over one summer's time. The creator of all creativity could not seem to think of one new idea. The one who had so gallantly shunned the lineup of lazy teachers at the side of the playground now sat on chairs most all day. Marlene thought that this girl had just put on a good show to get a good grade in student teaching, and now didn't care as long as she was on the payroll.

Then this new teacher asked Marlene to take her to the doctor because she wasn't feeling well. Mrs. Evans admitted that in her feeble thinking she pronounced this girl lazy. After many times of driving her to the doctor, Marlene finally told her that she would have to start riding the bus home from the doctor's office so she could go on her way. A few weeks later the girl died of leukemia.

Mrs. Evans spent many days agonizing over this situation because of her guilt in being so selfish and judgmental. But God used this to deal with her in an unusual and dramatic way and helped her to learn to give people the benefit of the doubt rather than judge them for their actions. While she realized that people cannot always go running to take everyone to the doctor in case the diagnosis is leukemia, she did learn that "a loving heart will cause people to reserve judgment and help others." It was a life-changing lesson forever burned into her heart and mind.

While Marlene was teaching school, she began work on a second master's degree. She would teach during the day and then go directly to Furman University after school. Many times Wendell would go with her; while she was in class, he would go to the library and study. Marlene often went home and cooked dinner, but sometimes when she got out of class about 6:30 p.m. they would go out to eat—occasionally to the Poinsette, but more often than not to an inexpensive steak house in Greenville where they could get a steak dinner for $1.05 plus tax. Marlene would finish work on her master's degree in educational administration and supervision several years later at the University of Chattanooga.

While Wendell was in graduate school, the Evanses had the opportunity to work in a church in Asheville, North Carolina, on weekends. It was quite a drive from Greenville, South Carolina, to Asheville every weekend in their old '49 Plymouth which had bald tires and holes in the floor through which water sloshed. They didn't feel that they had accomplished much during the few months they traveled back and forth through the mountains, but they had received valuable experience for later work.

A number of years after that experience, they happened to visit Bob Jones University and ran into a young lady who was a recent graduate of the school. She came running up to them and said, "Remember me?" Of course, they did remember her, for they had stayed in the home of her parents quite a few weekends during the time they traveled back and forth to Asheville. The young lady told them all about the fact that she was now teaching part time at Bob Jones while her husband was receiving his training to be a pastor. She explained their plans of starting a local church one day soon. Marlene said, "Carol, how did you happen to come to 'BJ?' "

She answered, "Don't you remember when you used to come and talk to me about the school when you stayed at our home?" She had been in the seventh grade that year. Wendell and Marlene had talked with scores of people who were in the eleventh or twelfth grade and were actual candidates for college. Yet, God chose to work in His own way helping that one girl to remember what they had said while she was in the seventh grade. It seemed as if He were saying to Wendell and Marlene, "Remember, I'm the One Who does the work!"

When Marlene went off to college, Kathryn and Doris missed her terribly and always waited anxiously for the next time she would come home. When she did go home to Nebraska, she was always very thoughtful and concerned that her sisters have nice things. One time she even took one of the girls to Lincoln and purchased her first foundation garments for her. Kathryn remembers a beautiful orange cotton skirt with a wide black patent leather belt that Marlene bought. Another time she bought a beautiful dress with matching shoes. Kathryn felt so "in" with the things Marlene got for her.

In Doris and Kathryn's eyes, Marlene was the most important person on campus—they were sure Dr. Bob Jones, Sr., depended on her greatly because they certainly did! Marlene wrote home often and told many interesting stories of her college life, which gave Doris a desire to attend Bob Jones. She did so during the time when Wendell and Marlene were still living in Greenville. Marlene had constant concern for Doris' welfare and seemed to think she should take her schoolwork more seriously. (Doris says she had the idea that college was all about going out in ministries and even taking the place for others when they needed to do extra studying!) Marlene tried to impress on Doris that she needed to study and even went so far as to go to her dorm and study with her for her tests. She was married and teaching, but unselfishly took her time to get her sister on the right track. Doris graduated from college and began teaching school in Michigan where she met Jerry Smith, the man who was to become her husband. Years later Doris and Jerry moved to Indiana where he still serves as the chairman of the education department at Hyles-Anderson College, and Doris is on the staff of Hammond Baptist Grade School. It was a thrill for Marlene that she and Wendell got to serve the Lord together with family members. Her investment in Doris' college years paid great dividends.

In January of 1959, with just one semester of doctoral classroom study left, Wendell accepted a call to pastor the Faith Tabernacle of Hendersonville, North Carolina. The church building was a log structure which seated about 250 people, though the regular church attendance was only about one-fourth of that number. They made the 40-mile drive to Hendersonville each weekend for church and also for the mid-week evening service. In May Wendell finished his classroom requirements, and the young couple moved to Hendersonville. Though it would prove to be a monumental task, he only had to write his dissertation to complete his doctoral work. With their college days behind them, Wendell began putting his time into building the only church he would ever pastor.

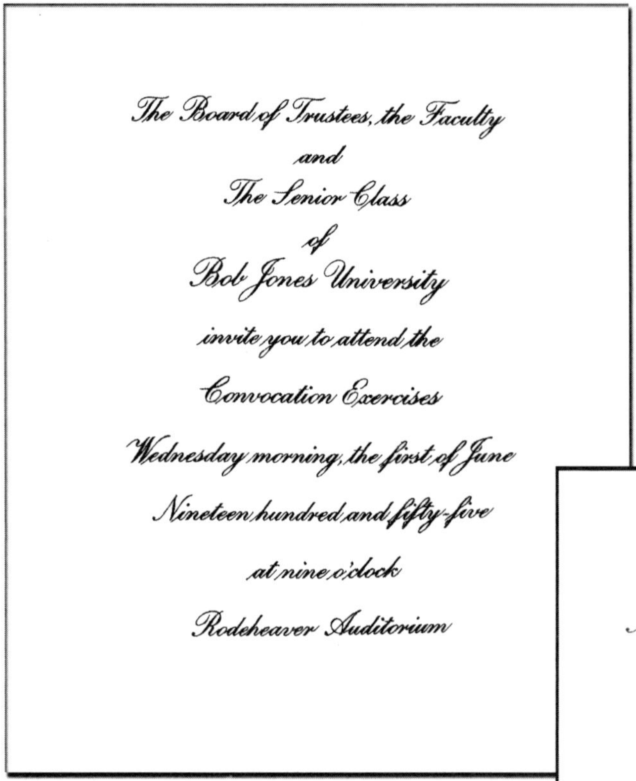

The Board of Trustees, the Faculty
and
The Senior Class
of
Bob Jones University
invite you to attend the
Convocation Exercises
Wednesday morning, the first of June
Nineteen hundred and fifty-five
at nine o'clock
Rodeheaver Auditorium

Left: Marlene's graduation announcement from Bob Jones

Pictures on page 85:
The young pastor's wife
A Zugmier family picture
(c. 1959)

Miss Marlene June Zugmier

Part Six

Hendersonville

After Wendell and Marlene moved to Hendersonville, she accepted a position teaching eighth grade at Valley Hill Elementary School. One of the most difficult situations Marlene had to deal with during this time involved helping a young lady choose to be admitted to a mental institution. The school in which she taught was comprised mostly of mountain children from a poor area. Nearly eighty percent of the eighth grade class was made up of children in tragedy.

One day the younger brothers and sisters of a beautiful high school girl came to tell Marlene that Sandy was in the hospital because her feet were frozen from standing in the river all night. She had tried to kill herself. Although they were not well acquainted, they had seen each other often as Marlene waited at the corner for the city bus to take her to town. Those chance encounters had not been pleasant, for Sandy had rudely turned her head from Marlene every time she called, "Hello!"

Thinking that perhaps the river incident was her chance to win the troubled teenager to herself and to the Lord, Marlene carefully planned her visit. She went to the flower shop and chose pretty, colorful tulips for Sandy. When she and Wendell walked into the hospital room, Sandy reared back as if someone had struck her. She cursed, spewed forth ugly words concerning Marlene's not caring about her, shouted accusations of her loving her sister more than her, and made firm declarations of her hate for Marlene. Sandy also expressed bitterness over the fact that she felt Marlene had undoubtedly been in cahoots with her parents because of the tulips.

After being hospitalized, Sandy refused to see or have anything to do with her parents. She had concluded that since Wendell and Marlene were bringing her tulips in January, her parents were getting to her through them. The truth was, Marlene had not talked to her parents and had no idea that Sandy's favorite flower was tulips. The florist just happened to mention the fact that new tulip plants were available.

After being there for some time, Wendell felt that possibly his leaving

Wendell and Marlene Evans

would help Sandy to be able to talk with Marlene. Soon after he left the room, Sandy broke and began sobbing. She insisted that she was never going to go home again because she felt that no one there loved her or wanted her. That began a two-hour session of letting out resentments of a lifetime. Because Sandy had turned her head from Marlene every time she'd called, "Hello," Marlene had said to herself, "Sandy hates me and can't stand the sight of me." During that two-hour long talking jag, Sandy admitted that she'd always wanted Marlene's attention, but thought that Marlene loved her sister. Sandy felt that no one who loved her sister ever loved her. This incident helped the young teacher learn that one cannot always take people's actions—especially negative actions—at face value.

A few days later Sandy went home with Marlene. It seemed there was no other solution since her parents said they could not afford to keep her in the hospital, nor could they get her to agree to go back home. Wendell and Marlene realized some years later that, as a young married couple, they had made a very unwise decision. They knew it had been a big mistake to have taken a teenager into their home, and they were grateful that God had protected them through this undertaking.

Sandy got back into school, and the next few weeks were filled with mood swings that left Marlene absolutely exhausted—not knowing if she would wake up the next morning to a laughing, sunny, pretty girl or be awakened at 2:00 a.m. by the sound of beating on the walls as Sandy yelled, "My mother is trying to get me!" Finally, the night came when Sandy grabbed a kitchen butcher knife to kill herself and then turned it on Marlene when she tried to stop her. She was a petite girl, but very strong in a wiry sort of way. God gave Marlene sense enough to refrain from trying to go after her and calmed her enough that she was able to say quietly and slowly, "Sandy, you don't want to do that. Put it down." Other words to that effect were used until she dropped the knife and ran into Marlene's arms. Who could ever know if Sandy would have actually attempted to take her life, or if she was just crying for help in order to not want to do so. It didn't matter. Either way, it was serious; something had to be done. Being young and inexperienced, Marlene made the mistake of promising she'd not let them keep her if Sandy would go to the hospital for something to calm her.

When they got to the hospital, the doctor immediately wanted to commit Sandy to a state mental institution. Marlene begged to take her home, saying that she could get Sandy to make that decision herself. The medical staff laughed at her as they said, "People in this state of mind don't make decisions like that." However, they finally agreed to let Marlene take her at her own risk.

Marlene later stated, "I was foolish. I was wrong. God in His loving care of the sincere but ignorant allowed me to talk to her all night long in such a way that she went to the doctor the next morning to ask for whatever help she needed. I did not gloat; I was grateful."

After three months of difficult treatment, Sandy resumed a fairly normal life. The last time Marlene heard from her twelve years had transpired since that awful night when Sandy had tried to take her life, and she was functioning well as a wife and mother. Marlene always felt that perhaps the fact that Sandy had been led to voluntarily ask for help might have been partially responsible for her seeming cure.

Nancy Perry

Faith Tabernacle paid the pastor according to how much money about 65 people put in the offering plate on Sunday mornings. The Sunday night offering was designated for the operating expenses of the church. The income Wendell earned as pastor was small, but the lessons both he and Marlene learned and the great people with whom they served influenced them for a lifetime. The years at Faith Tabernacle were a great starting point and played a very important role in their Christian service in years to come.

Nancy and Paul Perry were a faithful deacon and wife at Faith Tabernacle. Paul, an astute businessman in Hendersonville, owned and operated Mowers and Tractors, Inc. Marlene learned much from Nancy who loved to care for her family, take walks in the woods, arrange flowers, work in the yard, take kids on outings, and teach daily vacation Bible school. She was a very active person, and she and her husband had a good marriage, home, and business. Both were in love with the Lord and the church. Marlene saw Nancy lose a daughter, a husband, a house, a business, and her health all in a few years. Through all of this Nancy kept her love for Christ, her Christian testimony, and her care for others—even as she suffered the rest of her life with severe rheumatoid arthritis.

One year near election time, Paul Perry headed up the dry forces in a hotly contested beer and wine vote in Hendersonville, with the chief of police on the other side of the debate. During the heat of the battle, there was a big snowstorm in town. Paul had just begun to sell snow blowers at his place of business, and when he appeared on the Hendersonville city streets to volunteer one of his snow blowers, the chief of police said, "Paul, I don't understand you. Here we are bitter enemies, and you are down here helping me." This incident made a big impression on Marlene who had reacted so strongly about the Poinsette Hotel situation when she had been opposed by the ladies of the student wives' organization. Paul knew the secret of opposing an issue without hating a person and was very influential in helping Marlene master this profound truth!

The Perry's were not only a tremendous help and influence on Wendell and Marlene, they also became dear friends of a lifetime. In 1972 when Hyles-Anderson College was begun and dorms were being built at Baptist City, Dr. Jack Hyles gave some of the administrators the opportunity to name a dorm. Dr. Evans chose "Paul Perry Hall."

The Hardens were another faithful couple at Faith Tabernacle. Mrs. Harden was Marlene's buddy and took her to gather berries, find herbs, and pick flowers. Marlene was thrilled when she was able to provide a special event for Mrs. Harden as Marlene's sister Kathryn was married to Dick (a commercial airline pilot) who gave Mrs. Harden her first—and only—airplane ride.

Mrs. Harden was called "Baby" until she was asked her name in the first grade. She never knew where she got it, but "O'Neal" popped out. She was "O'Neal" for life. In her later years when Marlene and Wendell met her she was called "Granny Harden."

Marlene credited Granny with teaching her some really important lessons about life and people. One of those times was when Marlene watched Granny go through over 100 cards from funeral flowers the night of her husband's memorial service, only to break down when she came to the almost illegible writing of the name of the "town drunk," Vince Nelson. He had pushed garden roses through holes he had made in a piece of cardboard to read "George," her husband's name. Mr. Harden had been a well-known contractor, and the flowers at the funeral had been gorgeous and beautiful, but Granny had gotten really touched over

Faith Tabernacle
Hendersonville, North Carolina

some flowers from the town drunk. Granny Harden taught Marlene a lot by those feelings displayed over that poor old piece of cardboard.

Even greater was when she said, "Marlene, I can't talk to people to get them to accept Christ, but I'll go with you and do anything I can to make the way for you." She led Marlene through the woods to the houses in the hills, cooked big dinners, took goodies to sick people, pulled a possum by its tail out of tree, and anything else Marlene couldn't (or wouldn't!) do. She was the silent partner.

Years later, after Marlene learned from Fay Dodson at First Baptist Church of Hammond, Indiana, how to win souls using the Phoster Club plan, she realized she could have taught Granny how to be a soul winner. She once wrote, "Granny Harden, thanks for not putting down soul winning because you didn't know what to do and I didn't know how to help you."

One of Marlene's most interesting soul-winning stories took place in Hendersonville. When Wendell became pastor, he started a visitation night, a new ministry for the church. Marlene would usually go with one of the ladies in the church, and they would usually let her do the talking. One particular night Marlene knocked on a door and talked with two sisters who promised they would come to church on Sunday night, but they didn't have a way. Marlene promised to find them a ride, so on Sunday afternoon she called Paul Perry and asked him to pick up her two visitors. Paul picked the two ladies up, and when they arrived at church, Nancy used an old Southern expression as she exclaimed, "Oh, da law me! My husband just brought in Christmas Cactus and Easter Lily!" Nancy was referring to them by their professional names...they were prostitutes! Marlene attracted all types of people!

At Thanksgiving time Wendell asked Marlene to prepare a church Thanksgiving banquet for about 90 people. The first person she thought of to help her was a home economics teacher. Surely she would at least be able to give her some counsel as to how to accomplish this task. When Marlene talked with her and told her they were wanting a turkey dinner and indicated the time frame in which they had to prepare it, the teacher responded, "No, indeed. This can't be done."

Marlene was forced to turn to Granny Harden, who had not even finished grade school but was well known for her cooking. She was shocked to hear Granny say, "No problem. We'll need four large turkeys…" and go on to plan and organize the entire meal. Marlene pondered on these two different responses and realized that while both ladies had received an education in cooking, Granny had learned how it could be done while the teacher, who had a formal education, had learned how not to do things to the point that she was paralyzed if she did not have all the right ingredients, and especially time, on her side. Not only did this situation help to reinforce in Marlene's mind that "It can't be done," is not an acceptable way of thinking when there is a need, it also helped her realize that formal education is not the only kind of education. She saw that sometimes formal education is the least practical and the least useful of all types of education because of the attitudes it creates in its product.

It caused her to have the following philosophies of education:

1.   If your education or training helps you to relate to more people in appropriate ways rather than causing you to critique more people, you have received some excellent schooling.

2.   If your education or training helps you to feel you can be used of God more, you have been well taught.

3.   If you realize that the only thing that makes you different from the person with less formal education is that you sat through a bunch of classes, you are a fortunate formally educated person.

4.   If you come out of your formal training—high school, college, voice classes, piano lessons, or whatever else you might take—knowing you just have some of the tools you need to really start learning, you are a wise person.

These philosophies helped Marlene understand that formal education does not equal being smart. She had the uncanny ability to recognize great qualities in people such as talent, ability, and knowledge—whether they held a doctorate degree in their field of study or had not even finished first grade.

The work in Hendersonville flourished, growing from an average attendance of 65 to about 125 in the two years Wendell pastored the church. They had a high day of 135. Wendell and Marlene were young and dynamic, and they energized the youth work at Faith Tabernacle.

Above: Billy and Benny [McCrary]
McGuire listed in the Guinness Book of
Records as the world's heaviest twins
In this photo, the 19-year-old twins
still weighed 450 pounds each!
Below: Richard and Roy Perry

Marlene Evans
A Biography

They used their 1957 Chevy as a bus and picked up young people from the entire Hendersonville area for Sunday school and church. They also conducted youth activities to provide wholesome fun for the teenagers.

Among the young people they served and influenced, were the famous McGuire twins—Billy and Benny. At that time they went by their real last name, McCrary, but years later changed their name to McGuire when Japanese sportscasters had trouble with their name, pronouncing it "McQueery." The twins didn't like that, and so they changed their name to McGuire. They were to become the world's heaviest twins. The boys were normal in size until they were about four years old when they both contracted German measles. When they suddenly began gaining a disproportionate amount of weight, doctors told their parents that the boys' pituitary glands had been adversely affected by the sickness. By the time they were 10 years old, Billy and Benny each weighed about 200 pounds; at 16 they weighed 450 pounds; and at 21 about 650 pounds. When they were 16, they decided to put their size to use. They quit high school, went to Texas, and began working in rodeos. They eventually ended up in wrestling.

Benny and Billy were in eighth grade, and each of the boys already weighed about 300 pounds when Wendell and Marlene met them. Their parents were good Christian people. The boys had been saved at the age of nine and were faithful members of the youth group and the church services. Wendell gave the boys trumpet lessons during his tenure as pastor.

Both Benny and Billy died at young ages, Billy at 33 and Benny at 54. The famous twins continued to embrace their Christian testimony through the years. During their brief encounter with the twins, Wendell and Marlene had played an important role in their lives.

Also in the youth group were Paul and Nancy Perry's sons, Roy and Richard Perry. Both of the young men attended Christian colleges, and Roy is the pastor of an independent Baptist church today. Again, Marlene and Wendell's spiritual influence was long term and indicative of the influence they would have in years to come as they poured their heart and soul into the lives of young people.

After pastoring Faith Tabernacle for two years, Wendell resigned the church in January of 1961. With his many pastoral responsibilities, he had not found the necessary time to finish his dissertation for his doctoral degree. He also still entertained the dream he and Marlene had both expressed while at "BJ"—that of working in Christian education on the college level.

After his resignation, Wendell and Marlene moved back to Greenville, South Carolina, where they once again lived with Hassie McCarter. She had sold her farm and built a new house. She charged a little more than she had when they lived with her in the farmhouse. Dr. Evans used these months to do research for his dissertation. In June Wendell and Marlene moved to Nebraska where he wrote his dissertation while she spent the summer working for her dad. By this time Alvin Zugmier had sold the restaurant and bowling lanes and now owned and operated the Star View Motel of Axtell, Nebraska.

Wendell had almost given up the idea of being a college teacher because he was not a straight-A student. (He says he later realized that oftentimes straight-A students do not prove to be the best teachers because they sometimes have difficulty in relating to their students.) However, he began applying at Christian colleges seeking a teaching job. One of those institutions was Tennessee Temple College in Chattanooga, Tennessee, a ministry of the great Highland Park Baptist Church where Dr. Lee Roberson was pastor. He received word that he had been hired to teach in the seminary at Tennessee Temple, and the fall of 1961 found Dr. Wendell and Marlene Evans back in her beloved South—in Chattanooga, Tennessee.

Above: *Wendell Evans' ordination at Faith Tabernacle; March 1959*
Pictures on page 95: Three photos of Marlene Evans during her
Chattanooga years

Part Seven

Chattanooga

Wendell and Marlene arrived in Chattanooga just a few days before school was to begin. They moved into an upstairs apartment on Bailey Avenue about one and a half blocks from Highland Park Baptist Church. They could walk to church, which was ideal since they did not own a car at this time. Marlene never forgot that first Sunday morning walk to church when she was introduced to the bus ministry. She spotted the buses lined up on Bailey Avenue when she was still about a block away. She immediately started crying. She later observed, "Some people say that I 'get touched' easily. But, to tell you the truth, anyone who doesn't shout, yell, breathe a prayer, cry, or something when they see 1…2…3…4…5…6…7…8…9…10…11…12…13…14…15…16 buses lined up is 'teched' as far as I'm concerned. I counted them over and over. There were 16 that day!"

An interest in the bus ministry had been planted in Marlene's heart causing her to watch the student bus workers, check out the buses lined up on Bailey Avenue, and frequently direct her eyes toward the section where the riders all sat together during the church services. As far as she knew, only students worked the buses, and so Wendell and Marlene became heavily involved in other ministries of the church. God blessed the Evanses tremendously in their work at Highland Park. They gave themselves 100 percent, and everywhere they served, the ministry prospered and grew.

Of course, they loved the preaching. Dr. Roberson was a tremendous influence on Marlene with his emphasis on the victorious Christian life and the Second Coming of Christ, and this great man of God was soon added to her list of heroes.

Every Sunday was a big day to Dr. Roberson, and he used the Wednesday evening Teachers' and Officers' Meeting of nearly 500 workers as a platform to get them inspired about increasing Sunday school attendance and reaching goals. Highland Park Baptist Church was the world's largest Sunday school at this time and ran about 10,000 in attendance. Each month a different teacher of an adult Sunday school class was asked to be in charge of the Wednesday evening promotions.

When they had been in Chattanooga about a year, Dr. Evans was asked to take the responsibility of planning church services for the college students. He supervised five Sunday school classes and three student church services which involved organizing the preaching, teaching, song leading, and special music of those services. He continued in this capacity during the rest of their tenure in Chattanooga. Because of his responsibilities with the college services, Dr. Evans was one of those asked to be in charge of the Wednesday evening promotional time for a month. Marlene helped him plan and carry out his promotions, which gave Dr. Roberson the opportunity to see her in action. He immediately saw the tremendous promotional abilities Marlene possessed. He loved her ideas and was fascinated by her energy and her personality. He liked to do things big, and he had found someone who was like-minded. Dr. Roberson hired Marlene full time to be the Sunday school promotion coordinator.

The great architect, David Adler, said, "Make no small plans. They don't excite people. Make only big plans." Marlene lived by that philosophy in whatever she did, and the Wednesday evening Sunday school promotions were no exception.

Marlene had two young men who assisted her with the Sunday school promotions, Roger Ellison and Jimmy DeYoung. (Both of these men graduated from Tennessee Temple College. Roger Ellison eventually became vice president and later president of Trinity Baptist College in Jacksonville, Florida, and later pastored in Schroon Lake, New York. He is now a conference speaker.

Jimmy DeYoung worked for Word of Life, started New York City's first Christian radio station in 1982, started a Baptist church in Jerusalem with six people which now runs about 375, and is now a much-sought-after conference speaker on prophecy. The three would get together and brainstorm for ideas. Though Dr. Roberson was very conservative, he liked the fact that this team went "to the edge" and was creative and flamboyant with their promotions.

• They planned a Christmas promotion—Helicopter Sunday—where Jimmy dressed up as Santa and flew in by helicopter for the children. It was quite an event and promoted a lot of excitement as plans were

Above: David and Joy posing with Colonel Sanders during one exciting Sunday school program! Below: Mrs. Evans and Dr. J. R. Faulkner

| *Marlene Evans*
A Biography

made for the helicopter to land at the public school just across the street from the church.

• Jimmy ran the church radio station and was the morning announcer. He would use two voices—his own and the voice of "Uncle Josh." Mrs. Evans got the idea for "Uncle Josh" to speak to the kids, and so Jimmy dressed the part and visited each of the classes. Talking in the raspy voice of "Uncle Josh" before so many classes nearly killed his voice!

• Jimmy had hair similar to Dr. Roberson's, and so for one promotion they borrowed one of Dr. Roberson's double breasted suit coats for Jimmy, sprayed his hair gray, and introduced him as Dr. Roberson. They were a little hesitant about carrying out this promotion, but Dr. Roberson and all of the people loved it.

• One of the Sunday school promotions Marlene planned was Transportation Day. This was an annual event featuring a big parade with all types of floats and all types of vehicles. Dr. Roberson especially enjoyed this big day as he rode atop the big red fire truck from the local fire department! Marlene and Wendell both rode borrowed motorcycles for the event. One year Dr. Evans' cycle had a sticker on the back that said, "I like girls." He, of course, was the object of much teasing over this, and people delighted as he responded to their teasing with, "I do prefer them to guys!"

• Another Wednesday evening Marlene needed furniture on the platform to complete the stage for their promotion. She made plans to go home and be there when the men picked up the furniture from her house. Meanwhile, Dr. Evans came home and went in to take a shower before he went to church. When he came out from the shower, much of the furniture was gone! (Mrs. Evans later conceded that she didn't think it had been a good idea to remove most of their furniture before checking with her husband!)

Dr. Roberson was a planner and did not do things in a last-minute way. However, one year on the fourth of July, the program he had planned for the Training Union hour fell through. That morning in church in announced, "Tonight we will be having a wonderful patriotic program during the six o'clock hour. We'll be having patriotic music, special readings, and much more. You won't want to miss it!" Then he turned and looked at Marlene and said, "Mrs. Evans, you'll be in charge of that." He matter-of-factly went on with the church service as Mrs. Evans realized what a big program she had to orchestrate in just a few hours. At the end of the service, Dr. Roberson looked at her and said teasingly, "Mrs. Evans, did you listen to the message this morning?"

Mrs. Evans showed her loyalty and flexibility as she did organize a great patriotic program by enlisting the talents of music faculty, speech faculty, and other gifted members of the church—without one word of criticism or self pity. When the leader asked for something, she spent no time on deciding whether it could be done or if it was reasonable. She simply set about finding a way to do what the leadership requested.

It is to be expected that when someone makes things happen, there are always those who do not like it. This was true of Marlene's promotions. Some of the maintenance men did not appreciate her ideas and the work they involved, and so one of the men complained to Dr. Roberson's assistant, Dr. J. R. Faulkner. They weren't used to the demands required to carry out her ideas. Dr. Faulkner's response was, "Sir, your only questions are 'What does she need?' and 'When does she need it?' " Dr. Evans says that Dr. Faulkner's response had nothing to do with his own feelings or ideas about the matter. He simply knew that Marlene was doing exactly what Dr. Roberson wanted, and Dr. Faulkner's whole agenda was to find out exactly what Dr. Roberson wanted and to help carry out those ideas to the smallest detail.

For Basketball Sunday, Marlene had Jimmy and Roger come down the aisle from the back bouncing a basketball and throwing it back and forth to each other. One of the men missed the ball when it was thrown to him, and it landed in an elderly lady's lap. This dear lady was not a great fan of Marlene to begin with because of the promotions she organized and was not happy about the ball in her lap, but Dr. Evans says, "It didn't slow things down a bit!"

Marlene also helped with the Thursday evening visitation program. They met in a large room where there was first a dinner and then a big promotion time before the people went out visiting. Annie Ruth McGuire, a dear friend of Marlene, said, "We had a pep rally nearly every Wednesday and every Thursday. Dr. Roberson loved promotion and loved it that he had someone to make it happen the way he wanted."

Marlene always had a great love for the wife of each of her pastors and

Above: Mrs. Evans with Dr. and Mrs. Lee Roberson
Lower: The Evanses with the Robersons in the private dining room of Hyles-Anderson College

*Above: Mrs. Evans (standing) with
Mrs. Hyles (l) and Mrs. Roberson
Below: Beverly Hyles (standing),
Miss Annie Ruth McGuire (l),
and Marlene Evans*

found ways to show that love and admiration. Annie Ruth says, "Marlene brought out Mrs. Roberson much like she did Mrs. Hyles—she made big over her. Mrs. Roberson was not a person to seek public attention, and most of us ladies were more reserved toward her, but Marlene adored her preacher's wife and wanted to honor her."

She once used the Thursday evening visitation program to honor Mrs. Roberson. Marlene asked Barbara Eash to make big, beautiful doll cake for the event. Barbara did not have a lot of advance notice for this project, so Marlene went to her house just minutes before visitation to pick it up. Barbara said, "Please watch the cake!" as Marlene went whizzing out the door. She slung the cake into the car and hit the car seat with it. She hurriedly took the cake back in, had Barbara fix it the best she could, and then went on her way to visitation. Of course, when she presented it, she told the colorful story of how she had messed up the cake, and everybody loved it!

Not only did Marlene do big things on Wednesday evenings and Thursday evenings, she also did big things as president of her Sunday school class. Roundup Sunday, the biggest day of the entire year, was always the first Sunday in September, and Marlene would plan giant promotions for this special Sunday each year, such as bringing Mrs. Bob Jones, Sr., and other famous guests to the class. Mrs. Evans did not realize that Mrs. Beverly Hyles would be her pastor's wife in just three or four years when she invited her as a special guest. Dr. Evans recalls, "Marlene asked me if I would help host Beverly Hyles. We picked her up at the airport in a chauffeur-driven black Rolls Royce. A wealthy member of the church owned this 1920's model that was in mint condition, and Marlene wanted Mrs. Hyles to have red-carpet treatment."

Marlene learned much from Dr. Faulkner as she worked under his leadership in her promotional roles—especially regarding the matter of loyalty to leadership. He taught her the importance of helping the man of God so he could be used more fully. He directed her to ask herself questions such as, "Do you think this would please Dr. Roberson?" or "What would the Preacher think about this?" She later credited Dr. Faulkner for helping her to understand the biblical position of pastor and to elevate that position to its proper place. He is probably one of the main reasons that she was so "in tune" with her pastors and so consciously tried to do things they way they wanted them. She had been taught the concept of loyalty as she'd heard Dr. Bob Jones, Sr., say many times, "Don't be a disloyal skunk." He had a disdain for disloyalty and transferred that to Marlene. However, Dr. Faulkner strengthened her attitudes toward leadership, and especially the pastor, as he so beautifully manifested that character trait in his own relationship with Dr. Roberson.

Marlene hosted a weekly program for ladies on the church radio station WDYN. Her programs were varied but included interviews with well-known ladies such as her pastor's wife, Mrs. Lee Roberson; Mrs. Fred Brown, wife of Evangelist Fred Brown; and Mrs. Haskell, wife of Dr. E. C. Haskell who was the chairman of the deacon board at Highland Park. In the program she also included devotionals and teaching on subjects such as character, homemaking, child rearing, and so forth.

In the late 1960's Wendell was frustrated about his soul winning, and Marlene continued to have the desire to be involved with the bus ministry. They asked if they could have a bus route and were thrilled when they were told, "Sure!" Dr. "Cuz" Parker, head of the bus ministry at that time, sent Brother Pat Creed, a married student, out to train them. Brother Creed took them to Ringgold, Georgia, on the following Saturday and visited the homes with Wendell and Marlene.

Marlene recounted that first Sunday morning on the bus:

"I WAS so proud to board our own bus on Sunday morning, but actually I was scared to death that no one would get on when we stopped before homes and honked. We prayed and sang all the way from Chattanooga to Ringgold, and then we made our first stop where a mom and her nine children all trooped out ready to climb on the bus to our singing, 'Get on board, little children.' I bawled my eyes out."

Mrs. Evans made it a ritual to "sing" the riders onto the bus each Sunday and did so throughout the entire time she was in the bus ministry.

Wendell and Marlene started their route in the Welcome Hill area of Ringgold. A deacon and his wife, Mr. and Mrs. Buddy Thomas, helped them on the route. The route grew quickly; soon the Thomases started a

The Bus Ministry

Above: Mrs. T. G. Green
Below: Dr. and Mrs. Evans
Mrs. Evans "sports" her
beautiful mink!

second route in the Tunnel Hill area. A few months later another layman, Henry Nelson, helped Dr. Evans start two more routes—one in New England, Georgia, and one in Tiftonia, Tennessee. This gave them a total of four bus routes. These were not just Sunday morning riders. Dr. Roberson was a great believer of "three to thrive"—Sunday morning, Sunday night, and Wednesday night—and hence, the buses ran for all three services. While they did have Temple students work on their bus routes, an unusual aspect of the Evanses' work with the bus ministry was the way they pulled so many Highland Park Baptist Church members into their routes. Prior to this time it was mostly Temple students who worked the routes.

One of their bus kids was killed in a traffic accident when the car in which she was riding ran into the back of a semi truck. The family of this rider and other families on the bus routes consisted mainly of very poor, Appalachian people who had some unusual customs. One of those customs was "keening," a long, mournful wail grieving the death of a loved one. Dr. and Mrs. Evans went to visit the family on a warm Georgia night in April and could hear the poignant sounds of grief from the wailing family as they approached. It was a heartbreaking time, and yet bittersweet as the 17-year-old girl had attended church just one Sunday. She had loved Dr. Roberson's preaching and was so excited about coming back the next Sunday. She had told Wendell the Sunday before that she was going to have her little brothers and sisters on the bus the next week.

There were both great days and trying days on the bus route. At the time, they did not realize the extent to which their influence would reach. Marlene was excited to be a bus worker, and that excitement permeated every aspect of the route. She seldom waited for people to come out of their houses to get on the bus—or for other bus workers to get off and get the riders. She herself hopped off the bus and ran to the houses, excitedly hugging and greeting the children.

Mrs. T. G. Green, a prominent member of the church, had recruited Marlene to sell china. As was true with everything she did, Marlene excelled. One of the prizes she won for selling china was a mink stole, which she sometimes wore on the bus route. Marlene and her friend Annie Ruth McGuire, who was also one of the bus workers, laughed about the fur as it just didn't look right on the bus route. However, Judson

*Marlene Evans
A Biography*

Mitchell noted that Marlene "did not flinch when her mink stole was needed as a tool to pacify Randall Langford, a mentally handicapped boy who was very fidgety and nervous." It seemed Randall was calmed only by Mrs. Evans' tender touch, and in the cooler months he was calmed by "snuggling his less-than-slightly moist nose in the soft recesses of her mink."

Though Marlene was already a person who gave herself to people, she undoubtedly was influenced even more in this area by a deacon's wife who worked on their route. Brother and Mrs. Peduzzi were faithful workers, and Mrs. Evans would watch this woman, who was every inch a lady, discreetly hold a perfumed handkerchief to her nose with one hand while she wrapped her other arm around the smelly children.

Judson Mitchell was one of Wendell and Marlene's student bus workers when Vicki Jackson, Dr. Evans' work scholarship secretary, joined the route. Judson and Vicki began dating, and when they became engaged, Marlene saw a bus promotion in the making—and attempted to convince them to have their wedding on the bus! No one really took her seriously, but she had it all planned how Vicki could walk down the aisle and Dr. Evans (who had been asked to perform their ceremony) could do so on the bus. Vicki and Judson chose not to have their wedding on the bus; they were married at Lakewood Chapel just across from Camp Joy, the camp owned and operated by Highland Park Baptist Church. Dr. Evans did perform the ceremony and Mrs. Evans hostessed the reception.

Above: Vicki Jackson Mitchell
Below: Judson Mitchell

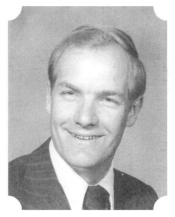

A lifetime friendship was formed between the two couples who worked together on this bus route. A few months after their graduation from Tennessee Temple College, Judson and Vicki were asked by Dr. Jack Hyles and Dr. Wendell Evans to join the staff of Hyles-Anderson College, where they served the Lord together for many years. Vicki worked very closely with Mrs. Evans, first as her assistant teacher and then as a part of the original staff of Christian Womanhood.

A few years later, after Dr. and Mrs. Evans had moved from Chattanooga to serve at Hyles-Anderson College, they received a most surprising report from Dr. Jim Vineyard. He was the bus director at First Baptist Church of Hammond, Indiana, at the time and had been speaking out of town. He had met a young man who had ridden on the Evanses' Ringgold, Georgia, bus route and who was now captain of a Fort Riley,

Kansas, bus route. When Mrs. Evans first heard this report, she was not told the bus captain's name. She thought and thought, "What kid from our bus route had become a bus captain—with 60 on his route?" She thought of John, but no…the first few months on the route he'd been a help, but the last year had been a catastrophe. It seemed he always had to be dragged onto the bus, after which he headed toward the rear of the bus with defiance and rebellion. But, to their surprise and delight, he **was** the one. Marlene realized then and there that it's no use to try to figure out what you have accomplished and what you have not. The Lord does it all anyway. This story was an encouragement to her to just keep on investing in people and to let God take care of the results.

Mrs. Evans made a difference during the two years she served in the bus ministry at Highland Park Baptist Church. Years later Dr. Roberson wrote, "As a bus helper in Chattanooga, she excelled as a soul winner and as a leader of others."

The Business Women's Sunday School Class

Probably the most life-changing event that happened to Marlene when they moved to Chattanooga was her decision to attend the Business Women's Sunday School Class. Marge Ogle, a member of the class, had invited Marlene to attend with her. Mrs. Evans was immediately captivated by the teacher, Louise Renaker. (Mrs. Renaker was a widow at Highland Park Baptist Church who, after being widowed for some years, met a widower, Olin Holbrook, whom she later married.) Though she had a difficult time believing Mrs. Renaker was for real, Marlene was very attracted to this happy and effervescent Southern aristocrat.

Mrs. Renaker was known for her delightful way of talking. In fact, as a single young lady she had worked at a dry cleaners and answered the phone as no other employee ever had. David Renaker would call the place of business where she worked and was always greeted with "Kelly and Powell" in that singing, delightful manner for which she was known. One day he decided he must meet the person on the other end of the line and drove to Kelly and Powell Dry Cleaners. There he met Louise; they dated, fell in love, and married.

Mrs. Renaker loved the Bible and had a burden for her ladies to not only love the Book she loved, but to live by the principles of that Book.

For that reason, she placed great emphasis on the tongue—including gossip and criticism.

Up until meeting Mrs. Renaker, Marlene really had not looked much to women. She found most young women's talk to be boring. She especially hated their gossip, probably because she saw its hurtfulness, and she just didn't respect young women her age, or even most women, for that matter. She somehow felt that women weren't going anywhere. Men were doing exciting things; the men she looked to were talking spiritual goals and getting things done for God. Marlene had a passion for God and loved being right in the middle of serving God. However, God knew that for Marlene to become all that He wanted her to be, she needed a heroine to combine with her list of heroes. And that is where Mrs. Renaker came into the picture.

Mrs. Evans would call her Sunday school teacher and complain about other women in the class and Mrs. Renaker would respond with, "Oh, Honey!"

Mentally Mrs. Evans would retort, "Oh, Honey nothing!"

Mrs. Renaker would continue, "But we just don't gripe! No! Christians don't talk that way!"

Mrs. Evans would respond with a firm, "I do!"

She had grown up as a "Daddy's girl" where her daddy had been gruff and blunt, and he "told it like it was." She had always admired this quality in him, and though she was more feminine about it, had mirrored this trait in her own life. She lived by the philosophy, "What you see is what you get," and felt she was doing people a favor by being outright honest with them.

Her Sunday school teacher's admonition was a whole new way of thinking for this lady who had grown up in the rugged Midwest. Actually, Marlene had a tough time believing that Mrs. Renaker was for real and that she really expected Christian women to talk differently. She was attracted to her, however, because down deep in her heart Mrs. Evans realized that this was actually the type of woman she had dreamed of when she wrote her ninth grade English paper.

One of the unusual aspects of Mrs. Renaker's way of handling problems—and a method Marlene was known for later on—was the way she took care of situations behind the scenes without exposing the person.

Above: Mrs. Louise Renaker Holbrook
Below: Fall Installation Banquet of the Business Women's Class (Arrow pointing to Mrs. Evans)

Marlene and other ladies in the class wanted to tell others and get it out in the open when there was a problem, but Mrs. Renaker taught them a better way. Mrs. Evans was sometimes frustrated as she watched Mrs. Renaker's methods, such as taking a lady out to eat when someone accused her of taking money from the treasury or dressing immodestly. Marlene's thinking was that this rewarded the wrongdoer's behavior. However, she eventually learned that people are not always guilty of that which they are accused; and even if they are guilty, protecting the person usually helps correct problems so much easier.

For the 11 years Dr. and Mrs. Evans lived in Chattanooga, Mrs. Renaker kept working with Marlene on her attitudes and her tongue, but Marlene also learned many other truths and principles from this great woman. One of the lessons she learned just by observing her was how to act when being honored before a group. When honoring came her way, Mrs. Renaker simply stood and smiled and looked at each person in the face, seeming to be just loving the ladies. She didn't act coy or simpering or say things like, "You shouldn't have done it," or "What do you want, a quarter?" This response helped Mrs. Evans tremendously when she herself was the object of honoring as the founder and editor of *Christian Womanhood.*

Since all real growth is slow growth, Mrs. Evans' learning of what Mrs. Renaker was trying to teach her was a long, slow process. However, Mrs. Renaker's teaching began to come through, and step by step Mrs. Evans began changing her talk; she made a concerted effort to be more and more careful of the words she used.

Marlene once acknowledged, "She was one my husband loved for me to talk with on the phone as she always gave me Scripture instead of gossip and criticism!" Mrs. Renaker corrected Marlene lovingly with Scripture almost every day in the 11 years she was in her class. Though she learned many important biblical philosophies and principles during their tenure in Chattanooga, this was probably the training which most qualified her to be catapulted into a ministry of which she had never dreamed.

Dr. Evans says, "Mrs. [Renaker] Holbrook always gave Marlene verses to back up what she was telling her. For a while I didn't realize how much Marlene was getting from Mrs. Holbrook. I just thought she was a sweet Southern Christian who knew the Bible. When I learned that Mrs. Holbrook prayed faithfully for us, I decided to let Marlene talk with her all she wanted!"

Wendell and Marlene had lived in Chattanooga less than a year when they decided to adopt. In June 1962 a case study for the desired adoption was begun, and the process was completed in December. Their case worker had told them they could plan for their baby—a girl between one and six months old—sometime after the first of the year, but more than likely it would be May or June.

Therefore, it was quite a surprise when Marlene received a call in January that they would be getting their baby (who had been born September 19, 1962) the next day. When they arrived at the adoption agency, the case worker who had called Marlene told Wendell that his wife had surely taken the news calmly. Wendell replied that he didn't really think she had been so calm. Marlene said, "I was so excited I had to keep overly composed, or I would have shouted at her. I just couldn't believe it was so soon. We were expecting to wait until May or June at least!" They walked out of the adoption agency on January 30, 1963, with their new bundle of "Joy." After seven years of marriage, Wendell and Marlene were thrilled to be the parents of an adorable, brown-eyed four month old whom they named Joy Lynn. Her baby announcements read, "I wasn't 'expected'; I was 'selected.'"

With the news of Joy's arrival, Marlene immediately resigned her teaching position to give herself full time to the responsibilities of motherhood. She did not go back to teaching until both of their children were in school more than six years later.

When Joy was three, Wendell and Marlene adopted a second child, David Lee, who had been born April 1, 1965. The adoption process was not nearly as long this time as their home had already been approved. They were equally as excited to get this dark-eyed baby boy as they had been to get Joy. However, they were not convinced he was nearly as impressed as they were with the whole deal! In a Christmas letter written just days after David's adoption became final on December 1, 1965, they said, "He showed that he couldn't care less by giving a big yawn in

The Adoption of Joy and David

Above: Joy's adoption, Marlene and the case workers
Below: David's adoption, Marlene with Joy and David's caseworker, Marilyn McAfee, September 20, 1965

*Part Seven
Chattanooga*

response to a proud statement by the judge." Baby David was not exactly what Joy had expected. She thought she was getting a playmate, not someone who would lie in a crib and sleep! But as the children grew, she did have a playmate; Joy and David got along famously!

With the passing of the years and the onslaught of "legal" abortions after the Supreme Court decision in <u>Roe v. Wade</u> in 1973, Mrs. Evans became more and more grateful to the birth mothers of her children. Those feelings of gratitude eventually led her to write the following words:

Thank You for Not Killing My Children!

I PREFER the name "birth mother" in referring to the mother of my adopted children (as opposed to "real mother" or "natural mother"). I feel pretty natural, and I feel as if I'm the real mother. I walked real floors at night when my children were sick, I worked to help pay real bills, and I felt real pain today as I awoke crying, missing my real children. (Joy is in Papua New Guinea, and David is in Germany.)

But there is no way I am the birth mother. I have no earthly idea what you went through to give birth to the baby who is now my child. I have something very important to say to you—"Thank you for not killing my children!" It must have occurred to you that there were places you could have gone to have that tiny fetus killed. Society was saying it was all right to do so.

To Joy's Birth Mother

Judy, in your case I now know you were frantic at the news of a new baby on the way. You were only 20 years old; you already had one toddler and one infant; your husband had begun drinking heavily and was, for all practical purposes, non-existent. You had no marketable skills nor a high school diploma. You panicked and ran. Thank you, thank you, thank you for not running to an abortion place even when you were so nervous and distraught. You, at that point, were so torn by conflicting pieces of advice, but you didn't have an abortion!

Judy, I don't know if we'll ever find your address again since you've moved once more. I don't know if you'll ever write to the Tennessee

Joy Evans

Marlene Evans
A Biography

Department of Human Services to see if there is anything in your file; therefore, I don't know if you'll ever see this letter. If you don't, I'm praying that God will let you know that I love you for not killing your Debbie Springfield—my Joy Evans Ryder. I pray for the peace of God for you—almost daily.

I prayed for you way before you and Joy had the few good phone calls you were able to have after she found out where you were before she left for New Guinea in January, 1987. I prayed for you at Joy's special occasions—her birthdays, salvation time, baptism, graduation, wedding, and so many more times. Of course, I thought of you as I stood by Joy's bedside when her baby was born.

How can I help but love you for giving me the opportunity to mother Joy?

To David's Birth Mother

I know almost nothing about you. We've tried to reflect our children's wishes in wanting to initiate a search for their birth parents. David has never expressed a desire to us to proceed in doing so. If he does, of course, we'll help him all we can. As of now, he's a year or so from the age that Tennessee has set for the opening of adoption records.

David Evans

I wonder…if you know Jesus as your personal Saviour…if you are well…if you are alive…if you think of a baby born April 1, 1965…if you were married…if you are married now…if you are divorced…if you were a young person on drugs as so many began to be in the '60s…if your baby was taken from you with your hardly knowing what was happening…and on and on.

I love you whether you're living a miserable life or a very settled and possibly even great life. I have no preconceived notions about either of my children's birth relatives. I told Joy to be prepared for a shack or a mansion when we went to meet her relatives. Of course, I'm speaking somewhat figuratively, but it might be as difficult to find a governor as it would be to find a prisoner. No matter what your life—I love you. Love—real love—doesn't depend on what kind of life the object of that love is living, although it's difficult to love you with a personal love, not knowing anything about you. I love you for not killing David Lee Evans, my son.

Above: And baby makes three!
Dr. and Mrs. Evans with Joy
Below: Wendell, Marlene, and Joy on
a family outing

The Robbery

If you could see the tall, dark, and handsome boy who has fast become the man of responsibility and character he is, you'd be so happy you did not kill him.

Marlene loved her children dearly and never forgot the fact that God had specially chosen those two babies for her and Wendell to rear.

Wendell and Marlene had moved from the apartment on Bailey Avenue to a house they rented in East Lake, a nice residential area of Chattanooga. The owners of the house had made it very clear that they could live there until they had children, at which time they would be asked to leave. And so, shortly after their getting Joy, Dr. Roberson let them move into a vacant girls dorm since they did not have a place to live on such short notice. At the time, Tennessee Temple Village was being developed where they were building duplexes to be used as ladies' dormitories. When the duplexes were finished, Marlene was asked to be a girls' dormitory supervisor, and Dr. and Mrs. Evans moved into one of those duplexes at 1812 Bennett. Marlene supervised five of the duplexes and was responsible for 58 dormitory girls. When Mrs. Evans became a full-time staff member at Highland Park Baptist Church as the Sunday School Promotion Coordinator, a doorway was cut into the walls dividing the two sides, and they were given the entire duplex.

It was in this duplex that a dating couple was visiting Dr. and Mrs. Evans. The young man made some derogatory remarks about Dr. Bob Jones or Bob Jones University. Of course, Marlene was well aware of the fact that the entire course of her life had been altered when she'd first heard Dr. Bob Jones, Sr., and she realized the impact attending Bob Jones University had on her life. She was not about to tolerate any such negative talk and asked the young man and his date to leave!

One summer day in 1964, Wendell returned to their home in Chattanooga after being in Knoxville all week while Joy and Marlene were visiting her parents in Nebraska. Wendell thought it was weird that Marlene would have left the door unlocked and ajar when leaving on a long trip, but he accepted the fact that it could happen. He didn't think much about it until he noticed a string of hangers down the hall, through the kitchen, and out the back door. Then he saw a big gaping hole in the window where they had just placed a new air conditioner. He hurriedly surveyed the rest of the house and found all jewelry, along with jewelry boxes, guns, cameras, silver, radios, record player, clothes, and a veritable storehouse of other goodies gone!

In the days and years following this event, though they had felt violated, it amazed Wendell and Marlene that they seldom missed any of those things which had been stolen. They realized how meaningless things really are and how important it is to live one's life for that which is eternal. It was at that time Marlene wrote the following thoughts and asked God to help her break ties with things for the rest of her life: "I enjoy things but have nothing I would not willingly give in order to be used of God. I want to join Paul in saying, '*Not that I speak in respect of want…I am instructed both to be full and to be hungry, both to abound and to suffer need.*'" (Philippians 4:11a, 12b) One had to be with Wendell and Marlene only a few minutes to realize that they took this biblical principle to heart—they definitely lived in a way that showed they practiced an adage they often quoted, "People are more important than things."

Marlene with Joy and David

Teaching

In the fall of 1961 Marlene began teaching in the Mary Ann Brown Cerebral Palsy Center with orthopedically handicapped children. She had just nine students, but even that small number required the help of a full-time assistant, Miss Harlow. She loved this work and once said, "These affectionate, fun-loving children made the work most enjoyable." She taught these children for a year and a half, and wrote about some of the children she taught.

"Darlin' Debbie"

A LITTLE girl I called "Darlin' Debbie" would come dancing in with her whole body in uncontrollable motion, fling the top of her head toward me and say, "See my stitches; I fell again." She soon had to add a football helmet to her otherwise immaculate and very feminine ensembles.

The floor of our schoolroom was made of three-inch wide boards, and we worked and worked trying to help Debbie come straight to the

(l-r) Debbie Workman (Darlin' Debbie) and Roger Burgess (a butter-ball topped with white ringlets)

front of the room down one of the three-inch boards. I'd say, "Come straight down the board to me, Deb." When she grew in ability to walk straight toward me, we clapped and cheered, which excited her to the point that she'd lose her balance again. We'd all laugh and have a good time, but I'd think, "How hard it is to grow!"

A Butterball Topped with White Ringlets

Roger, that fat, little, blue-eyed butterball topped with white ringlets, spent a good part of the day asking about a second roll at lunch. Every child could have a second roll once the first roll was eaten. Roger's head and arms flew back and forth most of the time, and they really went into action when he was anxious about anything. Therefore, he'd bob his head and arms at me wildly asking, "Do I get a second roll? Do I get a second roll? Do I get a second roll?" just as fast as he could spit out the words. My calm, supposedly reassuring words, "Roger, eat the roll you have first; then you'll get another one," didn't seem to penetrate—not for very long, anyway. It was the same every day as well as I can remember.

Alice Fay

It was Christmastime and Miss Harlow and I ventured into town to buy gifts for our orthopedically handicapped kids. As we were browsing, we were approached by a clerk who asked about their needs and tried valiantly to make good suggestions. Until we noticed the horrified look on her face, we hadn't realized how callously hard our remarks were sounding. Alice Fay was a fact of life with which we lived. The conversation went something like this:

Clerk:	"How 'bout getting all the girls some of these little house slippers with animals on them?"
Teachers:	"Oh, yes, they are cute. Let's get those! Oh, no, Alice Fay doesn't have any feet."
Clerk:	"What about buying little rings with the appropriate birth stone for each girl?"

Teachers: "Oh, yes, they are cute. Let's get those! Oh, no, Alice Fay doesn't have hands."

On the conversation went as the clerk suggested barrettes (Alice Fay had no hair!), singing toothbrushes (Alice Fay had no teeth), and more. A look of disbelief and then pity crossed the face of the clerk.

We had almost forgotten the tragedy of Alice Fay. As teachers, we had to block a few problems as we laughed with Alice Fay about how she was going to get her nubs down into the paste jar…helped her decide that she could wear a tight gold bracelet on her arm for a wedding band someday…and scolded her for beating all the other kids as she learned to walk the monkey bars with her arms. Alice Fay also had to be regularly reprimanded for trying to "hold hands" with a boy in the class!

Janie

In my class there was a little seven-year-old girl with cerebral palsy. Since she had come from a pre-school where the children had called the teachers by their last names, she called me "Ebans," not being able to pronounce the "v" in Evans.

She'd call, "Ebans," and I would say, "Mrs. Evans, Janie." This went on all year, but I might as well have "joined 'em" because I could not "lick 'em." She often forgot her words when I had her read, and she'd say, "It not matter, Ebans." That phrase became a regular part of my talking to myself.

Perhaps Janie shouldn't have taken that attitude about reading. However, maybe she knew, "It not matter, Ebans," because she died a year later….even now when I get all harried I say, "It not matter, Ebans." And it usually doesn't!

These children left an indelible impression on Marlene and were another piece to the puzzle God was using to form the attitudes and philosophies of a lady who was to influence hundreds and thousands in years to come.

After Joy and David were both in school, Marlene went back to teaching. One of the schools where she taught was Orchard Knob

Elementary, an all black school with about 1,500 students. Marlene taught the lowest achieving group of six first-grade classes.

In 1954 the Supreme Court had ruled in <u>Oliver Brown et al. v. Board of Education</u> that segregated schools are "inherently unequal" and ordered the desegregation of public schools. No one stirred for some time, but in the early 1960s the civil rights issue was forced, and race riots began occurring throughout the South. Four white teachers had been brought in to teach at Orchard Knob as part of the desegregation process. Marlene was one of the four, as well as Barbara Foster, whose husband taught and coached at Tennessee Temple. There was also one family of white children in the school.

While Wendell and Marlene were in Chattanooga, there were only two racial rampages that were of such nature that curfews were declared and the President mobilized National Guard troops to quell the riots. These occurred while she was teaching at Orchard Knob. It seemed strange to look out the schoolroom window to see convoys of National Guardsmen with guns and bayonets trained toward the school while helicopters constantly hovered in the sky above. Mrs. Evans' heart broke for the little children who came to school shaking after watching their neighborhood store, located just two blocks from the school, burn to the ground.

This was a tense time for everyone in Chattanooga. A 5:00 p.m. curfew was instituted and was strictly enforced. Tennessee Temple even had to change their graduation—originally scheduled for the evening—to the afternoon. There was a lot happening, and as usual, Mrs. Evans did not want to miss a thing. She was on the phone with her friend Annie Ruth when the National Guard arrived in Chattanooga. Annie Ruth's dad was listening to the radio and was giving a blow-by-blow description of the news report (Marlene Evans *loved* "blow-by-blow" reports.) which Annie Ruth passed on to her! Annie Ruth's nephew Ray, whom she reared, had gone outside to watch the helicopters. However, he was out after the 5:00 p.m. curfew, and when the police talked to him, he took off running. He was just sure they were going to take him to jail, so his feet barely hit the ground as he ran toward home!

God seemed to sweetly keep His hand of protection on Marlene in a special way during this traumatic time. She had a black teacher's aide

Carolyn Cothran

named Carolyn Cothran who was also a good friend and a very sweet Christian lady. Marlene drove Carolyn to her home in the housing projects after school each day. One day a dear lady friend who lived in her all-black project called Carolyn and said, "Don't let the white lady bring you home. They're waitin' for her." Another time that showed God's protection was the day an immediate evacuation was called. The black principal appeared at Marlene's classroom and made immediate plans to get her out safely. He and several of his men teachers were so kind and attentive. During these incidents, Marlene said she felt she had experienced a little of the feeling of having a table prepared in the presence of her enemies. It was definitely God's hand of protection, but it was also His blessing as she always treated black people with such dignity and respect. They knew she loved them, and they consequently watched out for her during this dangerous time in Chattanooga.

It was a well-known fact that Marlene Evans hated bigotry in any form. While others got great delight in racial slurs, fat jokes, and so forth, Mrs. Evans never found humor in any type of prejudice. Her work at Orchard Knob School definitely was part of the equation that helped define her attitudes of intolerance toward bigotry.

During their years at Highland Park Baptist Church, Marlene had some experiences with a few of its wealthy members, experiences that God used to test and to influence her. During her high school days, she had never felt "in" with the more popular students, so when some of the wealthier women of Highland Park Baptist Church began paying special attention to her and inviting her to their social events, she was quite honored. Though she still didn't feel she really fit in, as these were women who had money to buy things Marlene could not afford, eat at restaurants that were out of her price range, and do things socially that did not seem to fit her lifestyle, she got a certain "high" from the attention and acceptance these ladies provided. However, this life in the "fast track" was clouded by the fact that she had to shake off feelings of uneasiness that came from some of the ladies' remarks and actions.

When Marlene had enrolled at Bob Jones University, she almost immediately got a burden to win souls to Christ. She soon began to real-

Lessons from the Wealthy

ize that soul winning is the most important work in the world, and it is THE big reason God leaves Christians on this earth once they have trusted Christ as Saviour. Marlene had learned from her great leaders such as Dr. Bob Jones, Sr., and Dr. Lee Roberson the philosophy that every Christian ought to be a soul winner, so she was somewhat taken aback during an incident so big it became frozen in time.

One Sunday morning in the Business Women's Sunday School Class a beautiful, well-dressed lady was standing before Marlene as she was answering Marlene's question, "Will you be at visitation Thursday night?" This lady had been going visiting regularly, so Marlene was not prepared for the answer she gave. "We're working so hard now. We are paying for a church bus to operate, and we are not going out anymore."

Marlene later conveyed,

I WAS so bumfoozled that I was shocked into silence—a big deal for me! Since unsaved people were visited during the visitation program...I realized she was really saying, "We're paying for our soul winning to be done." In fact, she had said enough to make that very plain. She was already a rich woman and could buy most anything she wanted to buy. Of course, it was right and good that she and her family were paying to operate a bus, but she nor you nor I can pay money to get our personal soul winning done. My thinking is not important. It is a command of God for every Christian to go. "...Go ye into all the world, and preach the gospel to every creature." (Mark 16:15)

A few weeks later a second incident caused Marlene to reconsider her new friendships. Shortly after she had arrived at the home of one of these wealthy ladies for a social get-together, the hostess opened her cupboard door, and Marlene was astonished to see the shelves lined with bottles of liquor. She was even more dismayed when her host made an off-handed remark belittling Dr. Roberson and some of his convictions. She ached inside realizing that she was with the wrong group of people, and she knew she had a choice to make. She agonized over the decision and, after making a break with this group of ladies, looked back over the events that had caused her to get into this situation.

She realized that these ladies, most of them members of her Sunday school class, had asked her to join them because they wanted her fun. She saw that people who are living a double standard can't really make their own fun because they are living two lives. They were not happy people, and so they had invited her to provide fun for them. She also realized that those women would probably soon break their ties with Highland Park Baptist Church and the biblical standards of separation that identified them. She was right; those ladies and their husbands did leave the church. Marlene never gloated over the fact that she had been correct in her assessment; she was sad for the women. But she had learned some really important lessons. This was a pivotal experience for her as it was really the first time she'd had to pull away from wrong friends in such a marked way. God knew that Marlene needed that experience to be prepared to work with college girls in just a few years. It qualified her to help girls be able to choose right friends and also to separate from wrong friends.

These incidents did not cause Mrs. Evans to automatically "write off" wealthy people. She had friends of all ages, social classes, and abilities. It was not the wealth that caused her to separate; it was the attitudes and lifestyles these ladies had chosen as a result of their wealth. In fact, she was greatly influenced in a positive way by another wealthy member of the church.

Mr. McGilvray was the director of what was considered the world's largest Baptist Training Union—the 6:00 p.m. Sunday night meeting at Highland Park Baptist Church. During the summer when Marlene was not teaching, she worked in his family restaurant—The Texan—during the noontime rush. Many times she watched him feed "bums" at the side door as he took time from hosting people such as the mayor of Chattanooga at the front door. He treated both groups of people the same way—friendly and helpful. When someone once pointed out that the man to whom Mr. McGilvray was taking free food was drunk, he replied, "He's still got to eat."

Mr. Joe McGilvray

Often when Marlene would look up from her place on the first floor of the church to the balcony where the McGilvrays sat, she would see one of those "drunks" in church with him. Though Mr. McGilvray was a colorful character, there was no fanfare or hullabaloo connected with his bringing a "drunk" to church. He was a humble man who cared for every person in every level of society.

From *The Evangelist of the Highland Park Baptist Church, December 12, 1962*

*Marlene Evans
A Biography*

Dr. Evans was asked to be a part-time member of the Highland Park Baptist Church staff and run the Sunday evening training union. Mr. McGilvray was responsible for the adult training union, and Dr. and Mrs. Evans built the departments. Marlene was in charge of the beginners and primaries which included five departments (ages 4 through 8), and Wendell supervised the junior and intermediate departments (ages 9 through 16). Marlene's departments grew from 35 to over 200. Dr. Evans' departments tripled in size under his supervision.

Marlene began experiencing pain in her neck and thought it was just a "crick" in her neck, a minor nuisance that would last a week or so and be gone. However, the "week or so" came and went, and Marlene's pain and symptoms only increased. The pain began to settle in her arm which would tingle with numbness. She was working at Avondale School in Chattanooga at the time; and rather than "running after" children, she wanted to just sit and hold her arm. Actually, she would have preferred taking to her bed indefinitely!

Finally she went to the doctor and was diagnosed with degenerative disc disease. Surgery was scheduled for December 22, 1970. She would be spending eight days in Erlanger Hospital which would, of course, include Christmas.

Plans were made for Joy and David to spend six days in Hendersonville, North Carolina, with Paul and Nancy Perry. It was such a help to Wendell and Marlene to know the children were being cared for so beautifully by such dear friends. As always, Paul and Nancy thought of so many details, even down to washing the children's dirty clothes before their returning home and helping them to unpack once they got home. All of this care over her children gave Marlene such peace and helped her to be able to relax through the surgery and days following.

The surgeon explained to Marlene that a piece of bone would be removed from her hip. An incision would be made in the front of her neck, her vocal chords would be pushed aside, the disc would be removed, and that piece of hip bone would be placed in her neck to fuse the verte-brae together.

This was her first experience with sickness or surgery and the first time she would be hospitalized. Marlene was quite surprised at her reaction. She knew that the real Marlene Evans would have been very reactionary, fearful, and could quite easily have worked herself into a frenzy. However, she did not. The morning of her surgery she called her parents in Nebraska to let them know what was happening. She felt amazingly calm. The surgery was a marvelous success, and from the minute she awoke, Marlene felt better than she had in several years. The pain was gone.

Later reflecting on the experience, she credited her calm and peace to her Sunday school teacher who was now Mrs. Holbrook. She had often said, "Girls, some of you haven't faced much. Your parents are still living. You haven't been sick. You've always had everything you needed and a lot of what you just wanted. If you live long enough, you'll face some sorrow, sickness, or trouble. It's all right. Just get ready for it; there's nothing for a Christian to fear but the Lord. If you're twice born (John 3:3), you'll die only once. Nothing can touch you except it be allowed by the will of God—for your good and His glory. Everything is in His hands—He knows what we need. He'll allow it for us in His time, purpose, plan, and pattern. God's timing is perfect. He sends the rain and the sun, the tears and the smiles. You get ready to honor the Lord in suffering. It will rub off on people. He honors us as we honor Him—yes, especially in time of heartache. Scriptural promises will just pop up at you like popcorn. Get in the Word now and be prepared for whatever He allows in your life. If you suffer well, don't touch the glory. It belongs to Him. You can rejoice in the hospital bed, at the funeral home in the death of a loved one, or in the poor house. Philippians 4:4—'*Rejoice in the Lord alway: and again I say, Rejoice.*'" Mrs. Holbrook's nine years of teaching, correction, and acceptance had taken hold and were beautifully displayed by Marlene's actions and attitudes during this difficult time.

Mrs. Eva Reed, Annie Ruth McGuire's mother, stayed with Marlene at the hospital. Mrs. Reed was a very colorful and earthy woman who had grown up in northern Alabama. She was prejudiced toward Wendell; and anytime he would walk into the room, she would stop the conversation, look at him, and say in her low Southern drawl, "Well, there's Wendell." Mrs. Reed wanted Dr. Evans to have a spotlessly clean house, especially during Marlene's recovery time, so she would take a cab and go to their

Above: After surgery, Mrs. Evans (r) with Annie Ruth McGuire and Ed Jorges
Below: (l-r) Miss Annie Ruth McGuire, Mrs. Eva Reed, and Marlene Evans

house to clean. As she started to get out of the cab one day, the driver turned around and asked if she was in a hurry. When she answered, "No," he said, "I'd like you to go riding with me." Mrs. Reed was so taken off guard and so incensed about his inappropriate proposal that she got flustered and closed the door on her big toe. Of course, it was an incident that they all laughed about for years to come as they recalled her telling the story. That toe never healed, so it was a reminder the rest of her life what had happened. Her eyes would get really big as she would say, "My toe was killing me, but I was not going to let him know about it. I knew if he were interested in me, he was in really bad shape!"

Marlene's recovery, though quite difficult, was a blessed time for her as she rejoiced in how God's grace had been so sufficient for her. She realized it was not nearly what some people suffer, nor what she might face in the future, but this was her first real trial such as this, and she was seeing that her teacher was right.

What a beautiful Christmas present it was to experience His sufficient grace during this trial. It made her realize that His grace is sufficient for *all* times. It caused her to fall in love with Jesus all over again. God showed her that she didn't have to trust in her own ability to be a true testimony of His grace. God would do it for her through her. She had a new understanding of II Corinthians 12:9, 10, *"And he said unto me, My grace is sufficient for thee: for my strength is made perfect in weakness. Most gladly therefore will I rather glory in my infirmities, that the power of Christ may rest upon me. Therefore I take pleasure in infirmities, in reproaches, in necessities, in persecutions, in distresses for Christ's sake: for when I am weak, then am I strong."*

In a thank-you letter to her Sunday school teacher, she demonstrated once again how she loved to make a "happening" out of the ordinary: "Didn't we have fun in the hospital as we sampled goodies you brought up and had parties over my tray....The lovely candy dish with all the goodies for me to share with visitors and the hospital staff was a very appreciated gift. Don't you think it made my room really homey?" The ladies of the class had brought items such as a quilt and a throw rug to decorate her room. Making a hospital room homey was an idea she incorporated in the future, not only when she was in the hospital, but when others were sick. She would often do thoughtful and unusual things, such as send a case of Coke to a patient's hospital room for them to share with the nursing staff.

Her goal was always to "make things happen" in the patient's room. It is evident that God had a real purpose in allowing this trial in her life.

One of the difficult limitations which resulted from her back surgery was that of being unable to ride on the bus route. In order for her to at least be able to see the children, the driver would drive the bus by their house on Sundays so she could come out, get on the bus, and greet the riders. Marlene used her recovery time to dictate letters to the many people who helped her and encouraged her through her surgery and the days following. She also wrote numbers of letters to people on the bus route. In one such letter she was writing to Mrs. Helen Inman who had been sick. After some encouraging words about Helen's sickness, she said:

> "PRAY that I will be able to be back on the bus very soon as I am really getting itchy to be on again. I hardly want to see the kids or get on the bus when it stops at the house because I just want to crawl in there and stay with them! I know this is not the thing to do for I could be hurt and not be back on [the bus] for months instead of just a few more weeks. Hope to see you Sunday."

It was characteristic of Mrs. Evans to take care of herself following a sickness, surgery, or injury. She never seemed to use these situations to shirk her responsibilities, but she did use caution and wisdom to take the time necessary to heal before returning to those responsibilities. When she reentered, she wanted to be able to stay with the responsibility rather than having to take time off again because she went back too early.

Marlene also showed in her letters following surgery her uncanny ability to make everyone feel important. To Mrs. Elinore Hawkins she wrote, "I like you! Of course, everybody does, but you have been so happy and cheerful and, therefore, an inspiration to many of us as we come to our own times of difficulty."

This was the first of two such back surgeries Marlene would undergo. These surgeries resulted in her being very limited in what she could do. Whereas she had always been a very physically active person, she was no longer able to cook, do housework, and perform other physically demanding activities. This proved to be a particularly trying time for her as she had two young children.

Mrs. Elinore Hawkins

Her second surgery was in the spring of 1972, shortly before the Evanses moved to Indiana. It was a beautiful spring day when Marlene got out of the hospital. Dr. Evans knew her love for nature and made her return home especially memorable by taking her on a ride to see all of the beautiful dogwoods that were in full bloom.

She tried to find ways to continue to make things happen for her children, especially during her recovery time. David's birthday, April 1, came shortly after Marlene's second surgery, and she called upon her husband's work scholarship secretary, Vicki Jackson, to take David and several of his friends to a local ice cream parlor. David and Vicki both remember this event to this day. Vicki was instructed to let David get whatever he wanted, and he chose a huge banana split. It was a big deal to David that he could choose anything he wanted, even though he didn't eat nearly all of it. The huge banana split was also memorable to Vicki—especially because he didn't eat all of it. At first she thought, "What a waste," but she came to realize it was important to both David and to his parents that his birthday be a memorable one and that the few cents they spent on something he didn't eat was far outweighed by the fact that they had provided a memory of a lifetime for David.

Marlene Evans was a need filler. She lived her life watching for the needs of others and finding a way to supply those needs. However, she was often not able to meet those needs herself. It was then that she used her ability to "rally the troops" and find a way to meet that need by getting others involved and even making them feel it was their idea. Preson Phillips taught at Tennessee Temple College, and his wife Barbara taught in the Tennessee Temple Elementary School. She had a problem with her sweat glands and was very sensitive to the heat. She would get extremely sick when high temperatures made the classrooms unbearably hot for her. This had gone on for years, but when Marlene heard about it, she found a way to raise the money and purchase an air conditioner for Mrs. Phillips' classroom. Her response to this need was typical and was repeated hundreds of times, not only in Chattanooga, but for the rest of her life.

Marlene and her good friend Annie Ruth McGuire were quite responsible for their widowed Sunday school teacher's getting remarried at the

The Wendell Evans family

Her Ministry to Others

| *Marlene Evans*
A Biography

age of 70. Mrs. Renaker went to Florida each winter where she had met Olin Holbrook. Every time she was in Florida, they would sit together in church and spend time together. He was in love with her and she loved him, but she just wasn't sure she wanted to get married. Finally Marlene and Annie Ruth got on the phone with Louise and Olin. Annie Ruth says, "We talked them into getting married, and we set the date. It was a big affair! We planned the wedding and had Mrs. T. G. Green do the reception. (Mrs. Green was known for the receptions she planned and organized. She was also the teacher of the largest women's Sunday school class at Highland Park, the Grace Bible Class. Mrs. Green was a good friend of Mrs. Evans and a delightful person, but she was also a perfectionist. She would carefully inspect details of the work she had delegated, and it was not uncommon for her to have Marlene and me do the place settings over again when they were not to her pleasing. She wanted every detail done properly and beautifully.) After the wedding Marlene came to my house; we collapsed on the bed and said, 'What have we done? Have we done the right thing?' Then we looked at each other and said, 'It's too late now! She's on her honeymoon!'" It was the right thing, and the Holbrooks had many wonderful years together!

Mr. and Mrs. Olin Holbrook

Marlene was masterful at getting people to do things they wouldn't normally do or weren't sure they even wanted to do. She never did this for her own benefit; it was always for the good of others. One of these incidents was that she talked Annie Ruth into giving blood. She had never done so before meeting Marlene and never did so again once Mrs. Evans moved to Indiana, but Annie Ruth was a faithful blood donor as long as Marlene was there to encourage her!

Dr. Roberson went overseas while Dr. and Mrs. Evans lived in Chattanooga. It was his first time out of the country, and Marlene got the wild idea to meet him at the airport. Once again, she made this a big event! She had the red carpet rolled out and about 2000 people there to greet him when he got off the plane. There were so many people there it almost closed down the airport. They all loved it, but he didn't. The expression on his face showed that he was not at all impressed—with the big crowd, with the students being out of the dorms after curfew, etc. Marlene had not yet learned to clear everything with Dr. Roberson like Dr. Faulkner did, but this took her a step closer in learning this lesson!

Above: Sam and Addie Mills
Below: Mr. and Mrs. Clarence Evans

After Marlene had become an Evans, she'd met a whole "raft" of Iowa people all at once at a family reunion. Feeling slightly overwhelmed, she looked around and discovered a nice-looking man who was sitting as quietly as she was. He and Marlene began to talk and became pretty good friends. She found out he was Uncle Sam Mills and that he was married to Aunt Addie, Dad Evans' only sister. Marlene was later told that he was good to his family and a fine provider, but he had never accepted Christ.

Wendell and Marlene received word that Sam and Addie were going to visit Wendell's parents who had moved from Iowa to South Carolina to manage Kampus Kourt, a well-kept mobile home park where many "BJ" married students lived. Then, all four were traveling to Chattanooga to spend a weekend with Wendell and Marlene.

They all knew that Aunt Addie had prayed for Uncle Sam to be saved for over 50 years, but for some reason, Wendell and Marlene had not thought through that the ideal opportunity for Uncle Sam to get saved might arise during this visit.

In spite of this, it seemed that God had orchestrated the entire weekend, including Uncle Sam's visit to Highland Park Baptist Church on Sunday. People who knew Uncle Sam would have thought he wouldn't want to visit the Business Women's Sunday School Class with Marlene, but Wendell was leading the college church, so Mom and Dad Evans, Uncle Sam, and Aunt Addie followed Marlene. She didn't even think to ask Clarence and Sam if they wanted to visit a men's class. Married couples often visited her class with a loved one, so it was no big deal to the ladies of the class to have Clarence and Sam there.

Marlene had scheduled one of her little boys with cerebral palsy from her class at school to visit her Sunday school class and recite a speech entitled, "The Farmer and the Lord." That was the particular Sunday Uncle Sam was there. Though the scheduling of the farmer speech for the particular Sunday Uncle Sam was visiting was, humanly speaking, an "accident," Uncle Sam was, indeed, a very successful farmer. Marlene had not planned for the two events to coincide, but the Lord used that little boy to touch hearts, especially Uncle Sam's it seemed.

The class teacher, Mrs. Renaker, walked up to him and very excitedly said, "Oh, is this dear Uncle Sam?" Marlene hadn't thought to tell her he was a very reserved person, but it seemed he didn't mind. However, Mrs. Renaker was not the only one who befriended him. It was as if all of Highland Park came up to meet this man who was a very private person, but he appeared to take it all in stride and even managed to act as if he liked it a little bit.

That night Uncle Sam went back to church. Wendell was in the church orchestra. Marlene was on the aisle side of Uncle Sam, and his wife and Wendell's parents were on the other side of him. She really hadn't planned that she'd sit by him; it just "happened."

Finally, during the Sunday night sermon by Dr. Roberson, it began to dawn on Marlene that she was sitting by a man who was her friend. He was on his way to Hell because he'd never asked Jesus to take his sin away and take him to Heaven when he died. Dr. Roberson very seldom said, "If there's someone without Jesus sitting by you, turn to him and say, 'I'll go with you,' " but during the invitation that night he did just that very thing. Marlene immediately turned to Uncle Sam. There were already tears in his eyes. (He wasn't a person to show emotion.) She said, "Let's go," and he asked, "Shouldn't I wait until I get home?" Marlene answered, "No, we don't know that you'll get home." That was all there was to it. He and Marlene started down the aisle. Wendell happened to look up and saw them coming. He hurried down out of the orchestra to kneel and pray in front of the seats Uncle Sam and Marlene were directed to on the front row. Dr. Faulkner sweetly and slowly led him to Jesus, and a prayer of 50 years was answered as 72-year-old Uncle Sam trusted Christ.

A church lady asked Clarence, Wilma, and Aunt Addie if they wanted to go forward to be with Sam and Marlene. They did, and she walked forward with them. All of this commotion had caught Dr. Roberson's attention, which caused him to inquire about what had happened. He was thrilled over Dr. Evans' uncle getting saved after 50 years of his wife's praying and announced it to the church. That night was a time of great rejoicing at the altar and throughout the entire church!

Uncle Sam went home to profess his faith at Aunt Addie's church, which immediately became his also. He became a church usher, started having family devotions with Aunt Addie, and continued living for Jesus until He went Home to be with the Lord at the age of 99!

Above: Marlene enjoys boating with Art and Emma Tompkins on the Mississippi River
Below: Marlene enjoys getting cool in the Mississippi River also!

| *Marlene Evans*
A Biography

Wendell and Marlene met scores of people in their ministry at Tennessee Temple College and Highland Park Baptist Church. Some of these people became friends of a lifetime. Two such people were Art and Emma Tompkins, both of whom are now with the Lord. The Tompkins' daughter and son-in-law, Joyce and David Stroud, were in the bus ministry with Wendell and Marlene. Joyce and David were college students who, upon graduation, started a church in their hometown area of Aledo, Illinois, where Art and Emma lived. Brother David asked Dr. Evans to come and preach for him, and so began a friendship with Art and Emma, Joyce's parents, that blessed their hearts for years.

Art, who had almost reared himself on the Mississippi River, called himself a "river rat." He was an extremely entertaining, colorful character with many interests and a man who took life's "bumps" well. Following an ear amputation caused by cancer, he was fitted with a prosthesis that looked very much like his real ear. Did he wear it? No, he left it in the refrigerator (he said it was "too much trouble!"). Years later when he was just two hours from going to be with Jesus, the church pianist went to visit him in the hospital. As she walked in, Art said, "Lucy, die young."

Lucy asked, "Why, Art?"

"So you'll make a pretty corpse!" That type of humor and timing was typical of Art Tompkins.

He had accepted Christ as his Saviour in late middle years when his son-in-law and daughter talked to him after they'd come home from Tennessee Temple. He had not lived his life for the Lord at all. After he was saved, he spent the rest of his life driving and walking up and down hills finding his "partying buddies" to tell them what had happened in his life and how they could be saved. Many a time while staying with Art and Emma in the log home on the Mississippi River, Marlene would see a friend or neighbor stop by, watch Emma cook up one of her famous meals for him, and then listen as they'd talk to the person about Christ.

When Wendell and Marlene first met Art and Emma, they had no idea that the Tompkins' home would become such a respite and getaway for Marlene when she needed a few days away from her busy schedule. She seemed to especially enjoy spending time being pampered and catered to in her hectic days after the launching of Christian Womanhood.

Dr. Jack Hyles spoke in chapel at Tennessee Temple College every year, and in 1967 Dr. Evans decided to ask if he could drive him to the airport. Dr. Evans had never lost his dream of helping to start a college and said to Brother Hyles, "If you ever start a college, I'd be interested in being a part of it."

Dr. Hyles' immediate response was, "I'll never start a college, but if I ever do, it would be a preachers' school." This statement put Dr. Evans off as he had the idea at the time that it would be possible to have a fully accredited junior college and keep it fundamental. He basically forgot about starting a college with Brother Hyles until his good friend, Dr. Bob Billings, was in Chattanooga recruiting teachers for the Hammond Baptist School system. He breezed through to see Dr. Evans, and as he was about to leave, he said, "Oh, by the way, we're starting a college."

"Oh, you are?" Dr. Evans responded.

When Dr. Billings stated, "I sure know who I'd like to have for the registrar," the offer did not really interest Dr. Evans. Dr. Evans then asked who would be filling the academic dean position, to which Dr. Billings answered, "I don't know, but I'd like to have you."

In the following days Dr. Evans could not get the new college off of his mind, and so he called Dr. Billings hoping to settle the issue. At the end of their phone conversation, Dr Billings said, "We won't contact you as that would be unethical, but if God won't let you forget this, call me."

God did not let him forget, and so he called Dr. Billings who arranged for Dr. Evans to fly to Indiana in January of 1972. He stayed in the guest apartment at First Baptist Church and met with Dr. Hyles on Saturday evening. A man had been lined up to be the executive vice president, but because he had resigned, they asked Dr. Evans to take this position. The college catalog was to be published in February; the administration needed to be able to include the name and a writeup about the executive vice president, so they needed an answer soon. On January 20, 1972, Dr. Evans called Dr. Billings and accepted the offer.

When any of his staff members left, it was customary that Dr. Roberson barely mentioned the departure from the pulpit. However, things were completely different when the Evanses left Chattanooga.

The Decision to Move to Hammond

A Tennessee Temple student who was a photographer for **The Chattanooga News Free-Press** *took a picture of Mrs. Evans, David, and Joy for the cover of the weekend magazine at Halloween time.*

There was a huge going-away party for them, and Dr. Roberson was very involved with this send off. It seemed he was almost mesmerized by this dedicated and loyal couple who had completely thrown themselves into the work at Highland Park. Dr. Evans talked with Dr. Faulkner about Dr. Roberson's attitude toward their leaving, and Dr. Faulkner responded, "Wendell, I'll tell you what the difference is between you and some other folks who have left. You've always been loyal. We've never known you to criticize the bus ministry, the chapel ministry, or anything else here at Highland Park Baptist Church." Dr. and Mrs. Evans were rare and precious gems as staff members, and Dr. Roberson seemed to have a unique love and appreciation for this couple. Years later during one of the times he was preaching at Hyles-Anderson College, Dr. Roberson sat in Dr. Evans office and said, "You did the right thing in leaving Temple and coming here."

A big tea was planned. Wendell and Marlene knew of the plans and knew the time they were to be there. Everything was ready and the guests began arriving, but there was no Wendell and Marlene. Annie Ruth and others who had planned the party were quite nervous until Dr. and Mrs. Evans arrived. The party was a bittersweet time for them. They were almost late because their good friend, Paul Perry, had died unexpectedly, and they had gone to the funeral. They were excited about their future, but they were grieving the loss of their friend. Marlene especially was grieving the losses she would be experiencing with the move.

Marlene loved Chattanooga. Every time she came through the East Ridge tunnel to the sight of Chattanooga, she felt as if she couldn't get enough of it. The Evanses taught Joy and David to say, "That's my city," when they came through the tunnel. The people on their Ringgold, Georgia, bus route would cheer and clap for Chattanooga and the Highland Park Baptist Church when they looked down on it from I-75 on their way to church. She also loved Dr. and Mrs. Roberson, Highland Park Baptist Church, her friends, the South, and her Sunday school teacher. Though she was from Nebraska, Marlene had had a love affair with the South since she first studied it in her fourth and fifth grade history books. She had lived in the South (South Carolina, North Carolina, and Tennessee) 21 years—more than half of her life. It suited her well. She suited the people there. Southerners would tell her about their friend's son marrying a Yankee and say to her, "You know, they're different from us," or in the midst of cooking green beans, turn to her and say, "My uncle married a woman from the North who just throws in some salt, pepper, and butter with green beans, heats them up, and acts like she's cooked for her family." They never seemed to realize that Marlene was, in actuality, a Northerner herself!

Nonetheless, she supported her husband's decision to help start Hyles-Anderson College. She kept her doubts and questions to herself and never tried to talk him out of his decision. A few years after they moved to Indiana, she admitted to him that she really had questioned the move, especially as she watched him work for his friend Bob Billings. It was difficult for her to see Dr. Evans go from working directly for Dr. Roberson and Dr. Faulkner to working for his friend from the trailer park in Greenville. But she didn't say a word and soon realized how directly God's hand was in the decision.

The move to Hammond would prove to be a most traumatic change that would include giving up much of what she held dear, but it was a move that would thrust both Wendell and Marlene to the forefront of Christian education and fundamental Christianity.

Above: Mrs. Evans honored by Chattanooga friends
Left: The staff and faculty of Ridgedale School, one of the schools where Marlene taught in Chattanooga (Arrow points to Mrs. Evans)

Pictures on page 128:
Above: David and Joy
Below: Dr. and Mrs. Evans

Faculty Ridgedale School
Mrs. Horacek Principal - 1962

Photo by Harry Evans

Above: Mrs. Evans with the faculty of Avondale School
Right: Joy and David stand beside a snowman built
by Tennessee Temple students outside of the dining hall

Pictures on page 131:
Center: promo picture of Mrs. Evans in the '90s
Top right: a picture of Mrs. Evans in the '70s
Lower right: Mrs. Evans teaching

| *Marlene Evans*
A Biography

Part Seven

Hammond

Adjusting to New Surroundings

*D*r. Evans had already made the decision to move to Hammond when Marlene was invited to speak for the annual mother-daughter banquet at First Baptist Church in May of 1972. She stayed for the entire weekend and attended services at First Baptist Church for the first time on Sunday. Mrs. Cindy Schaap, who is now the senior editor of *Christian Womanhood,* attended that banquet and has the following memories of Marlene Evans:

"When I was approximately 13 years of age, a tan, blonde-haired lady about 40 years of age was invited to be the mother-daughter banquet speaker at First Baptist Church of Hammond. I remember being very impressed by her beauty, by her down-to-earth speaking style, by her vivacious personality, and most of all, by her 'way' with teenagers. When Marlene Evans talked to me, I did not feel like she got down on my level; I felt like she brought me up to hers."

Mrs. Evans made an impact on the ladies—both young and old. This was the start of a very wonderful relationship between Mrs. Evans and the ladies of First Baptist Church of Hammond, beginning with the Preacher's wife, Mrs. Beverly Hyles. Mrs. Evans once said of her pastor's wife, "Mrs. Jack Hyles is so beautiful, so glamorous, so ladylike, and has such talent, I cannot believe that she can be so warm and tender toward me that I am not intimidated around her." Mrs. Evans and Mrs. Hyles did have a very warm and loving relationship for the entire 29 years she was a member of First Baptist Church.

Dr. and Mrs. Evans joined First Baptist Church on June 2, 1972. Mrs. Evans loved the practical teaching and preaching she got each service. She was "in tune" with Brother Hyles' preaching right off the bat. It seemed that he picked up where Mrs. Holbrook had left off when it came to helping Mrs. Evans with her talk and with her human relationships. Mrs. Evans described herself as having been a very bossy, very opinionated woman, especially until she met Mrs. Holbrook. The preaching she heard from Brother Hyles on Sunday mornings and Sunday evenings and the teaching she received from the Wednesday evening Bible studies took

The Mrs. Evans Cindy Hyles Schaap first remembers!

| *Marlene Evans*
A Biography

her to a new level in her attitudes, in her talk, and in her relationships.

One of the key principles she learned from her Preacher was to not generate unnecessary controversies. She began to realize that arguing over beliefs and philosophies does nothing to strengthen relationships, and seldom, if ever, does it win someone to a person's way of thinking. This did not mean she was not true to what she believed. She never moved when it came to her standards and convictions. She just learned that she could be kind to those friends, loved ones, co-workers, and any-one else with whom she disagreed without losing her Christian testimony and without compromising what she believed.

The Evanses had driven to Indiana in their 1965 four-door Lincoln which had "suicide" doors—where all four doors open from the center of the car. The five passengers included Dr. and Mrs. Evans, Joy, David…and Joy's cat named Kitty. Dr. Evans had decided they would not bring the cat to Indiana, but Mrs. Evans said to him, "We can't take a little girl's cat from her!" Kitty moved with them.

The children had very Southern accents, and shortly after arriving in Indiana, they went to breakfast at Sauzer's Restaurant at the corner of U.S. Route 41 and U.S. Route 30 in Schererville. When the waitress asked what they wanted to eat, David said, "Haaam, biskits'n, graaavy." She had much difficulty understanding him; he finally got his ham, but he never did get his biscuits and gravy!

Their first place of residence in Indiana was the Holiday Inn on Cline Avenue in Highland. The college was in the process of buying a large frame house in Schererville right by Baptist City (the campus of Hyles-Anderson College) where the Evanses were to live until they found the house they wanted to purchase. However, there was a mixup in the paper-work, so they were unable to move into that house. They lived in five dif-ferent places before purchasing their home at 38 Risch Drive in Schererville, which they moved into the first of December.

From the Holiday Inn, they moved into the First Baptist Youth Center, located just a few blocks east of the church on Sibley Street in Hammond. This was a colorful atmosphere, to say the least. Dr. Evans says, "I was excited about the new school opening while Marlene was looking at railroad tracks and listening to loud music from the bar across the street!" They also lived in several staff members' homes while those

"I love you and want you to know as I think of you, a smile comes to my soul. So many need your infectious laughter and your wisdom."

Beverly Hyles

Dr. and Mrs. Jack Hyles

families went on vacation. During this time, Brother Norm Floyd, a maintenance man at Hyles-Anderson College, kept Kitty for several months until just two days before school started when they were able to move into the frame house as originally planned.

Dr. Hyles was quite concerned about Mrs. Evans during this time and kept asking Dr. Evans how she was doing. He was amazed at the attitude she maintained while having no permanent residence and having to live without most of their belongings. Her attitude during this transition was characteristic of a "different" woman. Though she was struggling on the inside with the move and the homesickness it caused, she worked to keep her attitude and thinking right and kept her mouth shut about anything she didn't like. Mrs. Holbrook's teaching held her in good stead during this transition.

The Evanses' belongings were moved from Chattanooga to Indiana by Mayflower movers who unloaded the truck on August 20, just two days before the college was to open. While still in Chattanooga, Dr. and Mrs. Evans had asked the driver and his assistant to plan to stay with them in their new Indiana home over the weekend in order to go to church. He replied, "If we don't get drunk"; to which they countered, "Please don't this weekend." They didn't! Those two guys, about 25 years of age, stayed with Dr. and Mrs. Evans, slapped up bed frames, made sandwiches, and even took baths in cold water as some of the utilities had not yet been turned on. Because it was the only soap they could find, the Evanses offered their guests an Avon blue cow made to hang from the neck of a child! The movers also went to church on Sunday morning and found numbers of things wrong with the service but stayed for the Sunday night service and talked with Dr. Evans about salvation into the wee hours of the morning. However, they pulled out Monday morning unsaved.

John, one of the drivers, kept returning every time he made a run to Indianapolis, the Mayflower headquarters. Usually, he would stay only two or three hours, but each time Dr. and Mrs. Evans would deal with him about his soul. Finally, Dr. Evans asked him why he kept returning when he knew what he'd get. He replied, "I feel like you love me."

About the fourth time he rolled up, Marlene thought, "The neighbors are going to think we're schizophrenic…can't make up our minds whether we're staying or leaving!" That visit turned out to be the time John went to church and then "hit the altar running," after which he spent a fun Sunday afternoon questioning Dr. Evans about his new-found life in Christ.

There was another fun part. Dr. Evans got to drive the Mayflower truck! He had always wanted to drive a semi-truck, and that Sunday afternoon he got his chance. He, with John in the co-captain's seat, drove through the Baptist City campus of Hyles-Anderson College. There was no audience as no one, literally no one, had returned from his bus route yet. How disappointing! Nevertheless, God had given them some extra fun through a wonderful soul-winning experience that weekend.

Immediately after arriving in Indiana, Dr. Evans became completely immersed in his work. There was much to be done before the opening of the college on August 22, and so he asked Marlene to go house hunting while he worked. When she told the real estate agent that they wanted trees on their property, the lady responded, "Oh, yes, we have what you're wanting, right over in Sherwood Forest!" When Mrs. Evans went to the house, she thought the trees must be in back for they surely weren't in the front. When she got to the back, she still saw nothing. When she asked, "Where are the trees?" the agent said, "Oh, right there!" Mrs. Evans' recollection was, "Honestly, they were almost a figment of the imagination. They were twigs. One of them had to be tied up to stand alone. There wasn't even one apiece for the four of us in the family!"

To a woman who was already nearly as homesick as she'd been when she went to Bob Jones University, these were difficult days. She missed the warmth and friendliness of the people in the South and would burst into tears anytime a stranger spoke to her or befriended her! She also loved trees (and the woods) and couldn't imagine living in a house where there were no trees in the yard.

When Dr. Evans' parents came to visit in the early fall, Marlene and Dad Evans went house hunting together. They looked at quite a few houses, but when they found a house in downtown Schererville (just a few blocks from where the college was located at that time), she was "sold." She later admitted that she did not have an interest in the house for the sake of the house. She wanted the house because of all the trees in the yard. She loved God's creation and wanted to be nestled right in the very center of it, trees and all! Dr. Evans says, "Marlene loved the trees around

Mrs. Evans always found respite in nature, especially the trees in "her" Smoky Mountains of Tennessee.

38 Risch, Schererville

the house; and I loved the pillars on the house, but I came to love the trees as much as she did!"

Those first days in Indiana were really quite difficult for her as she was trying to adjust to living in the North, but she later admonished, "Wherever God wants you is the most beautiful place in all the world. Don't ever forget it! The Devil will use your feelings to cheat you out of God's perfect will for your life if you give him half a chance."

The children were enrolled in Hammond Baptist Grade School for the fall semester, David in second grade and Joy in fifth grade. Mrs. Evans was asked to teach several courses at Hyles-Anderson College, and she was happy to oblige since teaching was her passion. She taught classes such as speech, educational classes, and psychology. After the school year was in full swing, the administration asked Mrs. Evans to also be the dean of women, and she accepted. Specialized ladies' classes were later added to the curriculum, and Mrs. Evans was asked to teach these classes which included Christian Womanhood and Women Used of God.

Her Influence Began Immediately

Almost immediately, Mrs. Evans began influencing lives dramatically. Shortly after the college opened, Mrs. Evans met a very lovely young lady in her twenties who was blemished on her face with a big, reddish-purple birthmark which was almost impossible to ignore. One had to really concentrate on her eyes to not be pulled straight to the bright red part of her face. When she walked down the street, people who would have not liked to look at this part of her face couldn't help but be drawn to the blemished area for that first look. She had experienced people's stares all of her life, of course. When Mrs. Evans asked, "Has anyone ever tried to do anything about your birthmark?" she looked at her and said, "No, in fact, no one else has ever brought it up to me." (She did not seem at all pleased with Mrs. Evans' question!)

Mrs. Evans plunged ahead hoping to rescue the relationship by showing her that she could really come through with some help for her. The Debbie Fox Foundation for birth defects and disfigurements had just been started in Chattanooga. Debbie Fox was a girl who was born without a face in Soddy Daisy, Tennessee, right outside of Chattanooga, and her story had been written up in *Reader's Digest* and *Good Housekeeping*. After

*Marlene Evans
A Biography*

numbers of operations, Debbie became quite a presentable young lady and no longer hid in her home. Mrs. Evans figured that if a girl with no face could get help, certainly a girl who had a pretty face with just a birthmark could get help.

The young lady finally did agree to go to a dermatologist with Mrs. Evans. After an exam by the doctor, they returned to the car. Not much was said all the way home. The doctor had told her, "If we did a skin graft or anything to cover the mark on your face, you'd be in worse shape than you are now. At least the skin you have there is good. There is not a thing we can do for you surgically, but there is a makeup you can get at Marshall Field's in downtown Chicago."

Mrs. Evans didn't have the nerve that day to say they'd go look at the makeup. In fact, when she looked at that bright, red birthmark she thought, "Yeah, makeup…what makeup could cover anything like that?"

After mustering up her nerve again, Mrs. Evans asked the young college student to go to Chicago with her to at least look into this wonderful makeup about which the doctor had told her. As they walked down State Street in Chicago, everyone looked at the unsightly birthmark.

The lady at the cosmetic counter referred them to the very woman whose picture was displayed there. Mrs. Evans could not believe that the saleslady who came up to help them was horribly marked. She would not have believed it if she hadn't seen the picture. This lady took them up four floors to a back storage room and began making up the young student. Mrs. Evans had all she could do to keep from jumping up and down and having a fit as the ugly birthmark disappeared before her eyes! She didn't even want to show that she was happy in case the young lady wasn't as happy as she was when she looked into the mirror. Mrs. Evans shouldn't have been worried!

When the sales lady got through making her up and showed her to a mirror, she immediately revealed her feelings of euphoria over the seeming miracle. As they walked out of Marshall Field's onto State Street, no one looked at them. It was probably the first time in that young lady's life that people did not take note as she walked by them.

This young lady was just one of numbers of people Mrs. Evans helped. She was sensitive to the needs of others and just *never* wanted others to suffer public embarrassment, humiliation, or teasing needlessly. She felt that people had enough to fight and enough struggles in life without allowing needless struggles to continue. In years to come, Mrs. Evans would help people get braces to straighten crooked teeth, have unsightly moles removed from their faces, replace thick, "bottle" glasses with contact lenses, and much more. She truly cared about people and showed it by her actions.

Speaking Opportunities

Dr. and Mrs. Evans began receiving invitations to speak. In those days they often spoke together and took the children with them as they conducted family conferences in local churches. Occasionally Mrs. Evans would receive invitations to speak at mother-daughter banquets. She received one such invitation from Barb Zarris whose husband George was a pastor in Aurora, Illinois. George and Barb were Tennessee Temple graduates and knew Dr. and Mrs. Evans from their days in Chattanooga.

Though she oftentimes had difficulty with directions, Mrs. Evans decided to take Joy with her and drive to the banquet. They had been driving for nearly an hour when Joy said, "Mom, are we going the right way? There's Soldier Field." Dr. Evans had taken the family to Chicago and down Lake Shore Drive numbers of times, and Joy recognized the Bears' football stadium. They were *not* supposed to be in downtown Chicago. Frustrated and lost, Mrs. Evans pulled over, flagged down a policeman, and exclaimed, "Sir, if you get me out of this city, I promise I'll never drive downtown Chicago again!" He did and she didn't! He had Mrs. Evans follow him to the expressway that would get her to Aurora, and she kept her word—she *never* drove in downtown Chicago again!

There was no "Student Recruitment" department at the college in those early days, but Dr. and Mrs. Evans recruited numbers of students for Hyles-Anderson College while out speaking on the weekends. One of these students was a 22-year-old registered nurse named Carol Frye. Dr. Evans was preaching for Pastor Louis Maple at East Maine Baptist Church in Glenview, Illinois. Carol was one of the church greeters and welcomed Dr. and Mrs. Evans when they arrived. Dr. Evans spoke that morning on, "What Sin Are You a Slave To?" Carol sat listening and thought, "I'm a slave to the medical world." After the service, she went to talk with Mrs. Evans. Carol was a charge nurse at Lutheran General Hospital in

DesPlaines, Illinois, and had contemplated going to medical school. She had even taken a few pre-med classes at Loyola University. Carol was at a crossroads in her life and admitted that to Mrs. Evans. As they talked, Mrs. Evans said, "Have you ever thought of Bible college?" Then she said, "Carol, why don't you come out to visit the college tomorrow?" At this same time there was a group of people talking to Dr. Evans. They were also interested in Hyles-Anderson, and Mrs. Evans immediately suggested that they all visit the college the next day.

When the group arrived on Monday morning, the college vice president, Dr. Max Helton, directed them to a classroom down the hall and said, "Mrs. Evans is teaching General Psychology. You can go there right now." Carol walked in, and the very first truth she heard Mrs. Evans teach was from Philippians 4:4. Carol heard her say, "You don't have to rejoice in divorce; you don't have to rejoice in sorrow; you don't have to rejoice in trouble; you are just supposed to rejoice *through* these things."

Carol loved what she heard that day, as did one of the couples who had visited the college with her, Dennis and Julie Hudson. Hyles-Anderson was just a few days into its second year of operation; the fall semester had just begun, and the option of late registration was still open. At the end of that day, both Carol and the Hudsons were students at Hyles-Anderson College. Carol signed up for all of the classes Mrs. Evans was teaching that semester.

Mrs. Evans had no idea that Sunday afternoon in 1973 that Carol would one day work for her as the assistant dean of women and also help her lead the college activities department. Neither did she know that in less than ten years Carol, who temporarily laid aside her nursing profession to work at the college, would be nursing Mrs. Evans through cancer and chemotherapy. Mrs. Evans had the burden to influence lives and help young people reach their potential. She simply wanted Carol's life to count for eternity.

These were busy days for Mrs. Evans, but God gave her a wonderful team of workers. Vicki Mitchell, the Tennessee Temple graduate who had been Dr. Evans' work scholarship secretary, was Mrs. Evans' assistant teacher. Melvin Meister was a married student at the college who wanted his wife to be around Mrs. Evans and to be involved at the college. Linda Meister began volunteering for Mrs. Evans and became her first secretary.

Promo pictures of four of Mrs. Evans' first team members: Carol (Frye) Tudor, Vicki Mitchell, JoEllen Lee, and Linda Meister (clockwise)

The Starting of Christian Womanhood

JoEllen Lee, a member of First Baptist Church, also volunteered to help Mrs. Evans. Then God added one more person to this list of helpers. Soon after Carol Frye enrolled at Hyles-Anderson College, she began volunteering her free time to help Mrs. Evans, doing whatever Mrs. Evans needed her to do. The college had no official activities department at the time, but Dr. Helton and Mrs. Evans saw the need for exciting activities and, therefore, planned many activities for the students. Carol was a special help to Mrs. Evans in this particular area as she helped get things set up for activities and then was responsible for cleanup after the activities.

The college grew quickly. Beginning with 301 students the first semester, it grew to 501 the second year and to 700 the third year. It continued to grow as pastors realized they could send their students to a Bible college where they would come home more loyal to those who had invested in them and were responsible for getting them to college, more energized about serving the Lord than when they left home, and with a greater knowledge and zeal to win souls to Christ as they came home and immediately got involved in soul winning and the bus ministry. As had happened with every ministry where Dr. and Mrs. Evans had served, things were happening at Hyles-Anderson College and at First Baptist Church of Hammond. The church had been declared the world's largest Sunday school by Dr. Elmer Towns in 1970 and, of course, was continuing to grow.

Even greater days were ahead for Mrs. Evans and her staff as Brother Hyles began having special sessions for the ladies at his annual Pastors' School, held the third full week in March. Mrs. Evans had a dream for ladies to be different and had shared that dream with the young ladies in her college classes, but she was about to be able to pass that dream to women all across the nation. God had chosen her "for such a time as this."

The late sixties and seventies were a time of tremendous turmoil in America as race riots, peace demonstrations, free love, and the women's movement were in the forefront of the daily news. The proposed Equal Rights Amendment caused confusion and fear in local fundamental churches. The role of women was changing in the world as they were being told they had rights—rights to kill their unborn babies; rights to leave their homes, their marriages, and their children to pursue a career;

and rights to dress as they pleased. America's future was dark, and it seemed that Christian women especially needed guidance as they had never before needed it.

Dr. Hyles was well aware of the battle for the homes in America and had a burden for this great land. He had started Hyles-Anderson College in response to his pleading with God to save America. He, too, realized the great need for America's Christian women to be rallied and helped. In 1975 Dr. Hyles asked Mrs. Evans to speak on the subject "Christian Womanhood" for the ladies who were to attend Pastors' School. A number of ladies would help her present material on how to win souls, how to teach girls to be ladies, how to be submissive to husbands, and how to organize their time in order to be a keeper at home and a church worker—all for the glory of God.

Pat Hays, a woman who had moved to Hammond in the summer of 1974 to put her three children into Hammond Baptist Schools, took a few of Mrs. Evans' courses that year, including Christian Womanhood and Women Used of God. She had sent notes to Mrs. Evans regarding her publishing the materials she was giving in class. Mrs. Evans responded by saying, "Mrs. Hays, I can't even write a letter. I surely can't write a book."

Promo picture of Pat Hays (Hehn)

Pat had a part-time nursing job, and one day Mrs. Evans received a $17.35 check in the mail with a note which said, "This is to go to help you put some of your teaching on tape." This was one half of Pat's shift pay for a night of work. Mrs. Evans had no plans to make tapes and so just ignored the whole thing. (She admitted that she did keep the $17.35!)

When Pat heard that Mrs. Evans was to speak at Pastors' School, she asked if she could drive her to the church every day so she wouldn't have to think about being late, parking, or anything else that might hinder her being with the ladies. Then she asked if Mrs. Evans was going to make some tapes since there are usually facilities for selling them at conferences. Following is Pat's account of what happened:

"Nobody will want to buy that junk!" is a remark that I will remember until my dying day. Can you guess who'd say such a thing? It was Marlene Evans! Can you guess what she was talking about? It was "The Five Sins of Christian Women" tapes. Let me tell you the story!

Dear Mrs. Evans:

Ordinarily I do not read women's magazines! I leave this with my wife.

But I made an exception. I just read your article entitled, "Enjoying More People." I want to thank you for this article, and I trust the Lord will give me more patience and grace in dealing with the many people I meet.

My wife and I are praying for you! I know that you have suffered much. In it all, you have given a glorious testimony to the grace of God. Many thousands of people have been blessed by your beautiful words and your smile.

Give my best regards to your husband. May God's richest blessings be on you.

Sincerely,

Lee Roberson
Chancellor

LR:gs

Once upon a time way back in March of 1975, Dr. Hyles asked Mrs. Evans to speak on the subject "Christian Womanhood" for the ladies who were to attend Pastors' School.

I knew what she was going to speak about. It could be only one thing—the sins of Christian women! Every time Mrs. Evans was asked to speak at mother-daughter banquets, the women were in for a surprise because I knew they expected to be told how good they were. But every time they were told, "Tonight, I am going to speak on 'The Five Sins of Christian Women!' " I knew what would happen. Mrs. Evans would have them laughing and crying so much that they would not even know they were having surgery done to their hearts and would never be the same!

There is something about truth that once you have seen it, you can't "unsee" it. And that is what made her message so powerful, for the Holy Spirit talked to you on the inside while she talked to you on the outside.

I was 44 years old, and I couldn't remember anyone ever being brave enough to tell Christian women they had sins. I remember hearing, "Now we all have sins," but it was always "we." So everyone always thought, "They have sins." I don't remember anyone saying or implying that the "we" meant "me"; of course, it meant the other person!

The first time I heard "The Five Sins of Christian Women," I thought, "How does she know all about me? Only the Lord and I know about it, and we haven't told anyone!" I knew I hadn't told. So that only left one Person, and that's why I knew she knew what she was talking about, for a voice inside me said, "She's right and you know it." Know what I said? "Well, Lord, either You told her or she's just like me, and that's how she knows!" But the truth is the truth, and I knew I didn't want to keep some of the ugliness at which I'd had a glance!

The main points of her talk are: 1) Gossip and a critical spirit, 2) Nerves, worry and depression, 3) Lack of love for husband and children, 4) Lack of Bible, soul winning, and prayer, and 5) Immodest and unladylike dress.

I asked Mrs. Evans if she would make a tape on "The Five Sins of

Christian Women" to sell at Pastors' School. She made one 60-minute tape and found she wasn't through. She made another and was still not through, so she just concluded with the third one.

I asked Mrs. Evans if I could order 100 sets (which meant 300 tapes). She said, "You can order 25 sets. Nobody will want to buy the junk. I said the same thing on several tapes; I've never heard such terrible yakking as I heard when I received the test tapes." But I begged and pleaded, and she finally said, "Okay, order 100 sets, but I surely hate to have them sitting around cluttering up the place!"

I remember driving back from the Duplitape Company with the tapes, feeling like I had millions of dollars in the back seat of my car. As I put the sets together (three tapes to a set with rubber bands), I remember praying over and over, "Lord, don't let me sell any of these tapes to the wrong people!" I put about 25 sets on the table that was assigned to us and went to hear Mrs. Evans speak three times that morning. She went back to the college, and I stayed at Pastors' School.

Preachers would pass by and ask about the tapes; I would name off the five points and then say, "Now if you buy these tapes and don't like them, I want you to bring them back. You see, only certain people are to have these. If you have a tape recorder with you, listen to one side and be sure they are what you want. Do you understand? These tapes are to be listened to and used! They will change the lives of the ladies in your church. If you are going to put them up on a shelf, please don't buy them."

Some of you are saying, "That is not the way to sell!" Maybe it isn't, but by the time Mrs. Evans came back for the evening session, I had sold 100 sets of "The Five Sins of Christian Women."

She couldn't believe it, but the money in my hand convinced her, and she let me order another 100 sets for the next day. (What is really a secret that I've never admitted until right now is that I had already asked Duplitape Company if they could make more up that night if I needed them!)

Some of you are saying, "That's what I call FAITH!" No, it was believing in what I had seen happen at mother-daughter banquets and to myself through these talks. I believed in the power of the mes-

Mrs. Evans labored over writing articles and talks.

sage of these tapes. My motive was not to sell a lot of tapes but to get the few tapes I had to the right people! And I felt that was a very sacred responsibility! What should have talked people out of buying actually caused them to buy them, I guess.

The second day the 100 sets came, and our Blue Berets (the teen girls' service group at First Baptist Church of Hammond) were helping put the sets together when Mrs. Evans sent for me to come to the room where she was speaking. When I got back, they had sold quite a few sets and I said, "You mean you sold them? I didn't get to see if they were the right people. And I didn't get to pray over them." (I must have thought I was the POPE or something!) One of the girls said, "But Mrs. Hays, here's the money; isn't it okay to sell them?" I assured her it was okay but decided I would try not to have to leave again.

The second evening session came, and Mrs. Evans asked how many tapes I had left. I showed her an empty table and a fist full of money. She was relieved that we were out of debt. When I asked her if I could order another 100 sets for the next day, she said, "Has anyone brought them back yet?"

I said, "No, and I told them they could; so I think I got them all to the right people!"

Doesn't that sound dumb? I am laughing as I sit here at the typewriter typing this for you to read. Whether it is dumb or funny or whatever it may seem to you, that is the way the first 300 sets of Christian Womanhood tapes were sold. God has used the voice and heart of Marlene Evans to touch the hearts and lives of women and girls all over America, Africa, Canada, and many other countries of the world.

You may figure it out any way you please, but these tapes on "The Five Sins of Christian Women" have remained the most popular of all of our tapes! Not only did we sell 300 sets [at Pastors' School] in 1975, but we have sold thousands since then! I guess that deep inside, we all know we aren't as good as we like other people to think we are…and we need help!

Above: Mrs. Evans and the Blue Beret
Below: "The Five Sins of Christian Women" talk (which is still available) would become a full-length book.

Marlene Evans A Biography

Mrs. Evans knew that women were whiney, gossipy, gripey, complaining, nervous individuals, but she didn't know how much they did not want to be until that week at Pastors' School. At the closing session of Pastors' School, Brother Hyles had a parade of workers. As Mrs. Evans walked up into the choir and looked out into the great audience of people, she started crying and sobbing uncontrollably. The "quiet needler" (as Mrs. Evans often referred to Pat Hays) didn't cry at all, but she watched Mrs. Evans and the women in the audience. They had asked lots of questions:

- "Will you come to our church to speak to our ladies?" Mrs. Evans had to say, "No," carefully limiting her speaking engagements because of her family and her work at the college.
- "Could Fay (Dodson) come teach us how to win souls?"
- "Does Connie (Brown) have a book that would help us to know how to help girls become interested in being ladies?"
- "If the girls do want to be ladies, how do you teach them?"
- "I live on the coast of Oregon, and everyone would think I was crazy if I wore a skirt. Can someone write me once in a while to encourage me?"
- "I didn't want to come here with my husband. He made me come, but I told myself I wouldn't listen to a thing you said. Now I want to hear a lot more and I can't."
- "I haven't stopped crying since I got here. I didn't know there could be love among Christian women like this! I don't want to go home."

The emotional strain and excitement of the week plus the cries of those ladies were the reasons for Mrs. Evans' sobs. Needless to say, she was emotionally drained when she reached home that Friday. She immediately had to put her efforts on getting ready to turn right around to go to Logansport, Indiana, where her husband was preaching that weekend. Mrs. Evans was getting the kids' things ready and was feeling as if she'd been chewed up and spit out when Pat called with, "What are you going to do about it?"

Mrs. Evans asked, "About what?"

Pat said, "Well, you're not just going to give those ladies what you told them in the meetings and then just leave them, are you?"

Her response was short and to the point, "Yep, I sure am. I've gotta go to Logansport." That night, the next day, and Sunday Mrs. Evans thought

Above: Mrs. Evans'
first promo picture
Below: her second promo picture

of those women. For some reason she kept thinking particularly of the one on the Oregon Coast who felt so alone.

When Mrs. Evans returned home Monday, she told Pat they were starting a paper if the Preacher okayed it. Mrs. Evans met with Brother Hyles, he did approve the idea, and they were off and running.

True to form, Mrs. Evans made this big. Pat had been thinking of a little one-page sheet paper to start in about six months so they would have time to work through all the details. But Mrs. Evans had other plans. If they were starting a paper, they were starting it now, and it was going to be more than just one 8½ x 11 sheet of paper.

One of the first people she called was her beloved Sunday school teacher from Chattanooga, Mrs. Holbrook. She said, "I'm writing about you for a paper that has to be finished tonight. God wants me to do a paper. You know I can't write. I can't even write a letter. You'll have to pray that I can write this thing." Mrs. Holbrook was thrilled at the news and encouraged Mrs. Evans in her new endeavor. She also promised to pray for her.

By God's grace the first issue, Volume I, Number 1 was tabloid size (11 x 17) and was ready to be mailed by May, 1975. Mrs. Evans was still skeptical and didn't believe women would be interested. She was shocked when the first edition sold out. The statement of purpose she had chosen was, "America's first newspaper designed to meet the needs of women and girls with the goal of inspiring and instructing them to be used of God in the home and in the local, fundamental, Bible-believing church." *Christian Womanhood* was officially "in business."

The paper was bigger than one person could handle, and so the *Christian Womanhood* team was formed. The original workers chosen were that group of ladies who were already helping Mrs. Evans. They included Carol Frye, Pat Hays, Jo Ellen Lee, Linda Meister, and Vicki Mitchell. This group of part-time employees and volunteers gave themselves to the work of Christian Womanhood. Mrs. Evans, of course, was the editor of *Christian Womanhood*, and Pat assumed the title and responsibilities of assistant editor.

At its one-year anniversary in 1976, *Christian Womanhood* had over 10,000 subscribers in 50 states and 15 foreign countries. Mrs. Evans wrote at that time about *Christian Womanhood* and her workers, "Not one of us could do without the other. We're a team! None of us feel much as if we should be leading *Christian Womanhood*. We're not your typical ladies—kind of a motley crew! Yes, we are, but God…! Our preacher says, 'The Lord delights in doing His work through unlikely candidates so everyone knows He had to do it. Then He gets all the glory.' By this standard, we qualify! To God be the Glory!"

After speaking at Pastors' School, Mrs. Evans began receiving invitations to speak all over the country. With her priorities as a wife and mother, her teaching responsibilities at Hyles-Anderson College, and her editing work with *Christian Womanhood*, there was no way she could begin to honor all of the requests. She talked with her pastor, and Dr. Hyles suggested that she host a meeting at Hyles-Anderson College. This would also be a way to promote the paper which she had started. Mrs. Evans and her staff immediately began planning the meeting.

Mrs. Evans was flying out of town for a speaking engagement, and she took her staff to the airport with her to use the time to plan for this meeting. They were brainstorming to find a name for the conference. Numbers of suggestions had been made including, "Wonderful World of Women." Mrs. Evans liked it but felt it was too wordy. She was not sold on any of the ideas they had discussed. A few days later she called Mrs. Holbrook and said, "I want a word for a ladies' meeting that is going to be unusual. I want the ladies to realize it is going to be something really fantastic when they see the title." Mrs. Holbrook immediately responded, "You want a **spectacular!**" Mrs. Evans loved it and the conference was named.

Mrs. Evans advertised the meeting for February 6 and 7, 1976, expecting that maybe 300 ladies would attend. The Spectacular was the first conference of its kind. Mrs. Evans was shocked when the registrations began pouring in. It was soon evident that the conference was going to be too big to be held in the college chapel, and so plans were made to move the Spectacular to First Baptist Church. Up until this time, there had been nothing for ladies, and for that reason, the response was overwhelming. With piles of snow and freezing cold weather, over 5,000 ladies from nearly every state in the union attended that meeting! Because of the overwhelming response, the decision was made that the Spectaculars

The Christian Womanhood Spectacular

A photograph from one of the annual Christian Womanhood Spectaculars

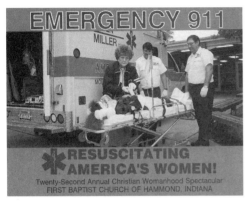

Brochures advertising the annual
Christian Womanhood Spectacular at
First Baptist Church of Hammond

were to become an annual conference at First Baptist Church. However, the time of year was changed from February to October, and a second Spectacular was scheduled for 1976.

Mrs. Evans considered that first Spectacular a miracle. She wrote a prayer of reflection about that conference.

MAYBE I'm confused, but it seems to me that the February 1976 Spectacular was a miracle. You know that we planned on having only a couple hundred women come to our college chapel…I told You people wouldn't come from far away for just a 24-hour period. That wouldn't show common sense. Whoever heard of someone flying to Indiana from Alaska for a one-day conference? They didn't even know what the thing was all about! When they did come, they shouldn't have stayed for all that happened to them. Lord, remember when I was a waitress and would rather wait on three tables of men than a table of women?

Lord, You have to know how hard it is to handle a bunch of women. You know that I was quaking in my boots when I got up on the platform. I told them I didn't want to hear any griping, gossiping, or whining all the time they were there and that they could have a refund if we heard anyone indulging in such. I always thought that this should be a rule of Ladies' Aid Societies or anything else. I never have liked the idea of sitting around with a bunch of women talking about some poor old woman who drinks a beer or smokes a cigarette when we're sitting there spieling out more foul stuff than they are probably taking in. Oh, don't get me wrong…You know how I hate smoking and drinking, but I guess I even hate this worse because smoking and drinking don't seem to be the problems of most Christian women. I've always seen "No Smoking" signs up in Christian gatherings, but I never have seen "No Gossiping" signs. I wonder why we're so hung up on smoking. Most of us don't smoke, but all of us gossip!

Is this the trick of the Devil? Remember when I told them that they weren't supposed to take any time washing their hands, putting on make-up, or anything else but were supposed to get right back into more meetings? I also told them they'd be going to their motel rooms at midnight and coming back at 6:00 the next morning. That isn't even educationally, psychologically, or physically sound. It's really stupid. I don't even know how You got women to put up with all that. Since people were flying in from Maine and Florida, it just seemed so urgent that we give them everything that we possibly could. The thing was, I didn't even know why they were coming. I'm still not sure what happened. I must be the dumbest child You have. Maybe You took something that shouldn't have worked and made it work so I could continue having the dream.

Of course, the dream she was talking about was the dream she'd had when she wrote her ninth grade English paper. Mrs. Evans had a dream to see different women, women who didn't gossip, criticize, and tear up churches with their negative talk. She had a dream to see different women who dressed modestly, loved their husbands, were faithful soul winners, and made a difference in America. She was seeing this dream start to become a reality.

With all of the fame and attention that came with being the editor of *Christian Womanhood* and the leader of the Spectacular, Mrs. Evans "kept her feet on the ground" so to speak. She saw people treating her differently the minute she walked onto the platform that very first Spectacular. She had listened to her leaders enough to know that fame and popularity are fleeting. She once said, "Dr. Roberson taught me to enjoy and appreciate any honoring that came my way but not to put too much weight on it as those things come and go." She also remembered that "Dr. Roberson also talked about listening to criticism long enough to filter some good on which to work, but to not pay too much attention to it."

The first Spectacular ended on Saturday afternoon. Sunday morning after Sunday school while Mrs. Evans was waiting for church to begin, she turned to Carol Frye and said, "All these people came to the Spectacular, but they are not the ones who are really important to me. I'm glad all these people love me, but what really matters is my family." It was in that pew that she planned her first "Family Spectacular," a tradition that continued until her Homegoing.

Her parents, Dr. Evans' parents, Aunt Lela, Louise Holbrook, and

Family Spectaculars

A snapshot taken at one of the Family Spectaculars

The Second Christian Womanhood Spectacular

Marlene Evans speaking at a Christian Womanhood Spectacular

Nancy Perry had all come from out of town to the first Spectacular. She wanted to show her love and appreciation for their support and wanted to let them know they meant more to her than those thousands of ladies who had come from all over the country. She took her entire family and loved ones to the Holiday Inn in Merrillville, Indiana, to eat lunch after church. She sent Carol Frye out to purchase gifts for each of her loved ones. After the meal as she presented the gifts to each of the people, she acknowledged that she realized she would never have been in the position of influence to have a Spectacular if it had not been for the love, influence, and support of that small group of people. Marlene Evans never forgot her roots, and she never forgot her family. She reserved a place in her mind, in her heart, and in her life for her loved ones; and no people, no positions, no titles, no responsibilities, and no opportunities were ever allowed to infringe on that place.

The response to the second Spectacular was even more overwhelming than the first. Mrs. Evans realized early on that all of the ladies would not be able to fit into the auditorium of the First Baptist Church, and so, again, there was a change in plans. While most of the ladies would sit in the church auditorium, the rest of the delegates would go to the Hammond Civic Center. To Mrs. Evans' amazement, over 7,000 ladies registered for the meeting. Several thousand of those ladies sat in the Civic Center and watched the Spectacular on closed-circuit television. Rose O'Brien and Barbara Foster (the same Barbara Foster who had taught with Mrs. Evans in Chattanooga during the race riots and who now taught at Hyles-Anderson College) emceed at the civic center and worked hard to make it personal and fun. It seemed that the delegates in the Civic Center had some advantages, such as getting to see all that was happening at the Spectacular better on the screen than the folks who were seeing it in person at the church. (Delegates in the civic center said they even saw the teardrops fall down the cheeks of Mrs. Jackie Dark, the wife of the former manager of the Oakland Athletics, Alvin Dark, as she spoke.) The entire meeting was, by all accounts, a great success as hundreds and thousands of lives were influenced for eternity.

Probably the greatest reason that Mrs. Evans' speaking was so influential was that she was so real. She once said regarding speaking to women:

> GENERAL stuff (like "I've had my problems.") doesn't move me a whole lot. Tell specific incidents when you struggled or made a mistake and tell what you did to fix the problem.

She had the wisdom to see that all the "general stuff" ladies had said for years had not changed lives, and she knew that women needed to be able to relate to the speaker. On the other hand, she also warned ladies who spoke not to get up and "tell all"—about situations or sins from their past that would hurt their own marriage or loved ones. Mrs. Evans always kept a balance of being real in her speaking while also being appropriate and careful in what she said.

An example of her being so real was written in *Christian Womanhood* one month:

> LORD, I guess You heard me say that snide remark the other day, so I might as well get down to me. I'm supposed to hate all this stuff. Yes, I teach against it. If I, who am supposed to be going toward a goal of being different, came out with that remark…oh, it wasn't so bad. It was just a little off-hand comment that implied something selfish about someone. The thing is, it wasn't even true. I still have some resentment in my heart about that person from a long, long time ago. I guess I still hate someone. Now, You see why I'm having nightmares about my dream. How can I ever hope to see a change in Christian women?

Mrs. Evans consistently worked on her words the rest of her life. She asked God to give her a love for all people. Anytime she discovered that she had wrong attitudes toward anyone or used hurtful words, she would immediately confess it as sin. She strived to be an example of a different woman in order to influence other ladies to be different also. Mrs. Evans would go on to conduct a total of 27 Spectaculars. These conferences never became "ho-hum" for her. She wanted each one to be different (with new ideas, new decorations, and so forth) than the previous meeting. She wanted to give the ladies a reason to come back the next year! She often said that she wanted her staff to help her make the Spectaculars

Spectacular Themes

Cameo ~ Changed Lives Forever
Four Seasons
Different Women
Pyramid '78
Broken Things
Holiday 1980
Broken Things II
Classics
Spectacular of Miracles
Celebrate '84
Cracker Barrel Spectacular
Rainbows in a World of Clouds
Spectacular Homecoming '87
Digging for Gold
Christmas Reunion Spectacular
Turn the World Upside Down
Carousel of Commitment
Managing Life's 3-Ring Circus
It's Not Too Late!
Homecoming
Survival
Emergency 911
Three Strikes and You're Not Out!
Living Like Royalty Mid Evil Times
I Need a Vacation!
Home Is a Healing Place

a "youth conference for ladies." She wanted fun, entertainment, music, and most of all, life-changing teaching. To that end she worked and chose themes she felt would accomplish her goals.

The Spectaculars continued each year as Mrs. Evans' influence also continued. After the second Spectacular she began conducting conferences called Mini-Spectaculars in churches throughout the nation. Hundreds and thousands of lives, homes, and churches were influenced and changed as Mrs. Evans spoke in these meetings. She went to each conference with the goal of being used of God. There was purpose in everything she did. Sometimes it was her speaking publicly that seemed to make the greatest impact during a conference, and other times it seemed God had sent her to a church to especially help one individual or couple.

- She went to speak at one church where a lady had been openly criticizing the pastor and causing trouble with the members. As Mrs. Evans spoke at this conference, this lady came under great conviction, her life was changed, and to this day she is a loyal member who serves the pastor and the church faithfully.

- A very lovely and proper lady was hurting over her daughter's recent marriage. This young lady had grown up in a Christian home but had somehow gotten involved with an unsaved young man and married him. The mother was heartbroken and wanted nothing to do with this man who had "stolen" her daughter. Mrs. Evans questioned the lady on the man's interests, and when she found out he had a motorcycle, Mrs. Evans encouraged her to get the young man motorcycle magazines, ask questions about the motorcycle, etc. She explained that if the man was ever going to trust Christ, he had to first see Christ in his in-laws. This was a turning point in that family's relationship with their son-in-law and daughter.

- When Mrs. Evans arrived at another church to speak, she found a very heavy-hearted pastor and his wife. One of their children had made a mistake which they felt would forever ruin their Christian testimony and the testimony of the church. Mrs. Evans sympathized with them, cried with them, and tried to help them know some practical steps to take to

Christian Womanhood Mini-Spectaculars

Above: Speaking at Bayview Baptist Church in Washington, Illinois

Pictures on page 153:
Top: Mrs. Evans flying to her first Mini-Spectacular in Briscoe Run, WV Center: Mrs. Evans (r) at a Mini-Spectacular in Columbia, Tennessee, Lower: In Great Falls, Montana

Marlene Evans A Biography

correct the problem. She had a few hours after the meeting before her plane flew out and suggested a very fun and crazy idea to the pastor and his wife. In those few hours Mrs. Evans got those people laughing so hard they were crying. They later said that this was a turning point for them. They knew Mrs. Evans cared, and they had been helped by her suggestions; but their hearts were so heavy. They had not laughed in days, and that laughter was medicine to their souls.

• A lady who helped plan and coordinate the meeting at which Mrs. Evans was speaking was ready to leave her husband. He had been diagnosed with cancer and had consequently undergone chemotherapy. It seemed that the chemotherapy completely changed his personality, and he had just quit talking. There was very little communication in the home. He even quit attending church. Mrs. Evans could relate to this man since she herself had been through cancer and chemotherapy. She spent time with this woman after the meeting, helping her to understand her husband and giving her ideas of what to do. She continued to counsel the woman over the phone from time to time, and today this dedicated Christian couple is faithfully serving the Lord full-time. That lady credits Mrs. Evans with the saving of her marriage.

• At another conference, the coordinator was discussing all of the improvements that had been made in the church during the previous year, which included beautiful new pews. The lady then stated that the pastor was going to use the old blue chairs which had been in the church auditorium as a promotion the following Sunday. She said, "I'm not bringing a visitor because I don't want one of those old chairs."

Mrs. Evans immediately picked up on this disloyalty and lack of support to the preacher and said, "Why wouldn't you want that chair? You don't understand how important they are to the preacher, do you? When that preacher looks at those chairs, he remembers people who sat in those chairs. He remembers that there was a day when there weren't enough people to pay for pews, and he knows how God has blessed this ministry."

By the time Mrs. Evans finished, that lady was under great conviction to support the pastor and get visitors to church on Sunday. She still has one of those chairs in her home!

In all, it is estimated that Mrs. Evans spoke in over 300 ladies' meet-

"STREAMS IN THE DESERT"
Carol Tudor, Laura Baker, Mrs. Middleton, and Mrs. Evans

Lisa & Marcia Schearer, Mrs. Evans, Carol Tudor, Loretta Walker

ings in nearly every state of the union and several foreign countries including Germany and Canada. Some meetings were quite large with several thousand delegates, and some were quite small with 30 or 40 ladies. There were many meetings where she spoke annually—some for over 20 years. But the size never mattered; Mrs. Evans gave her best at every conference, and in so doing, influenced thousands of lives.

The Death of Mrs. Evans' Mother

January 6, 1978, Mrs. Evans' mother, Helen Zugmier, went to Heaven. Mrs. Evans left immediately for Nebraska. No sooner had she reached her home in Nebraska than Mrs. Earlyne Stephens, bursar of Hyles-Anderson College and sister to Dr. Jack Hyles, called to tell her she was praying for her and the family. She so sweetly listened when Marlene told how Helen had not been very sick but just told Alvin, "I'm going to die," closed her eyes, and went to Heaven.

Earlyne exclaimed, "Now, that's first class!" Those were appropriate words that suited a need for Mrs. Evans at that moment. They finalized her acceptance of the shock as she became so thankful her mom wasn't called on to suffer more than she already had in her life.

The Evanses' son David was a special comfort to his mom during those days of grief. When Alvin and his three daughters left for the cemetery to choose a lot, David whispered, "Try to find a place by a tree." David and his mom shared mutual feelings with their love of trees. During the funeral David sat behind his mom and passed her mints, gum, and Kleenex with squeezes of the hands, which all told her he was watching her and was with her.

The Sunday following Helen's funeral, Mrs. Evans couldn't believe that her ears were hearing right when organist Elaine Colsten began playing, "When They Ring Those Golden Bells," for her offertory number. Immediately after the service, Mrs. Evans made her way to Mrs. Colsten to tell her that it was the main song sung at the funeral. Mrs. Colsten responded sweetly, "I know." It was her way of saying, "I love you and haven't forgotten your heartache."

The death of Helen Zugmier left Alvin Zugmier living alone. He did so for several years, but a romantic relationship formed with a lady he had known for years, Hazel Soneson. It is sometimes difficult for adult chil-

Mrs. Helen Zugmier

Marlene Evans
A Biography

dren to see a parent remarry. It can be an uncertain and difficult time as they think of having a stepparent, wondering if that person will try to take the place of their parent, etc.

When Mrs. Evans got word of her dad's interest in marrying Hazel, she immediately got on the side of the marriage. She counseled her dad, planned the wedding to be held at the Hyles-Anderson College campus, and started calling Hazel "Mom." There was never a moment's problem between this stepmother and stepdaughter. Mrs. Evans continued that relationship even after her dad went to Heaven.

Above: The Evans family the day of Mom Zugmier's funeral
Left: Marlene's Dad and his wife, Hazel

Dean of Women

Marlene Evans was not the typical college dean of women. She saw potential where others saw impossibility; she saw hope where others saw failure; and she saw a future where others saw a past. She believed in people when others had written them off, and she even hired people to work for her when others thought she was crazy!

One person she hired was a young maverick named Leslie Simpson who had come to Hyles-Anderson College from a very difficult home situation. She had been saved just a brief time before her enrollment, and though a very sensitive young woman, she says she "had learned to mask her hurts by a sense of humor and attention-getting antics."

Leslie says today, "I had loved my student teaching days at Hammond Baptist Grade School and was hoping to get an offer to teach. I was

Above: Mrs. Evans rides a motorized
bike with Leslie Simpson
Below: Brother David Sielschott, a
staff member at the college, attached
a sidecar to his motorcycle to take
Mrs. Evans for a ride.

crushed when rather than a teaching offer from Hammond Baptist Grade School, I was offered a job with the activities department at Hyles-Anderson and a position as a dormitory supervisor. (I found out years later that there had been a teaching offer at the grade school, but Dr. and Mrs. Evans had vetoed it because they felt I needed to be at the college.)" Both the activities department and the ladies' dormitories were under Mrs. Evans' supervision.

When I asked Mrs. Evans why she had hired me, she answered, "You were like a little kid with a blow torch. You have all this talent and ability, but you didn't have the maturity to use it properly. While others were watching you ride motorcycles across campus and tear up the dorms with your practical jokes, I was looking at the three years in a row you won the First Baptist Church contest for bringing the most visitors on the bus route. I was looking at the fact that you collected hundreds of dollars to keep students in school—when you didn't have money yourself! I was looking at the fact that when a student came into a class and said, 'Does anyone want to write to an older preacher who is lonely?' you accepted the challenge. (That lonely old preacher was the great Dr. R. G. Lee, with whom she formed a strong and lasting friendship.) I knew you had it in you to do great things, and I wanted to give you a chance."

Leslie made mistakes as a young staff member, but Mrs. Evans kept working with her, and she has now been serving the Lord full time for nearly 25 years. She is a Christian school teacher, she is married to a fine Christian man, and is rearing two godly children. This is just one example of the hundreds of young people Mrs. Evans believed in and helped to reach their potential.

Mrs. Evans had the ability to motivate people to do things way beyond what they ever imagined they could do. She was a "dream merchant" who looked past the masks, the hurts, and the antics and saw potential and hope.

When Mrs. Evans took a chance on Leslie, she had no idea that Leslie would be the one person most responsible for most of the books Mrs. Evans published. Leslie spent hundreds of hours assembling articles Mrs. Evans had written to put together *Redbirds and Rubies and Rainbows;*

Comfort for Hurting Hearts; *Help, Lord, They Call Me Mom*; *Marriage Without Divorce*; *Kids Without Chaos*; *Teens Without Turmoil*; and *Sickness Without Despair.* Mrs. Evans never invested in people with the idea that they were going to help her someday, but it did seem that many of those in whom she invested the most were able to turn around and help her in some tremendous ways.

Typically, when there is a problem with a group of people, if there is any communication at all, it is usually caused by those involved simply airing their gripes. As dean of women, Mrs. Evans had a most unusual way of handling room problems in the ladies' dorms—no doubt a method she learned from her Sunday school teacher, Mrs. Holbrook. Loretta Walker, wife of Evangelist Kevin Walker and a graduate of Hyles-Anderson College, tells a tremendous lesson she learned about handling room problems when she was a dormitory student.

*A dormitory supervisors' luncheon with Mrs. Evans
(l-r) Kris Matthews [Grafton], Mrs. Evans, Mary Purdum, Jane Sullivan [Grafton], Arlys Cooper, Pam Zweifel [Scholten]*

"There were ten of us in our room, and we had one girl who had a problem with personal hygiene. She did not take showers and did not do her laundry. It was not uncommon for her to go through her laundry basket, pull out an outfit, iron it, and wear those dirty clothes over and over. Finally, two of the roommates had had enough and took the girl to the shower room, turned on the water, and threw the girl into the shower, clothes and all! Of course, Mrs. Evans heard about the situation and called us into her office to discuss the problem. In my mind, I was not part of the problem because I was very busy with student teaching, work scholarship, the bus route, and so much more. I was seldom in the room, so I figured my being at the room meeting was just a formality. I also thought Mrs. Evans would go around and have everyone tell their complaint so we would all know each person's frustration. Boy, was I wrong!

Mrs. Evans began by stating that each of us was responsible for the attitudes and atmosphere in the room. She also briefly addressed the problem of the young lady's being thrown into the shower as she quietly stated, 'I've heard that several of you threw one of your roommates into the shower, clothes and all. I don't of approve of what you did, and I hurt for this girl. This didn't happen overnight. It is a problem that has escalated over a period of time, and we need to find ways to fix it. I'm not in the room like you are, so I would like for each of you to tell what you can do to make things better in your room.'

That was a new teaching for me. As the girls talked, I realized that I was part of that room; therefore, I was part of the problem and also part of the solution. When Mrs. Evans came to the girl who had been thrown into the shower, the young lady said, 'I am the problem.' She went on to tell how many hours she was working because she did not have money for her school bill, and how she did not have money for laundry or laundry detergent.

Hearing her words made the other girls realize that this girl needed their support, not their judgment and ridicule, and they began weeping over their insensitive behavior toward her. This rallied our room together behind this girl and helped bring real resolution to the problem. The biggest thing we all learned was that whatever situation we are in, we are part of the problem if there is one, and we are always part of the solution."

When Mrs. Evans first became dean of women, some of the dormitory supervisors were older and quite set in their ways. A few of these women resisted the suggestions and ideas of their younger leader. One woman, especially, caused problems and let others know she was not behind Mrs. Evans. One of the dormitory supervisors was a church staff member, and so one day, without telling or asking Mrs. Evans, she decided to tell Preacher about the problem.

Mrs. Evans had no idea why Dr. Hyles was calling her into his office and was surprised to find that it was to discuss the problems she was experiencing with the most difficult dorm supervisor. After asking a few questions and discussing the situation briefly, he told Mrs. Evans he would move the lady to a different area of responsibility. As she was about to leave the office, he said to her, "I don't ever want this to happen again."

Mrs. Evans was taken aback. She had not gone to Brother Hyles about this lady. In fact, she had not even discussed it with anyone, including the church staff member who had told him of the situation! At first Dr. Hyles' words seemed unjust to her since she had not initiated the meeting. However, she stopped and decided not to allow herself to dwell on such thoughts. She told herself that God had allowed this situation for

Mrs. Evans is presented a watch by Brother and Mrs. Hyles commemorating 25 years of service to Hyles-Anderson College.

Marlene Evans A Biography

a purpose and then made a vow that changed her life. She said, "As much as is possible, I'll never be in trouble with another woman the rest of my life." And she stayed true to that vow. She worked the rest of her life to "live peaceably with all women." She never compromised her convictions over this statement, but it did cause her to sometimes tolerate negative behavior from workers or give up plans and ideas that she wanted, but she had made a decision based on what the Preacher wanted, and she stuck to that decision.

"As much as is possible, I'll never be in trouble with another woman the rest of my life." —Marlene Evans

In 1992 Mrs. Evans resigned as the dean of women at Hyles-Anderson College. She had already been through cancer and chemotherapy in 1982. By now she was experiencing increasing pain and fatigue from degenerative disc disease and arthritis and felt she could no longer perform that duty in the way that would be best for the students. More than likely, the ovarian cancer that would claim her life was already lurking in her body, complicating her other diseases.

Belinda Gaona, who was a teacher at Hammond Baptist Junior High School, was asked to become the dean of women. Belinda says of Mrs. Evans, "She never gave me one moment's trouble! She *never* questioned anything I had done; she *never* gave suggestions as to how she would handle a situation; and I *never* heard one critical word from her or from someone else quoting her.

She simply walked away from it—leaving me her entire staff and her office. I didn't want her office, but she said, 'That is the dean of women's office. It belongs to you now. I don't need it.' With that she moved out, and so after a few days, my staff began redoing her office.

When Brother Hyles got wind of what she had done, he called me in and said, 'I don't want her to lose her office.' I agreed with him, and so, we moved out and she moved back in. She was there for me if I wanted to ask her questions, but she always made me feel that I was doing a great job!"

Mrs. Evans' resignation and subsequent treatment of her successor was a class act!

Belinda Gaona

Mrs. Evans loved teaching and counted every opportunity to teach as a privilege and as an opportunity to influence another life. She took her classes seriously and never stood before her students unprepared. She despised "boring" and went to great lengths to be sure her classes were interesting, exciting, and life changing.

Sometimes, however, her attempts to make things happen got just a little out of control. One of the principles she always tried to teach her Educational Psychology students was that while many people can observe the same event, many of those same people perceive that event differently. To demonstrate this truth she asked Dr. John Olsen, the campus host, to come into her classroom one particular day and pretend to have a heart attack. And so, according to plan, Dr. Olsen walked into the classroom unannounced, acting as if he had something to say to Mrs. Evans. He suddenly clutched his chest, groaned, and fell to the ground. One of the more alert students in the class realized that he had probably had a heart attack, immediately ran from the classroom, and called 911! Minutes later an ambulance careened up to the front of the college with its siren wailing and its red lights flashing. The E.M.T.'s ran into the entrance and asked where the patient was located. Of course, the security department was clueless and could not figure out why someone had called 911 without their knowledge. Someone had not followed proper college procedures!

The puzzle was soon solved, and the ambulance quietly drove away. However, new procedures were soon put into place to prevent such a thing from happening again. In the future, Mrs. Evans was always careful to inform the security department of any such anecdotes that were to take place in her classes, and students were made aware that any calls to 911 should first be cleared by the security department!

JoJo Moffitt, Mrs. Evans' assistant teacher for 25 years, tells a wonderful illustration how Mrs. Evans didn't just teach with her mind; she taught with her heart. One particular day Mrs. Evans talked about relationships with parents. After class she was walking out the door of the classroom and saw a girl openly weeping. She put her arm around the young college student and listened intently as the girl told the heartbreaking story that she had never even met her father. Mrs. Evans helped this young lady find her father, got him to come to the college to meet that girl for the first time, and then won that man to the Lord. Mrs. Evans never just stood up in class and taught a principle; she helped the students find ways to put those principles into practice.

Another time Mrs. Evans taught in her Christian Womanhood class about soul winning, from the book *Pattern for Living*. She gave the plan of salvation, and three girls were saved right in class. Then Mrs. Evans asked, "How many of you have a mom or dad you are concerned about who are not saved?" Many raised their hands, and Mrs. Evans asked Mrs. Moffitt to take the young ladies to the different staff offices she had pre-arranged to let the girls call their parents. Numbers of parents were saved through this effort. Mrs. Evans realized that the most effective teaching was followed up by action on the part of the listeners.

Mrs. Evans had a passion for teaching and wanted to transfer that passion to her students. In order to get across her philosophy of using the five senses in teaching, she asked the students in her Educational Psychology class for the following: they were instructed to go to the area on the campus behind the gym the next day. Everyone who played instruments and had them at college was asked to bring them to class. Other students were asked to bring marshmallows, chocolate bars, and graham crackers. Mrs. Evans had already contacted Brother Mark Pfeifer, who was in charge of the grounds department, and had arranged for him to build a campfire. The following day she programmed an old-fashioned "singspiration" as she had instrumentalists play while the students sang. After a time of singing, she let the students give testimonies. It was a life-changing experience for those students as they saw how using the five senses—taste, touch, smell, sight, and hearing—paved the way to change the entire atmosphere of the class.

Another time she was teaching on the principle of "burying the past" in order to move forward in serving God. She had JoJo Moffitt contact Brother Ault, a funeral director who is a member of First Baptist Church, and asked him if he would bring a casket into the class as she was teaching. After she had talked a while, she instructed the students to write down anything in their past they needed to bury. At that point she gave the signal for Brother Ault to enter the classroom with the casket, and she asked the students to put their pieces of paper into the casket.

Mrs. Evans with her assistant teacher, JoJo Moffitt

Mrs. Evans and Carol Frye Tudor in their "Sunday finest!"— ready for an activity

Working with College Activities

Mrs. Evans was an awe-inspiring teacher and made a difference in the lives of thousands because she refused to conduct "average" classes. She wanted to make a difference, and she realized that making a difference required going the extra mile every day, doing things "average" teachers just don't do. She especially wanted her speech classes to be inspiring and exciting. She realized that if the students graduated from college unable to effectively communicate the truths they wanted to teach, their ministry would end in failure and defeat.

For that reason she really put pressure on her speech students to produce. Brother Dan Wolfe, who was so intrigued and influenced by Mrs. Evans when he was a teenage delegate at Pastors' School, says, "It was said in the dorms, 'if you want to get an A in Mrs. Evans' speech class, do something wild and crazy—the wilder the better!'"

One day JoJo Moffitt and Mrs. Evans were walking down a college hallway toward speech class. Suddenly they both spotted a horse being led down that hallway. Dr. Evans and Dr. James Jorgensen, the college vice president, were walking in front of Mrs. Evans and JoJo. Dr. Jorgensen turned to Dr. Evans and said matter-of-factly, "Doc, somehow I have the feeling your wife and JoJo Moffitt have something to do with this horse!"

They did! JoJo, as Mrs. Evans' assistant teacher had worked diligently to motivate the students to "do wild and crazy things" in planning and presenting their speeches. On this particular day, at least one student had caught the spirit as he was going to demonstrate how to groom a horse.

Mrs. Evans had been greatly influenced by her Sunday school teacher, Mrs. Louise Holbrook and her emphasis on Philippians 4:4 and being a rejoicing Christian. At the end of every class period, Mrs. Evans quoted Philippians 4:4 with the students. The students walked from the classroom saying, *"Rejoice in the Lord alway: and again I say, Rejoice."*

In the fall of 1975 Carol Frye was hired on staff at Hyles-Anderson College. Mrs. Evans and Dr. Max Helton had been in charge of the student activities up to that point, but with Carol's hiring, an activities department at Hyles-Anderson College was officially formed.

Mrs. Evans was an idea person and had proven throughout her life that she was qualified to lead this department of the college. As with any other area where she had served, her thinking about activities was not the norm, not the status quo.

Though it seldom happened, a snow day was declared at Hyles-Anderson College. Everyone seemed thrilled to have a day off, including the activities department workers. Brother Bill McSpadden, who was now also on the activities staff, was shocked when Mrs. Evans called and asked what they had planned for the day. He was speechless. This was a day off! But Mrs. Evans did not think it should be a day off for the activities workers; this was a day for them to go into high gear!

She said, "Brother Bill, kids need things happening, or they'll get into trouble. When there is nothing planned, they are left to their own devices. I'm counting on you to make things happen. I have big dreams for what you can make happen today." It was not long until the activities workers would joke and say, "Her dreams are our nightmares!" and they never again wished for snow days!

Mrs. Evans had a great sense of humor and loved using humor in skits and programs. But she also had very clear ideas of what types of humor she wanted used. During the annual Youth Conference at First Baptist Church of Hammond, the activities department was put in charge of skits. In one of the skits, the "Lone Soul Winner" had come onto the platform, pulled his gun, pointed to different areas of the auditorium and said, "I'm going to shoot and ricochet the bullet off that buck-toothed guy right there, and then off that fat girl up there…" Someone told Mrs. Evans about this skit. She said nothing until the next activities department meeting. When the meeting started, she sat and cried. She was finally able to talk about the skit and the fact that any boy with crooked teeth in that auditorium felt the Lone Soul Winner was making fun of him, and any girl who was even 10 or 15 pounds overweight felt that everyone had looked at her when he made the statement about the fat girl.

Mrs. Evans hated bigotry of any kind, whether it was racial slurs or making fun of someone's physical features or mental capacity. She explained to the workers that she just never wanted any individual to

"Mary Jane" (a.k.a. Mrs. Evans) and "Jeff" (a.k.a. Carissa Grafton) ready for fall fun!

Above: Dan Wolfe (l) and Bill McSpadden up to some of their usual shenanigans

Lower: Mrs. Evans and Carol Tudor have fun at Pipes and Pizza to the delight of the girls on Carol's dormitory floor.

| *Marlene Evans A Biography*

have a good time or a laugh at someone else's expense.

By this time, none of the activities workers were laughing. In fact, they felt very much like crying, but Mrs. Evans was not a person to stay on the negative. Rather, she rallied the workers to come up with a list of guidelines to help them know exactly what was appropriate and what was not appropriate when it came to humor in their skits and programs. At this meeting Mrs. Evans was doing the very thing Cindy Schaap credited her for when she first heard her speak in 1972. Mrs. Evans did not get down to the level of others; she pulled them up to her level. Her teaching and example to the activities workers took their productions and activities to a new level of greatness as they realized they did not have to rely on making fun of people; crass, risque humor; or any other inappropriate subjects for their laughs. For all of these years and until this day, the activities department continues to adhere by the guidelines they wrote that day.

There was another way in which Mrs. Evans was not the typical dean of women—her fun. A pizza establishment had opened in Lansing, Illinois, just about 30 minutes from the college. When Mrs. Evans heard about Pipes and Pizza, she just had to go check it out. An old theater had been renovated and made into a pizza parlor. A young man named Dave had been hired to play the organ each night, and Mrs. Evans soon had a great relationship with this gifted musician. This was no ordinary organ Dave played. The Barton organ controlled all sorts of instruments including cymbals, drums, whistles, and many other sound effects. She was "nuts" about the place and often took groups of people with her so they could enjoy the "Pipes and Pizza experience" too. On nights Mrs. Evans was there, she made the atmosphere even more exciting with her clapping, her laughter, and her way of getting the entire crowd to participate and sing along with Dave's organ music.

Soon Mrs. Evans encouraged two of her activities workers to help make the Pipes and Pizza activity even more exciting by asking them to bring costumes. Brother Bill McSpadden and Brother Dan Wolfe would change costumes according to the song Dave was going to play next. For example, when he played the "William Tell Overture" (the theme from the Lone Ranger), one would put on a mask, the other would wear an

Indian headdress, and they would pantomime to the music. All of this energy caused a raucous happening.

Several months after the opening of Pipes and Pizza, Dr. Evans flew to Florida with Dr. Hyles for a speaking engagement. Dr. Evans relates, "We had returned to our motel, and as we walked onto the elevator, Brother Hyles brought up the subject of Pipes and Pizza. He mentioned a complaint letter he had received from the manager about the conduct of some of our people, and especially about the way a staff member had taken over the place. I looked at him and said, 'Preacher, that was Marlene.' I did not expect his response! He turned around and began pounding his hands against the carpeted walls of the elevator. He laughed and laughed, and when he regained his composure he said, 'Wendell, I'm glad I've got a dean of women who gets in trouble that way. The kids need a woman who gets in trouble for being a little rambunctious. They don't need a wallflower!' " Though Mrs. Evans continued to take groups of people to Pipes and Pizza after she heard of Brother Hyles' response, and though she continued to have fun with Dave and the crowd, she did try to contain herself a little bit so he never got a second report of her behavior!

Mrs. Evans loved happenings— including her reign as "queen" at a Mini-Spectacular parade in Turner, Maine

Whenever Mrs. Evans was asked to speak at a conference such as Pastors' School, she would usually ask the workers in the activities department to help her. One year Dr. Hyles asked her to speak on Jesus, the Shepherd. She got excited about this and asked the workers to dress up as shepherds and walk down the aisles of the church auditorium with little sheep. And so, the activities workers got busy getting shepherd costumes and finding a local farmer who would loan his sheep to this worthy project. Mrs. Evans also asked Mrs. Hyles to sing the song, "Gentle Shepherd."

The day came for her speaking, and though there were some difficulties in picking up the sheep and getting them to stay in the El Camino they had driven to the farm (they had to return to the college and get a pick-up truck with a camper top on it to contain the sheep!), all went pretty well until…they got back to the college with the sheep. They were supposed to keep the sheep until it was time to drive in to the church. The workers put the sheep in the screened-in porch, but the animals soon poked a hole in a screen and ran outside. The workers were immediately chasing little lambs around the college lake! They finally corralled the lambs and put them in a classroom (to the surprise of the teacher when he walked into the room after chapel!) where they stayed until they were loaded back onto the truck.

Once at the church, the shepherds carried the lambs down to the front of the auditorium where Mrs. Evans asked them to put the sheep down and let them walk. While Mrs. Hyles was beautifully singing "Gentle Shepherd," the sheep went crazy as they suddenly began running in the auditorium bleating, while they also "relieved" themselves, leaving little brown deposits on the carpet!

One of the workers later stated, "Those sheep raised holy havoc in that auditorium!" The shepherds were frantically trying to recover their lost sheep as Mrs. Evans, who always tried to take advantage of the "teachable moment," stepped to the mic and said, "Isn't this just like us? Don't we run away from the Shepherd when He's trying to protect us?" The sheep were finally gathered and the speech was finished, but there was still work to do. The carpet had to be cleaned, and order had to be restored in the auditorium! To be sure, this was one of her more memorable speeches—at least with the activities staff—and one she always enjoyed "reliving" with them!

While there were numbers of activities provided for Hyles-Anderson College students, Mrs. Evans programmed them to be different. A few of the activities she suggested were:

• "Behind Every Graduate There Stands…" She wanted graduates to have an opportunity to publicly thank their parents and others who had invested in them throughout their college years. She did not want graduates to make general statements like, "My mom and dad have always been there for me." She wanted the graduate to tell specific ways his parents had "been there." The more spectacular the presentation, the better! She liked awards, plaques, flowers, and more! She also had the activities staff work with the graduates to help ensure that the presentations were first class.

• Hyles-Anderson College Valentine Banquet. For years both Dr.

and Mrs. Evans worked with the program cast to help them learn to "really come out of themselves." Dr. Evans worked with the musicians, and Mrs. Evans worked with the actors. Mrs. Evans wanted the cast members to move and to be expressive as the play was presented. Again, she wanted a first-class program.

• Summer Series Under the Stars. Mrs. Evans got the idea that not enough was happening for the handful of summer school dormitory students. She asked the activities staff to host a six-week series to be held outside in the courtyard with a different program each week. These programs included everything from a piano concert to a comedy skit night. This series of programs did provide great entertainment for the students, staff, and even members of First Baptist Church of Hammond.

• Christmas Fun. Mrs. Evans also had great empathy for any students who were not able to go home at Christmas. Therefore, she helped the activities workers go to great lengths to be sure students did not sit alone and depressed in the dormitories. Gifts were presented by Santa and Mrs. Claus to both the guys and the girls. A special homemade breakfast, a delicious lunch at a fancy restaurant, and other fun activities were planned. Christmas was definitely not a day off for the activities department—though Mrs. Evans always made sure they were recompensed for the time they gave on Christmas day.

Though Marlene Evans was a great speaker, she was not an eloquent speaker in the traditional sense of the word—silver-tongued and smooth. But she was eloquent in the fact that she conveyed meaning, feeling, and mood as she spoke. She was colorful both in the words she spoke and in the visual aids she used. She had a disdain for the words average and normal when it came to communicating principles and truths to others. She, therefore, attempted to use the five senses in trying to get across what she was trying to teach or express. As she would often say, she wanted to "assault the senses" when planning an activity, speech, production, or party.

Her greatest visual aid seemed to be people. She would often honor people when she spoke, but it was never for the single purpose of bringing honor to someone. She honored in order to teach. She made her

Marlene Evans the Speaker

teaching dramatic and interesting in order to make an impact for a life-time and a difference for eternity.

• During a Spectacular, she had Keith Frye brought to the platform by paramedics. He was Carol Frye's brother, a man in his late twenties who had contracted a severe case of multiple sclerosis. Keith had been away from the Lord for several years until the sudden attack and grave diagnosis had caused him to return to the God of his childhood. His mother, Bertha Frye, had prayed for him the entire time he was away from God. He could barely speak and, in fact, spoke just one line, but it was powerful. His statement, "Ladies…never…give up…on…your…back-slidden and unsaved…sons!" not only brought tears to the entire crowd but changed the attitudes of many ladies toward their rebellious children.

• Young Jackie Odom, whose father is a pastor in Naples, Florida, had been diagnosed with a brain tumor. She went through some tumul-tuous times with her disease, but on the platform of First Baptist Church told the ladies at a Spectacular, "I can tell people about Jesus with my lit-tle green Bible." Of course, her words resulted in many ladies' deciding that if this young, sick girl could win souls, they certainly could too.

Mrs. Evans was a developer of people. Spiritual reproduction was the heartbeat of her teaching, her speaking, and her writing. As a speaker, she did not just want to speak to ladies; she also wanted to develop other speakers. One of the main ways she would get others to begin speaking was to have them tell a story as a part of her speech. Often it would be young lady staff members at Hyles-Anderson College whom she would bring to the platform. They would be nervous and did not want to say the wrong thing; so the first time she brought them to the podium, they would often turn to her and say, "I'm not sure what you want me to say." She would smile, keep her teeth together, and without moving her lips, declare, "Just talk and I'll help you. Don't ask me what to say!" Nearly everyone whom Mrs. Evans helped to learn to speak has a similar story (this author included!). She didn't want "dead space" during a speaking time; she just wanted the person to start talking, and then she would direct her to know what she wanted by asking questions.

Mrs. Evans helped develop numbers of speakers—many of whom

Marlene Evans and Carol [Frye] Tudor
interview Heather Vogt

never dreamed they would ever be able to stand up before a crowd and speak. Many of these ladies are now speakers at the annual nationwide Spectacular at First Baptist Church of Hammond, and many also speak at ladies' conferences throughout the country. Mrs. Evans never wanted to be the only ladies' speaker available. She accomplished her dream of wanting to reproduce herself so that numbers of ladies could be used to influence other ladies' lives, homes, and churches for the cause of Christ.

Mrs. JoJo Moffitt had been asked to speak at Pastors' School. This was her first time to speak, and she diligently wrote out her speech. JoJo is a very conscientious person, and so she worked and reworked her notes. Shortly before she was going to speak, she said to Mrs. Evans, "Would you mind coming to my session? I'm a little nervous about speaking since this is my first time, and I'd really like you to help me know what I should change for the future." JoJo says, "I had about 40 points that I gave in my 45-minute speech. After I finished, I went directly to Mrs. Evans and she said, 'JoJo, you gave such good material!' I replied, 'I know but the people were sleeping! What do you suggest?'

Mrs. Evans was so careful as she hesitantly said, 'Let's see, how about the next time just use four or five points and then give an illustration with each point.' She never put me down for the first boring speech I gave. She only encouraged me and gave me just a little bit of coaching at a time to help me learn to speak before a crowd with humor, interest, and principles that would help them for a lifetime."

Whenever Mrs. Evans spoke, heard someone else speak, or conducted an invitation, she always seemed sensitive to the Holy Spirit's conviction in her own life. One of these times was when Mary Purdum and Kris Grafton, two Hyles-Anderson College staff members, traveled to Michigan with Mrs. Evans for a ladies' conference. After Kris spoke on soul winning, Mrs. Evans gave an invitation, during which time she asked the ladies to promise they would contact someone during the weekend and tell him how to go to Heaven when he died (or they could get someone else to contact the person). Immediately Mrs. Evans got burdened for

Mrs. Evans, a speaker of speakers

Above: Mary Purdum
Below: Mrs. Evans speaking at a summer spectacular at Hyles-Anderson College

Uncle Dean, her dad's brother, who was in the hospital with terminal lung cancer.

Mrs. Evans asked Mary to try to contact a preacher in Beatrice, Nebraska, to go see Uncle Dean and make sure he was saved. Mary made several phone calls to information to get the hospital phone number. The hospital staff told her he had been released and gave Mary the phone number for the nursing home to which he had been sent. She called the nursing home to be sure he was actually there and also to get an update on his condition. When there was no answer at a Baptist church she called, Mary decided to contact Aunt Lela Forsyth and tell her that Mrs. Evans wanted a preacher to go see Uncle Dean. Aunt Lela called her niece and got the name of Pastor Joedeman.

Mary then called Pastor Joedeman at 8:30 p.m. Saturday night from Temperance, Michigan, where she was staying with some friends. He answered the phone by saying, "Jesus saves. Can I help you?" Mary began to explain to him the complicated story of just how she had come to call him. She soon found out that not only did this preacher know Jesus saves, but he knew how to tell someone else how to be saved.

Pastor Joedeman said he would try to go to the nursing center that night if he could get in. Mary gave him the phone number where she was staying and asked him to call her collect and tell her what happened. As she hung up the phone, it seemed too good to be true that he could go that same night, but she prayed it would work out. Uncle Dean had stopped eating and drinking, and there was no telling how much longer he would live. It was possible that the next day would be too late.

At 9:30 p.m. the phone rang. Mary's friend Debbie said, "Why don't you answer it? It's probably the preacher for you." Mary sat on the edge of her chair as Pastor Joedeman told her how Uncle Dean had been ready and willing to trust Jesus as his Saviour and to make sure he was going to Heaven. He said he had thought he had things right with God, but Uncle Dean told Pastor Joedeman he really wasn't sure he would go to Heaven. Pastor Joedeman told Mary, "I took him down the Roman's Road. That's the best way I know." She was thrilled to hear that Uncle Dean did pray and ask Jesus to save him.

Mary immediately called Mrs. Evans to tell her the good news. Mrs. Evans was speechless. She was so glad she had become burdened about

170

Marlene Evans
A Biography

Uncle Dean at that meeting in Michigan because in a very short time he went Home to be with the Lord.

It was so typical of Mrs. Evans to be tender to the speaking and preaching she heard. While she could have thought, "What would these people think if I make a decision at this meeting?", she did not. Rather, she always seemed to be open to what the Holy Spirit wanted her to do as a result of any invitation—her own or someone else's!

One of the greatest characteristics of Marlene Evans was that she could laugh at herself. She almost seemed to delight in some of her antics, and used them to help people to relate to her, to help them learn to laugh at themselves, and to help bring humor into her speaking to keep people's attention. She was able to find humor in everyday experiences and sometimes even found humor in the midst of very serious problems.

There was a period of time when the Evanses started receiving some prank phone calls. The caller(s) would dial their number, and then when anyone in the family would answer the phone, there was complete silence. This went on for some time, and Mrs. Evans finally called the phone company to see what could be done. The company employee instructed her that the next time she received one of those calls she should simply state, "Operator, this is the party with whom I'm having the trouble."

At this time, because of Dr. Evans' college responsibilities, the Evanses had two phone lines in their home. One was the regular family line, and the other was for Dr. Evans' use as college president.

Soon after Mrs. Evans called the phone company, she was using Dr. Evans' phone to dial out when the regular phone line rang. She picked up that phone, and there was silence. She hung up both phones and dialed again. The same thing happened, and by this time she remembered what she had been instructed to do and said very confidently, "Operator, this is the party with whom I'm having the trouble." She hung up both phones again and dialed a third time. When her other line rang for a third time, she suddenly realized that she had been dialing her own number! She would tell this story and have the ladies laughing hysterically, after which she would apply it to her speech by saying, "I was that problem party, and usually the problem is with us!"

Marlene Evans Knew How to Laugh at Herself

When Mrs. Evans flew to one particular ladies' conference, she was unable to get a flight back home immediately after the meeting on Saturday. She did not want to miss any church services on Sunday and was, therefore, forced to fly home on Monday. The meeting was not too far from her dad's home in Kearney, Nebraska, and so, after the meeting she asked the pastor if she could borrow a car in order to go visit her dad. The pastor graciously and willingly agreed to loan one of his cars to her, and she was off to Kearney.

On the way to Nebraska, Mrs. Evans decided to stop at a mall and purchase some gifts for her dad. She parked the car, went into the mall, made her purchases, walked out of the mall, and…had not the foggiest idea for what car she was looking! She couldn't remember the color, the make, or any other detail about the car. She went from row to row looking for the car and finally went to security. They were not much help as they couldn't get the answers they needed when they asked, "What color is the car?" "What kind of car is it?" "Where do you think you parked?" (Keep in mind, she was "directionally challenged"!) And so, she just kept walking through the parking lot looking for a clue. She finally found the borrowed car when she spied a King James Bible lying on the back seat. She tried the key and was thrilled to find it worked! As she later shared this incident, her listeners giggled and laughed as they related to her experience.

Mrs. Evans was diagnosed with ovarian cancer in 1994, after which she made some changes in her eating habits and also started taking a number of vitamin and mineral supplements that could possibly help extend her life. One particular morning she was home alone when she took her supplements along with her regular medication, which included some large pills. She evidently did not drink enough water as she put all the pills in her mouth at once instead of taking a few at a time. The pills got stuck in her throat, and she was afraid she was going to choke to death.

Immediately she remembered how her good friend Bertha Frye had called 911 when she was home alone and had a seizure. Afraid that she

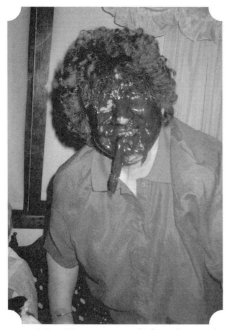

Mrs. Evans enjoyed chocolate pudding and gummy worms with her grandkids!

would be unable to communicate when the paramedics arrived, Bertha had unlocked the front door and written what had happened on a paper plate. And so, Mrs. Evans immediately called 911 and then found a paper plate and wrote what had happened. As she later told of the incident, she seemed so proud of herself for thinking so clearly at such a scary moment. Then, to the delight of her listeners, she would tell about the paramedic's arrival. "Within minutes, a big, tall, handsome stranger rushed in, ran up the steps, and threw his arms around me! I didn't know that's what you got when you called 911!" The ladies always roared at her version of the helpful paramedic's administering the Heimlich maneuver!

Above: Mrs. Evans and Bertha Frye
Below: Always excited

Mrs. Evans could also laugh at herself through surgeries and illnesses. She would tell one story about her infirmities and then say, "You've just heard about my hands. Hang on and you'll get the whole 'organ recital!' "

One particular time she told about the tremendous fluid building that occurs with ovarian cancer. Then she quipped, "None of this is fat; it's all fluid. I'm actually a very delicate, skinny girl!"

Mrs. Evans showed how real she was and how much she could laugh at herself when she wrote an article entitled "Bibs for Adults?" She was refreshingly honest and able to admit her weaknesses, which only seemed to increase her appeal to women.

Bibs for Adults?

I SPILL! Yes, I do! I get teased all of the time about some food or drink splattered down the front of my dress. Iced tea is one of my favorite drinks, and I like it served with lots of ice. By the time I get to the bottom of the glass, the ice falls all over the sides of my mouth and splashes down my front. People love to tell me that I shouldn't miss a mouth the size of mine.

There are several ladies I have known who have the same problem, and I love to point out the fact that they all give themselves to others. You see, they are so busy looking intently at and listening to

Proof that bibs are for adults!
Below right:
Proof that Mrs. Evans was always in
the middle of something!

their family and friends that they are not thinking of their food or clothes. (My friends don't accept that reasoning very well!)

Because I do have this problem, like it or not, I usually tuck in my napkin at the neck as babies or the sick or the senile wear theirs. Oh, spaghetti or rib eaters also are allowed a bib in certain restaurants.

Well, you would think I had committed the unpardonable sin. If some of you haven't been sure what that sin was, I'm here to tell you. Some folks think it is wearing a napkin hanging around the neck!

I have thought and thought about this matter.

- I save lots of cleaning bills and wear and tear on my clothes by wearing a napkin at my neck.
- I know of no verse in the Bible which interpreted means, "Thou shalt not wear a napkin at thy neck."
- There is no law against wearing a napkin at my neck, so it is not illegal.
- I have never gained more weight than usual when I wore my napkin at my neck; therefore, it is not fattening to wear a napkin at my neck.
- I have never caused an accident by wearing a napkin at my neck. It must not be dangerous.
- I do not believe wearing a napkin at my neck is any way immoral.

I have been intimidated for years by a dead woman—Emily Post. Why don't we get horrified over gossip spread at lunch instead of the wearing of a napkin around the neck at lunch?

Mrs. Evans had learned the truth of Proverbs 17:22, *"A merry heart doeth good like a medicine: but a broken spirit drieth the bones."* She not only administered that medication to herself, she also helped those with whom she came in contact as she administered that medicine to them also.

Marlene Evans
A Biography

Marlene Evans Took Others Seriously

A great factor in Mrs. Evans' influencing so many people was that she took others' needs, desires, hurts, and wants seriously. She never put down something someone said as insignificant or unimportant. In fact, to the smallest detail, if it was important to someone she loved or someone with whom she was counseling, it was important to her.

January 8, 1981, was the day Evelyn Smith (the mother of Mrs. Evans' brother-in-law, Jerry) went to be with the Lord. Because Evelyn was important to her sister Doris, she was important to Marlene.

After her funeral, Jerry Smith stopped by Marlene's office to talk about the funeral and burial for his mother. While they were talking, Jerry said, "It's probably silly, but I wish I knew if her shoes were on. Because of all her health problems, Mom hasn't been able to wear shoes for years. She liked to wear nice shoes. I gave them to Mr. Ault (at Bocken Funeral Home), but I forgot to check to see if they were on. I wouldn't ask him now. If they weren't on, it would make Mr. Ault feel bad, and it really doesn't make any difference."

Mrs. Evans related Mr. Smith's comments to Carol Frye who immediately questioned, "If it really doesn't make any difference, why did he say all that?" Mrs. Evans realized that was true and called the funeral home at once. "Mr. Ault, this is probably silly. My brother-in-law wants to know if his mother's shoes were on. If they weren't, I won't let him know I called. If they were, I can give that little piece of information as a surprise gift." Mr. Ault assured her that those things are not a bit silly. "In fact," he said, "they're very important at the time of the death of a loved one." He let Mrs. Evans know in no uncertain terms that Mrs. Smith's shoes were on! Mrs. Evans was thrilled to relay that bit of comforting information to her brother-in-law.

Above: Wendell and Marlene Evans with Jerry and Doris Smith (standing) Below: Jeff and some Malaumandan people greet Mrs. Evans at the airstrip. Inset: the mission supply plane

It was so typical of Mrs. Evans to really listen to people and to learn what was important to them. Once she knew what was important to someone, she did all she could to make those wishes come true. Her son-in-law and daughter, Jeff and Joy Ryder, are missionaries to Papua New Guinea. Mrs. Evans learned that the pilot who was bringing in their sup-

plies every few weeks liked a certain candy bar that is not available in the United States. Coffee Crisp bars can only be obtained in Canada. From that time on, any time Mrs. Evans was in Canada she would pick up a few of those candy bars and have them shipped to the pilot. Hers was a small gesture, but the fact that someone cared enough to get him the one unique candy bar he really liked spoke volumes to this pilot.

One year Mrs. Evans traveled to Alaska in December to speak at a ladies' conference. Shortly after she arrived in Alaska, a volcano erupted, shutting down the airports and nearly all modes of public transportation as the atmosphere was filled with volcanic ash. Mrs. Evans was stuck in Alaska for so many days she feared that she would not be home for Christmas. She was in contact with her family and encouraged her dad to go ahead and make the trip from Nebraska, insisting that they not change the originally scheduled family Christmas. She finally did get home, but not in time to have her Christmas shopping done for their celebration at Jerry and Doris' home.

Mrs. Evans always did her research, so she knew exactly what each person wanted or needed down to the last detail—color, size, brand, etc. She and Dr. Evans went ahead to the party after she gave Carol Frye and Jane Grafton a detailed shopping list. She instructed them that after they purchased a few gifts and gift wrapped them, to quietly open the Smith's front door (which would be kept unlocked) and carefully slide the gifts under the tree. In the Smith's bi-level house, the living room was up the stairs and to the right of the front door. The Christmas tree was located in the corner by the front door. Rather than a wall between the steps and the living room, there was a railing, so it was easy for Carol and Jane to inconspicuously deposit the gifts. Also to their favor in their race against time was the fact that the gift opening was no hurried event when Mrs. Evans was involved. Each person opened one gift at a time, everyone took the time to look at it, words of gratitude were expressed, etc. The opening of each individual gift was a happening unto itself.

Carol and Jane would deliver three or four gifts at a time and then return to the mall. Only Doris and Mrs. Evans knew what was going on behind the scenes and laughed conspiratorially as Alvin finally said, "It

Above: Mrs. Evans, her dad, and Doris having fun at a family Spectacular. Below: Mrs. Evans receives a lavender wig to the delight of Jerry Smith and his daughter Dianne

seems like gifts keep magically appearing under that Christmas tree!" It was an especially memorable Christmas for the family that year as everyone felt so loved and special when they realized Mrs. Evans had seriously taken their wishes and needs and found a way to get those gifts for them in such a short amount of time.

Mrs. Evans also took people's emotional needs seriously. One Sunday morning she was sitting behind some college girls. She suddenly realized they were making fun of a gentleman sitting in front of them. It was obvious by their gestures that the man had trouble with personal hygiene.

Mrs. Evans had no patience with others making fun of the less fortunate. After Sunday school she decided to make a statement to those girls without saying a word to them. She decided to demonstrate to those young ladies how they should be treating that man. She moved forward two pews, sat down beside Stan Wicks, and soon learned he was a ward of the state. He was a simple man with childlike faith. He had no family and lived alone in a small apartment just a few blocks from the church.

Above: Dr. and Mrs. Evans in action at a family Memorial Day party. Below: Mrs. Evans and Stan Wicks

A warm friendship soon developed between Stan and Mrs. Evans. They often sat together in church, and eventually she even invited him to a family holiday gathering. (This was most unusual because she so protected family time.) Stan's presence did add color and interest to their already festive get-togethers!

Stan felt so loved and accepted by Mrs. Evans that when Mrs. Evans was ushered to her front row seat as the mother of the bride at Joy's wedding, Stan soon followed. He walked down the center aisle and sat right next to Mrs. Evans!

When Stan passed away, Mrs. Evans immediately got concerned about his funeral. She just did not want him to have a pauper's casket and a small service with a handful of people at the funeral home.

Big plans were made for Stan's memorial service to be held at First Baptist Church. A nice, modest casket was chosen, special music was planned, and Mrs. Evans invited everyone she talked to! Stan Wicks, a poor, simple, somewhat unkempt man, had a funeral second to none at First Baptist Church!

There was only one oversight. Mrs. Evans confessed, "Somehow it never dawned on me that all these things I helped arrange had to be paid for!"

With the help of her generous and forgiving pastor, the money was raised and the funeral expenses were covered. Mrs. Evans always seemed so pleased she was able to give this indigent man unconditional love, friendship…and a beautiful funeral!

The Words of Marlene Evans

Anyone who knew Marlene Evans knew that her words were above reproach. She used such caution and discretion in choosing her words. She also used caution and discretion in leaving much unsaid, especially the negative. Mrs. Evans' care in choosing her words was one of the great distinguishing factors in her being a different woman.

Carol Frye Tudor tells of an instance regarding Mrs. Evans' talk.

Mrs. Evans and Carol Frye enjoyed talking and playing at a meeting!

ONE day I was driving away from the college, and I glanced over to see Mrs. Evans driving in the lane adjacent to me. I slowed down and waved to her, trying to get her attention.

Mrs. Evans was obviously talking out loud, and she was gesturing with her hands as she talked. I looked to the passenger side of the car to see with whom she was talking. The seat was empty! I kept trying to get her attention, but Mrs. Evans was enthusiastically talking away while staring straight ahead. The whole situation hit me as funny—I mean, I knew she loved to talk, and we loved to get together to talk. But this was the ultimate! She wanted to talk so much, she was enjoying talking to an empty car! She was obviously desperate!

Later I made a sarcastic remark about it, and she said, "Carol, I was practicing talking."

"What do you mean—practicing talking?"

"I want my words to count for eternity," she said. "I don't want to hurt people. I want to influence every person I'm around, so I have to practice what I am going to say."

Loretta Walker recalls traveling to a ladies' meeting where Mrs. Evans planned how she would respond to keep from hurting another's feelings. A year earlier when they had traveled to this particular meeting, she had been experiencing a lot of pain with arthritis and degenerative disc disease. She had needed a wheelchair so she would not have to walk through the airport. At this time she was feeling markedly better and had the strength to walk. She said to Loretta, "If the pastor is at the gate with a wheelchair, say nothing; I'll use it. I don't want him feeling embarrassed by telling him I don't need it." Mrs. Evans cared more for the feelings of others than she cared for her pride—riding in a wheelchair when she didn't need it.

Jane Grafton once asked, "Mrs. Evans, how do you always know what to say to people? You always seem to have just the right answers, especially for delicate or critical issues."

I PRACTICE what I'm going to say, and I try to think ahead what I'm going to face in conversations or situations, and then I plan my words. I often write down what I want to say, and then I practice and practice and practice it (sometimes saying it over 100 or more times) so that if the situation happens, I am prepared and don't say something I'll later regret. I like to have my "press release" memorized if I need it.

Mrs. Evans was well known for her "press releases." She always wanted to be careful, especially in sensitive situations, not to tell more than should be told. She was especially careful not to tell more information than someone wanted to be told. One time a family member had some health issues. Because it seemed many people had opinions on the subject, Mrs. Evans called the family member, talked through exactly what that person wanted told, and that became her "press release." If more questions were asked, she simply repeated the "press release." She was careful to protect others' wishes and their privacy.

Mrs. Evans often said, "Get your stance." The beauty of her planning what she was going to say prevented her from having to pick up the pieces and avoid all the ramifications from spewing out the negative. She always tried to be prepared in what she would say, whether it was in answer to a critical remark or to the news of an unexpected pregnancy where her stance was always, "Oh, that's wonderful!" She was not for abortion, and she never wanted a child to hear, "You weren't wanted." She decided many subjects that were "off limits." She was careful to never overstep the boundaries she had set. For example, she never made thoughtless comments to single ladies such as, "When are you going to get married?" She never asked unkind questions to childless couples like, "When are you going to have a baby?" As a result, Mrs. Evans seldom had to apologize for her words. She talked with purpose; she planned her conversations, and she planned her words. It was evident that she was very principled in her speech and in her conversation.

Dr. Evans says, "After Marlene had listened to Brother Hyles for a few years, she became so wise that many times she didn't even tell me her negative feelings on things. While she was sanguine in her relationships, she became so wise about holding her tongue. Though I am very careful about not telling things that should not be told, if anyone ever spilled the beans it would have been me. There was a little sanguine that would come out of me once in a while, and I would tell her something that was not supposed to be told. Later we would laugh as she would tease, 'You know what a blabbermouth you are.' It would have surprised people, but one of her great characteristics was that she knew how to keep secrets. Sometimes Brother Hyles would say to me about a particular issue, 'I don't even want you to tell your wife.' He didn't know it, but he didn't have a worry. If I had told her, it would never have gotten out. As a mature woman, she was very circumspect in her talk, in choosing her words, and in choosing what not to say."

While Mrs. Evans loved to talk—and "talked the positive to death" as someone once stated—she was also a great listener. It was interesting to watch her listen as she often gave her undivided attention to the speaker. She chose to be interested in other's interests and stories. This took great discipline—as she once confessed when she was speaking about the importance of being a good listener, "Sometimes my lip quivers I want to talk so badly!"

"One of her great characteristics was that she knew how to keep secrets."

Marlene Evans
A Biography

But people talked to her when they would talk to no one else because she had learned the art of being a good listener.

Mrs. Evans was a self-described "opinionated woman." She gave a talk one year at the Christian Womanhood Spectacular entitled, "I'm Not Compatible with Anyone!" where she told many of her likes, dislikes, preferences, and idiosyncrasies. The ladies laughed uproariously as she told how she liked her pizza. She explained how she could never figure out why, when people ordered pizza, they waited until it arrived to wash their hands, sit down at the table, and pray before the pizza ever arrived so she could eat her pizza the way she liked it—**HOT!**

Though she was careful not to express the negative, she felt in most situations she was definitely a person who knew what she liked. She did like to wear perfume that kept its scent all day long. In her later years, "Beautiful" by Estee Lauder became her fragrance of choice. She once told how this came to be.

W̲HEN Christmas 1985 came rolling around, Linda Meister, my secretary of seven years, who is now serving as a pastor's wife in St. Amant, Louisiana, invited me to come speak to her ladies for their Christmas party. Knowing my penchant for perfume all too well, Linda, who is allergic to scents, decided to call Carol Frye to see what my latest "poison" was. Upon being questioned by Carol, I nonchalantly answered, "Oh, just so it's beautiful."

The room in Linda's home which she had so carefully prepared for me had a bottle of perfume called "Beautiful" on the stand by the bedside. Certainly I enjoyed it but wondered why I was given that particular perfume since I'd never before heard of it. Linda told me that's what I had wanted.

People began asking me that question I'd always wanted to hear: "What are you wearing? You smell so good."

Haven't you walked by ladies who moved in a cloud of flowers and thought, "How come I never smell like that? Now, I'm not talking about reeking of "Blue Waltz" or some other dime store fare. I'm talking about fields of daisies and shades of lilies of the valley.

Marlene Evans' Favorites

I was told "Beautiful" was composed of the scents of 2,000 flowers. My, I felt elegant!

Upon returning to Hammond and asking Carol how I had happened to get "Beautiful," she said, "You said, 'Just so it's beautiful.' " I doubled over laughing as I let Carol know I had never before heard of "Beautiful."

Now it's up to Carol to be supplier as her little mis-communication (not mine!) has me hooked on the stuff. What an expensive habit! She and the girls of Hyles-Anderson College gave me three huge bottles of the stuff for my birthday in November, so I should be okay for a year.

Since every day is a special occasion for me (I'm alive!), I run out of those little bottles all too quickly.

Misunderstandings are usually the reason for the trouble we get ourselves into in human relations, but I'm capitalizing on this misunderstanding on Carol's part and am playing it for all it's worth. She thinks I'm taking full advantage of the situation.

Do I ever do anything dumb? No, never! But those around me do!

Mrs. Evans also loved to eat out at restaurants. She had known Dan Evins, founder of the Cracker Barrel restaurant chain, when Dr. and Mrs. Evans still lived in Chattanooga. One can only imagine the excitement Mrs. Evans displayed when she heard the Cracker Barrel restaurants were coming north. When Cracker Barrel opened in Lafayette, about 95 miles south of her home in Schererville, Indiana, she was ecstatic and drove there to eat just as soon as she could fit it in her schedule.

She was doubly thrilled when she learned that a Cracker Barrel was being built in Hobart, Indiana, just about 20 minutes from her house! (She was sure it was in response to all of the requests she had sent to the corporate headquarters!) She learned the date of the grand opening and reserved the round table in the corner for the entire day. (Those who worked with her teased her about her "doctrine of the round table." She liked round tables as opposed to square or rectangular because round tables enable everyone to be able to see everyone else, which, of course, makes for better conversation and involves the entire group. She so

Mrs. Evans had her own Cracker Barrel waitress apron. Notice her name and the four stars!

Marlene Evans
A Biography

impressed this "doctrine" into Brother Dan Wolfe that after becoming the managing editor of *Christian Womanhood*, he placed a **round** table in his office to be used as the conference table for planning meetings!)

Mrs. Evans arrived at the Cracker Barrel bright and early on the day of the grand opening, even before the restaurant doors were opened to the public. She (im)patiently waited until the doors were unlocked, and she immediately headed for that big round table. She had her secretary make up a schedule for the day and had invited different friends and groups of people to come at different times. She stayed from the minute the restaurant opened that morning until it closed that night. She even received bouquets of flowers which were delivered to Cracker Barrel congratulating her on its opening! This was so typical of her to make such a big deal out of the positive and create so much fun for so many people.

People knew of Mrs. Evans' love for Cracker Barrel—so much so that Renee Cox, wife of Pastor Jack Cox of Durham, North Carolina, even presented Mrs. Evans with some Cracker Barrel stock one year at her annual Mini-Spectacular. Mrs. Evans was thrilled with this gift and let everyone know that she owned stock in "her" beloved restaurant.

Above: Mrs. Evans with Brother and Mrs. Jack Cox at a Mini-Spectacular in Durham, North Carolina
Below: Mrs. Evans loved to receive gifts!

Mrs. Evans had fun with her favorites. Her response to someone picking up on any of her favorites was always such a delight to every individual involved. As much as she enjoyed receiving any of her "favorites," she never put down gifts that were not in that classification. In fact, she was thrilled when *any* gifts came her way.

Mrs. Evans did not keep all of the gifts she received. She believed that a person should give a gift with no strings attached and that the receiver should be able to do as she wished with a gift. (That is the philosophy and attitude she always had when she gave gifts.) Therefore, she often used gifts she had received to show gratitude to volunteers (such as the cleaning crew who faithfully came to her house every week after she was diagnosed with ovarian cancer), to her employees whom she felt went above and beyond the call of duty, etc. To Mrs. Evans, gifts were a tool to show gratitude, to encourage someone, or to meet a need.

Dr. and Mrs. Evans visited the Ryders in Papua New Guinea, and the people dressed in full regalia for the Evanses.

When her first grandson, Jordan, was just seven months old, his parents, Jeff and Joy Ryder, were making final plans to leave for their first tour of missionary work in Papua New Guinea. Mrs. Evans was a person who loved deeply and had a very close relationship with her daughter Joy. When asked what Mrs. Evans' real feelings were about the Ryders leaving for Papua New Guinea, Dr. Evans admitted that he really didn't know. He said, "Marlene was so expert at not talking her negative feelings that I never knew anything negative she felt about their leaving."

Now Mrs. Evans had no negative feelings about the fact that Jeff and Joy were giving their lives to serve the Lord full time. She was thrilled that their lives would be spent taking the Gospel to unreached tribes in New Guinea. But she knew this would mean that thousands of miles would separate her from her loved ones and that they would seldom get to talk with each other. Unless there were medical problems, she also realized she would only see the Ryders about every five years.

Mrs. Evans did not let life happen to her. When she knew a hurt or something negative was coming down the pike, she made plans to prevent depression and to help get her mind on the positive and on solutions. Such was the case when Jeff and Joy were making final preparations to leave the United States.

Dr. Evans was leaving to preach out of town immediately after Jeff and Joy flew out of O'Hare Airport, where family members would bid them farewell. Mrs. Evans had known she would return home to a big, empty house and knew that if she stayed home alone, her mind would be on the loss she was suffering.

So, several days in advance she made plans to stay at the college. She had a nice big recliner placed in the office and also had her secretary schedule appointments all evening so she could counsel when she returned to the college from the airport. Mrs. Evans' office had a restroom, so she packed a small overnight bag and, after her last counseling appointment, slept at the college that night. The next morning she had more counseling sessions scheduled before classes were to begin, so she had breakfast (her favorite meal of the day) brought in to her. She always had a plan to get beyond the hurt of what was happening.

During one particularly difficult time in her life, Mrs. Evans had just received some very devastating news. In the next few days Carol Frye took note of the fact that Mrs. Evans had laughed numbers of times. She was puzzled by the fact that Mrs. Evans could have such a great attitude and spirit when she was grieving over the news she had received a few days earlier and said, "Mrs. Evans, are you really happy?"

Mrs. Evans' answer puzzled her even more as she stated, "Yes, I saw a redbird this morning."

When Carol asked her to explain that statement, she gave her reasoning. She could either spend her days and sleepless nights worrying about the ramifications and outcome of the bad news, or she could fill her mind with God's goodness and sleep peacefully as she trusted Him to care for the difficulties of life. Mrs. Evans was not good-spirited by accident. Her positive attitude was on purpose as she decided what types of thoughts would fill her mind.

Once Mrs. Evans' love of redbirds was discovered, it was not uncommon for someone to mail a photo of a redbird or a redbird calendar or some redbird memento almost weekly.

One time Mrs. Evans and Carol Frye were flying to Minnesota to speak at a ladies' conference in Pine City, located north of St. Paul. They got up very early in the morning and left for the airport at 4:00 a.m. They arrived at the airport early, went to eat breakfast, got busy talking, and suddenly realized that they had missed their flight! They walked to the gate, and of course, the plane was gone. Carol was livid! Here she was supposed to be helping Mrs. Evans, and she felt totally responsible for the missed flight.

Immediately Mrs. Evans said,

Carol, we just need to have "instant peace." It does not matter that we missed our flight; it will work out. Anger is a wasted emotion and only causes us to be fearful and upset. We determine our emotions by how we think. We cannot change what happened, and therefore, we can decide to have "instant peace."

When Carol went to the desk and questioned the airline employee about another flight, she was told they would have to wait for several hours. Carol says that she was still angry and frustrated, so she bought a newspaper and hid her face behind it for a long while. Then when they got to the meeting, Mrs. Evans had Carol tell the story! She says, "My pride wanted to blame Mrs. Evans for the missed plane while I blamed myself. But as I started to tell the story, I realized that Mrs. Evans never wanted anyone to be angry at self, and the words she had given me at O'Hare Airport had been so right. Anger is a wasted emotion, and we really can have 'instant peace' if we decide to have it."

Partying with a Purpose

Below: Marlene and her sister Doris party!

Marlene Evans A Biography

One of the areas in which Mrs. Evans changed dramatically, especially after the age of 45, was that she got to the place where she had a goal for every social event. Whether it was a family get-together, a wedding reception, a Valentine banquet, or a high school open house, she would ask her husband, "What is your goal for this [event]?"

Dr. Evans says, "My goal was just to go and have a good time, and I'd reply, 'I don't have a goal.' She would respond, 'Could you have just one?'

This was a woman who had enjoyed parties and social events the entire time I had known her. The Business Women's Sunday School Class in Chattanooga would have a big Christmas party where the husbands were invited. It was just a big social time where everybody had fun. But about age 45, after being under Brother Hyles' preaching and teaching, she started wanting to make a difference everywhere she went. She wanted to touch everybody there. She tried to think through what each person needed and then attempted to meet those needs. She was always on that trail of having goals to help people. That is why people responded so much to her. They knew she cared. She reached her goal of touching lives at social events, and lives were changed as a result of it. I now find myself doing the same thing when I am going to be with people. I find myself thinking through what the people at that social event need from me."

Mrs. Evans did try to really think through what individuals needed from her. In 1989 there had been a terrible public attack on her preacher and on the ministry of First Baptist Church of Hammond. Negative articles falsely accusing Dr. Hyles and First Baptist Church of some unsubstantiated grave sins and mistakes were written up in the newspapers, and even made the national evening news programs. This was the first time many younger staff members had experienced such events, and Mrs. Evans realized this as she attended a Memorial Day picnic just days after the attacks began.

After the meal, Mrs. Evans sat with several couples and some single staff members and answered their questions regarding the attacks. The discussion had nothing to do with details of the attack or with the staff members thinking Brother Hyles was guilty of the accusations. Rather, the staff members had no "point of reference" to realize that their preacher and their church could survive these wicked allegations. Mrs. Evans calmly told them of a time while she was at Bob Jones University how some disloyal employees had made an attack on Dr. Bob Jones, Sr., and the college. She explained how every great ministry eventually comes under attack by the Devil, and that God is always on the side of the falsely accused. Mrs. Evans helped guide those young staff members and gave them hope in the midst of some very dark days. Of course, her words were proven to be right as the ministry of First Baptist Church continued to grow. She influenced those staff members and helped them stay steady during a very tumultuous time in their ministry.

Mrs. Evans also had very strong feelings that a birthday party ought to honor the person who was celebrating his or her birthday. For that reason, she encouraged people to come to a party "ready to talk about the person." She was also very specific in what she expected when each person talked. She did not want general statements such as "I really love Susie. She's a blessing to me." Mrs. Evans wanted the guests to explain in detail why they loved Susie and tell exactly how she had been a blessing!

If, during the course of the event, the conversation got sidetracked, Mrs. Evans carefully and wisely brought the attention back to the honoree. In the beginning she would "program" this type of talk with each of the guests in order to make things happen as she wanted, but eventually, unless the event was with a new group of people, those who knew her or worked with her pretty much knew what she expected at parties! This type of honoring people was a great tool in helping to build relationships as parents, children, friends, and loved ones gave meaningful words of what others meant to them.

The Zugmier girls—Kathryn, Doris, and Marlene—wanted everyone in Kearney, Nebraska, to know their dad was 80!

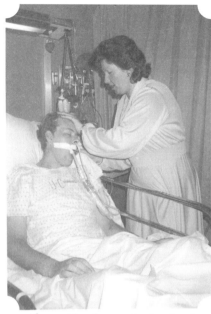

Above: Carol cares for her brother
Keith who was stricken
with multiple sclerosis.
Below: David, the birthday boy!

Marlene Evans
A Biography

Mrs. Evans also never let things that went wrong ruin a party. One time she and some of her family members went to the home of Carol Frye's parents, Bud and Bertha, for the Sunday afternoon birthday party of her brother Keith. This was when Keith was a truck driver and away from the Lord, before he had multiple sclerosis. Carol had ordered an adorable "Linus and Lucy" cake for the party as Keith had often referred to her as "Lucy, the bossy older sister." Several of Carol's friends were going to ride to church with her that morning and went to her dorm room to help carry gifts and decorations for the party to her car. The cake was inside a box that she handed to one her friends. She then handed her another package, and that young staff member placed her Bible on top of the cake box. The top caved in, and the top of the beautifully decorated cake was smeared!

Carol tells that she was quite upset and when she arrived at the party after church, immediately let Mrs. Evans and everyone else know what had happened. Mrs. Evans was not about to let a smashed cake ruin the party. She had a goal of reaching Keith Frye and helping him return to the Lord, and so, when the cake was brought out after the meal, she made a cute remark, grabbed a handful of cake with her hand and stuffed it into her mouth. She soon had everyone laughing hysterically, and especially Keith. He could not believe that a Bible college president's wife was so down-to-earth. Several years later after Keith had gotten right with the Lord, he brought up this incident as one of the turning points in his attitude toward faithful, dedicated Christians. Mrs. Evans' fun and her attitude toward a smashed cake had made a difference in the life of this young rebel.

Dr. and Mrs. Evans' son, David, recalls a most memorable birthday party his mother provided for him on his first "Indiana" birthday, less than a year after they had moved from Chattanooga. A few days before his birthday David asked his mom if he could have a few friends over after school on his birthday. She told him "Yes," and he looked forward to a great time with his friends. However, on his birthday he came home from school to find his entire class waiting for him. What a time they had as

Mrs. Evans had arranged such events as donkey rides down Risch, the street on which they lived! Mrs. Evans loved to help anyone have a good time and a great party, but she especially wanted that for her own children and found ways to make it happen!

Not only did Mrs. Evans seem to have an agenda when she attended parties, she also had an agenda on family vacations. In 1981 Dr. and Mrs. Evans took their children, Joy and David, on a family vacation to Yellowstone National Park. Mrs. Evans realized that with her children quickly approaching adulthood, this might well be their last family vacation. She wanted it to be fun and memorable. There was little Mrs. Evans seemed to enjoy more than nature, and so she helped program the counting of animals and other natural beauties on this trip. The family kept announcing what they saw, and Mrs. Evans made sure it was recorded. When they returned to Indiana, she had her secretary type up the list of sights they had seen and put copies in her children's files to be sure they would have these for a lifetime!

Above: Joy pets one of the goats in Yellowstone.
Below: David with his folks at Yellowstone

Evanses' Family Vacation
Monday, July 27–Saturday, August 1, 1981

YELLOWSTONE NATIONAL PARK

1	skunk	23	moose
1	woodchuck	15	mule deer
1	badger	17	bison
1	eagle	15	deer
1	pelican	97	elk
1	owl	3	marmots
1	coyote	3	mountain goats
1	snowshoe rabbit		
1	pronghorn deer	183	animals (rare to us)
?	chislers		
?	Canada geese	*as well as*	
1	grizzly bear	mountains, geysers, lakes, woods, and waterfalls!	

Marlene Evans' Personal Struggle with Cancer

Dear friends of Mrs. Evans: Mrs. Mrs. John R. (Lloys) Rice (l) and Miss Viola Walden (r)

Marlene Evans A Biography

In July of 1982 Mrs. Evans discovered a lump in her breast. At once her mind went back to her mother who had been diagnosed with breast cancer 30 years earlier. She immediately made an appointment to have the lump checked. As she and Carol Frye left the doctor's office a few days later, she said, "Dr. Cal says, 'It's cancer until proven otherwise.' Let's go eat breakfast, Carol."

Carol was stunned. "How can we go eat at a time like this?!" she questioned.

Mrs. Evans grinned and said, "What? Do you think I'm going to stop eating just because I may have cancer?"

Carol had not expected this type of response from Mrs. Evans, and as they sat down to eat at Zorba's Restaurant, she asked uncertainly, "Mrs. Evans, aren't you going to ask, 'Why me?' "

Her answer to this question was no less astonishing than her response a few minutes earlier. "No! I'm going to ask 'Why not me?' Just because I'm a Christian doesn't mean I can't or shouldn't get cancer." These attitudes were typical of Mrs. Evans through her entire cancer journey.

A few days later on August 6, 1982, Dr. Dennis Streeter performed a radical mastectomy. She went through the surgery well, but her mind was not on herself. Her mind was on her family. It was Aunt Lela's birthday that day, and a big party had been planned. Mrs. Evans had purposely not told Aunt Lela about the impending surgery because she wanted her to be able to enjoy her party to the fullest.

While still a little foggy from the effects of surgery, Mrs. Evans got on the phone with Aunt Lela and in a very upbeat tone of voice said, "Happy Birthday, Aunt Lela!" She went on to ask about the party—who had attended, etc., and then very casually brought up her surgery. She mentioned that she'd had "…just a little mastectomy."

She once wrote about her first cancer diagnosis,

I BELIEVE that the first step to take when the doctor says, "It's cancer!" is to run to Jesus and to the Bible for great gulps of Scripture. Don't panic or go into hysterics. Don't yell and scream. Don't walk—**run** to Jesus. You can stave off fear this way.…I know from experience that you can fight off the fear by going directly to the Scriptures. Some people have said, in referring to me and the way I have responded to the diagnosis of cancer, that I am a remarkable woman. I am not remarkable; I do have a remarkable God Who has given me a remarkable Book to help not just me, but **every** Christian respond in a remarkable way!

Mrs. Evans was in the hospital for five days, but just a day or two after surgery she'd had her "fill" of hospital food. She called Carol Frye early one morning and said, "I cannot take any more yellow jello!" She told Carol she had flushed her jello down the commode and asked her to bring her a "real" breakfast from Bob Evans—one poached egg, one slice of bacon well done, whole wheat toast with butter, orange juice, and a coffee. In the days following until she went home, she had a number of meals delivered, including a Cornish hen under glass deliciously prepared by Miss Arlys Cooper, the gourmet cook who had worked for the Evanses for many years.

Mrs. Evans' cancer was in her lymph nodes, and so chemotherapy was recommended. In Rochester, Minnesota, Mayo Clinic doctors prescribed a six-month regimen of chemotherapy. Mrs. Evans asked a number of questions, one of which was about her prognosis. Her oncologist responded, "We will be ecstatic if you live three to six years."

On the way home from Mayo Clinic, Mrs. Evans planned her funeral. She decided who she wanted for her pall bearers, who she wanted to sing, what songs she wanted sung, and other details including the food to be served at the funeral dinner. This would not be the last time she planned her funeral. In fact, in years to come it became quite humorous since she outlived nearly all of her original pall bearers!

Mrs. Evans started her chemotherapy in November of 1982. This would prove to be a very difficult and trying time for her. She later gave a speech about her treatment and entitled the tape, "Chemotherapy: Through Shades of Hell."

She had been warned that she might get sick to her stomach from the chemotherapy, but she'd always had a strong stomach and really didn't think she would. On the evening of her first treatment, Leslie Beaman brought Mrs. Evans a delicious homemade meal which included spinach lasagna. Dr. and Mrs. Evans were in the basement of their home enjoying

"*God must love you very dearly to trust so much pain and sorrow to your care. I just read this: 'Humanly speaking, we may grow a bit uneasy at times, but there comes the blessed assurance that Jesus lives within, that the Holy Spirit is our Companion, and that our Father watches over us.'*

That is safety and security, and I say with the Scotsman, 'who ever heard of anybody drowning with his head that high above the water!'"

—Viola Walden

[Excerpt from a note of encouragement to Mrs. Evans]

Above: Some of the "styles" Mrs. Evans enjoyed while wearing wigs. Below: JoJo "guiding" Mrs. Evans in the classroom.

Marlene Evans A Biography

Leslie's meal, and Carol was upstairs cleaning up the kitchen. Dr. Evans walked up the steps and calmly said, "Carol, Marlene needs you."

She thought nothing of it since he was so calm. She made her way to the basement where she began running into "puddles" on the floor. She followed the puddles to the bathroom where Mrs. Evans was leaning over the commode. Mrs. Evans looked at her with surprise and said, "I guess my stomach isn't as strong as I thought!"

Mrs. Evans would teach on Monday mornings, after which she would go get her chemo treatment and then go home to bed. For the first 48 to 72 hours after each treatment, she was sick about every 30 minutes to an hour. Wednesday or Thursday she would return to work and teach through the next Monday morning.

The chemotherapy had many side effects. Some, such as losing her hair, did not seem to be a big deal to Mrs. Evans. She realized she could simply get a wig until her own hair grew back. One of the more difficult side effects for Mrs. Evans was the effect it had on her mind. She suddenly could not remember things and had a very difficult time getting her words. Her assistant teacher, JoJo Moffitt, was such a tremendous help to her at this time. JoJo never left Mrs. Evans' side as she would stand to teach. She helped her remember where she was in her notes, helped her remember what she was trying to say, and prompted her with key words. Mrs. Evans later noted that there would have been no way she could have taught on the days she did if she'd not had JoJo by her side.

During these days of chemotherapy, Mrs. Evans kept her regular schedule as much as possible. She even continued to go speak at ladies' conferences. In December she flew to California with Carol Frye to speak at a conference. She was bald by this time and had already purchased several wigs, but as they walked through a flea market with the pastor and his wife, Mrs. Evans spied a hot pink Afro wig. As their plane landed in Chicago, Carol encouraged Mrs. Evans to switch wigs and put on the new one she had purchased at the flea market. She giggled and without hesitation made the switch!

What a sight for this classy woman in a conservative business suit, nice pumps, a feminine blouse, and beautiful jewelry to be wearing a hot pink wig. But they had fun with it! A tall, thin black man with a big Afro came up to her and said, "Sister, I really like your hair! Did you dye it in honor of the Christmas season?" They laughed with him and with others all the way through the airport, but the best was yet to come.

When Mrs. Evans arrived home, she walked up the steps to see a very shocked expression on Dr. Evans' face. Then he chuckled and said, "Well, Marlene, if you can have some fun out of being bald, I'm all for it!" He knew the struggles she had faced with her cancer treatment and was very supportive and thrilled for any fun she could have with it!

Never Question God

Through all of this time, Marlene Evans never questioned God, and her attitudes were nothing short of amazing. Rather than focusing on the negative—what she was not able to do and what she had lost—she worked with amazing discipline to keep her mind on anything positive—what she was able to do and what she had *not* lost. She also concentrated on what she *could* do as she worked on solutions. She could do nothing about losing her hair, but she could purchase several wigs—including the cheap $10 hot pink Afro that gave her and many others lots of laughs.

She said during those days,

> Being angry at God is a waste of time and energy because when your mind is concentrating on anger at God, it cannot be focusing on solutions. Get your mind off the bad and onto the good. Get your mind off of what you can't do and onto what you can do!

For nearly two years after her chemotherapy treatments, she was very quiet and withdrawn. (Chemotherapy weakens the immune system, causing its recipients to feel very negative and depressed.) Dr. and Mrs. Evans had always enjoyed having breakfast together, but during these long months Mrs. Evans had nothing to say. She later told Dr. Evans that for every one positive thing he would say, she could think of ten negatives! The great thing was, she kept her mouth shut. It was evident that her vibrant, upbeat personality was gone, but she was careful to not talk all the negative thoughts she was thinking.

When the effects of chemotherapy on her mind lasted for so long, she began to think that she should give up her responsibilities of teaching at Hyles-Anderson College and her position as dean of women. However,

"The knowledge that God is far wiser than any of us helps to keep me going. We have to allow Him to work His perfect will in our lives in whatever way He chooses…even through a seeming tragedy like cancer. Some people allow the Lord to use them and their tragedy to make a difference for others. Being really used often results in lives being changed that would never have been changed. Knowing that He loves me and has a plan for my life makes me able to keep on keeping on."
— *Marlene Evans*

[Excerpt from a letter written by Mrs. Evans]

"You vill bloom again!"

Mrs. Evans with Dr. Frigas

Ovarian Cancer, Stage 4

1994

before making a decision that drastic, she decided to see her coordinating physician at Mayo Clinic, Dr. Frigas, a Greek man with a distinct accent. After asking her some questions, he realized it would probably be more hurtful for her to be at home alone than to continue her duties. However, knowing that she could not face all the administrative duties caused her to say, "But, Dr. Frigas, I'm hurting my workers."

He immediately answered, "You vill bloom again!"

Oh, what comfort and encouragement those words were to Mrs. Evans! She did not get better all at once, but every time she began to doubt if she'd ever be well again, she'd think, "I vill bloom again!" God used this good doctor to give beautiful words of hope that helped a patient on her long and lonely journey.

Mrs. Evans returned to her oncologist at the cancer clinic in Merrillville, Indiana, every year for checkups to be sure the cancer had not returned. While those around her wanted to celebrate her fifth anniversary of being cancer-free, she did not. She'd heard of so many women celebrating their fifth anniversary only to experience a recurrence of cancer and die six or eight months later.

When she made it to the ten-year mark, her oncologist said, "Why are you still coming here to have checkups? You are considered cured." Mrs. Evans was surprised by that statement, but she never let herself believe it. She always felt in the back of her mind that the cancer would return. She didn't dwell on that negative possibility, but she'd had so many people in her family, including grandparents, aunts, and uncles, who had died of cancer that she just always believed it would come back. She did all she knew to do and was careful to get her annual checkups each year. However, as much as she took all the preventive measures she knew to take, the cancer was lurking within her body in a much greater way than anyone imagined.

For months Mrs. Evans had been experiencing some bothersome symptoms including heartburn, fatigue, and pain in her thighs. One of the greatest symptoms she described as "fire in my gut." At times the pain was almost unbearable. She had even visited several physicians including a gynecologist, who all gave her a clean bill of health. This is not surprising since there is no foolproof test for the kind of cancer she had. It is often referred to as "the silent killer" of women.

In the beginning of April 1994, she traveled to speak at Hopewell Baptist Church in Napa, California, where Dr. Mike Ray is the pastor. Jane Grafton had gone with her that weekend and had noticed how little Mrs. Evans seemed to be eating. On the flight home Mrs. Evans put her seat back to sleep. As Jane sat and looked at this great woman who had been so influential in her life, she was bothered by how distended Mrs. Evans' abdomen seemed to be, especially considering how little she had eaten that weekend.

A few days later Mrs. Evans discussed her symptoms with Carol Frye, who called Dr. Cal Streeter. He immediately ordered an ultrasound of the abdomen, so Mrs. Evans asked Jane Grafton to drive her to Methodist Hospital in Merrillville, Indiana, for the test. A few hours later Dr. Cal told Mrs. Evans, "Get a surgeon. You have ascites; your abdomen is full of fluid."

Jane drove Mrs. Evans back to the college where they went to Carol's office to meet with Carol and Kris Grafton, the head nurse at Hyles-Anderson College. Kris and Carol both knew that more than likely, the ascites indicated that cancer would be the diagnosis. It was decided that Mrs. Evans should go to Mayo Clinic, so Kris Grafton called Dr. Frigas' secretary, a sweet Christian lady named LaDonna Mourning, to set up an appointment.

The next morning found Carol (who had driven Mrs. Evans to Mayo Clinic) and Mrs. Evans in West 15, the floor where her physician of 15 years was located. Though patients are usually called to the desk over the P.A. system and then shown to their exam room, Dr. Frigas walked into the waiting room to greet Mrs. Evans. Mrs. Evans saw him coming and rushed toward him. She was relieved to know that her case was now in the hands of the Mayo Clinic physicians.

Mrs. Evans went through a week of testing after which she was told she had ovarian cancer, a very devastating diagnosis. Surgery, which would give a clearer picture of the diagnosis, was then scheduled. Mrs. Evans called her husband immediately, who then contacted their children, David who was living in Texas at the time and Joy who was in Papua New Guinea.

"Our Saviour's touch has still its ancient power, and when human help has done what it can, we may still press through the crowd and touch Jesus. Spurgeon said, "God is too good to be unkind, too wise to be mistaken, and when you cannot trace His hand, you can always trust His heart."

—Viola Walden

[Excerpt from a letter written to Mrs. Evans]

October 17, 1994

Dear Mrs. Evans,

It is not hard to admire you these days. You are hanging in there like a trooper. Keep doing it. We need you. I need you. Everywhere I go I meet people who know you and love you and are praying for you. I am one of those. God bless you.

Sincerely,

Dr. and Mrs. Hyles with
Dr. and Mrs. Evans

She also called her dad and her sisters. After each phone call and before the next, Mrs. Evans would take a few minutes to regain her composure. Though she realized the diagnosis after the surgery was probably not going to be good news, she tried to stay calm and low key as she made each phone call.

Once she had notified her family, she turned to Carol and said, "Let's go eat." They walked out of the Mayo Clinic building, and Carol followed Mrs. Evans across the street to the Elizabethan Room, a very classy restaurant with strolling musicians. Mrs. Evans wanted to be "pampered" to help get her mind off the negative news she had just received.

By the time they had finished a delicious and relaxing meal and returned to their room at the Clinic View Inn, flowers had already begun arriving and phone calls were coming in. Hyles-Anderson graduates, pastors and pastor's wives, fellow staff members, and friends from all over the country had heard the news and immediately wanted to express their love and support to their beloved friend. Though her heart was heavy from the news she had received, Mrs. Evans loved all this attention. She said to Carol, "I feel like Tom Sawyer. I'm getting an opportunity to see my own funeral. Very few people ever have the chance to hear their friends express how they really feel about them. I had no idea people would respond in this way." But suddenly the thought hit her that people might give flowers and words then and not at her funeral. And so, as phone calls continued to come in she would tell people, "I love your flowers, but don't think they take the place of sending them to my funeral. I want lots of flowers then too!"

Every phone call was meaningful to Mrs. Evans, but one call stood out above all the others—a call from her pastor, Dr. Jack Hyles. The switchboard was "jammed" with calls, and numbers of people had trouble getting through as they kept getting a busy signal. When Brother Hyles finally reached Mrs. Evans, he said teasingly, "If you'd quit gossiping on the phone, I could get through!" Mrs. Evans responded with her distinct hearty laughter. She was so thrilled to hear from her preacher. She later said, "Brother Hyles' phone calls couldn't take away the diagnosis of cancer, but they did cause me to feel very special, which lessened the pain of the diagnosis."

She also said, "It's truly amazing that being insulted by Brother Hyles can make you feel special, but it does! Somehow he builds you and encourages you at the same time he is teasing you." When Brother Hyles asked if she was going to take chemotherapy again, she answered hesitantly, "I don't know, Preacher. You know how that medicine makes me act so crazy!"

His quick response tickled her as he teased, "Marlene, don't blame the medicine! You were crazy long before you ever took chemotherapy!"

Surgery was scheduled for Thursday, April 21. True to form, Mrs. Evans did not spend time thinking about herself or worrying about the outcome. Rather, she spent the time giving Carol Frye very specific instructions as to what she wanted to happen in her room. She realized from the phone calls and flowers she had received in her motel room that there would be visitors and phone calls in her hospital room also. She wanted every visitor and every caller to know of her appreciation for their care and concern.

Dr. and Mrs. Hyles came for a surprise visit to Mrs. Evans at Mayo!

She said to Carol, "As sick as I'll be, I'll know if there are hurt people in my room." She *always* wanted *everyone* treated right! She not only wanted people treated right, she wanted her room to be a place of building and encouragement. Her last words to Carol before leaving for surgery were, "Don't forget, as sick as I'll be, I *will* know if there is tension in the room. I'm counting on you to see to it that visitors are well cared for!"

Dr. Evans and Carol waited in her room during the surgery. Carol was busy decorating the room with posters and cards when suddenly Dr. Evans' mouth dropped open and he stopped talking mid-sentence. Carol turned to see why he looked so stunned, and she was as shocked as he was to see Dr. and Mrs. Hyles standing in the doorway. They had flown to Rochester, Minnesota, just for Mrs. Evans' surgery. They arrived too late to see Mrs. Evans before surgery, but they were also there to support Dr. Evans. The time passed quickly as Dr. Hyles and Dr. Evans bantered back and forth and told the latest jokes they had heard. When Mrs. Evans got out of surgery, pastoral visiting privileges were sought for Brother Hyles to be able to see her in the recovery room. Unfortunately, Brother Hyles was unable to see Mrs. Evans, but before returning to the airport Dr. and Mrs. Hyles were able to be with Dr. Evans as he listened to the surgeon's report.

Dr. Williams, a tall, lanky, bearded man who had 35 years of surgical experience, told Dr. Evans that he had been able to remove about 96 percent of the cancer. The surgery had been quite extensive and had included the removal of a tumor the size of a large cantaloupe, the omentum (the protective covering lining the abdominal cavity), and the scraping of her abdomen in an attempt to remove as much cancer as possible.

Dr. and Mrs. Hyles had to leave for the airport, but their presence had been a tremendous blessing and encouragement to Dr. Evans. After they left the room, he turned to Carol and said, "It's unbelievable that Brother and Mrs. Hyles would take a whole day to fly to Minnesota just to be here for Marlene and me when he spends so much of his life in airports and on planes!"

Mrs. Evans' recovery was slow, but it went well. Her diagnosis was ovarian cancer, stage IV. She was to begin chemotherapy three weeks after surgery; but due to complications with the healing of her incision, treatment was delayed for two weeks. At that appointment Mrs. Evans asked Dr. Hartman, "What is the natural course for this disease?"

She answered, "Studies show that women with stage IV ovarian cancer usually live two to five years after the diagnosis. The devilish nature of this disease is that it will come back in full force eighteen months after diagnosis."

This was a grave diagnosis, but Mrs. Evans took it matter-of-factly. When Mrs. Evans and Carol left the clinic, they got in the car and drove home. Carol knew Mrs. Evans would want an upbeat atmosphere, so she put on quartet music; they "sang" their way home to Indiana. They also "re-planned" Mrs. Evans' funeral. During this second planning they discovered that many of her original pallbearers had gone to Heaven!

Marlene Evans was a rejoicing Christian who kept her mind on the positive. That did not mean she put her head in the sand and ignored problems. Quite the opposite was true. When there was a problem, such as cancer, she learned all she could regarding the prognosis and nature of the disease, researched to find her options, made a decision as to what would be the best choice of treatment, and then started the treatment. She faced problems head on so that she could free her mind to think on good and right things.

After two more weeks of rest and healing, Mrs. Evans began her six-month chemotherapy regimen at Mayo Clinic on May 25, 1994, where she would receive one treatment each month. One of the more positive

Above: Mrs. Evans with Dr. Hartman, her Mayo Clinic oncologist
Below: Mrs. Evans relaxing in her hot-pink, warm wig

Marlene Evans
A Biography

aspects about this second bout of chemotherapy was that new drugs had been developed since her 1982 regimen that would help with the side effects, especially the vomiting. After each treatment, she would take a very expensive, football-shaped pill called Zofran every two to three hours. There was much discussion over the shape and price of the pill—$17.25. Each treatment required about $258.75 in Zofran medication to prevent vomiting. One night immediately after Carol administered the Zofran, Mrs. Evans vomited it back up. Carol exaggerated the cost of the pill as she said, "Well, there goes that $20 football down the drain!"

Mrs. Evans smirked as she quickly responded, "Does the price rise when it comes back up?"

Mrs. Evans made specific plans for each Mayo trip to keep them interesting and to keep her mind off of the main reason for the trip—her chemotherapy treatments. She mapped out favorite restaurants such as the Machine Shed in Rockford, Illinois, for a roast beef dinner and Burnstadt's European Café in Tomah, Wisconsin, for rhubarb pie.

By the fall of 1994 Mrs. Evans was quite weak from the four chemotherapy treatments she'd had. Though she was weak and feared that she might not be able to meet her teaching responsibilities at Hyles-Anderson College, she had an even greater fear of lying home in bed alone every morning. She decided to go ahead and teach that fall. JoJo Moffitt, her assistant teacher, took care of all the attendance records and paper work involved in teaching, leaving Mrs. Evans free to just come in to the classroom and teach. Carol Frye would go to Mrs. Evans' house each morning and help her get ready and then drive her to the college.

On one particular day Mrs. Evans seemed so weak and depressed that Carol suggested she stay home. Mrs. Evans declined stating, "I will not think good if I lie in bed. If you can get me to school and I can teach my classes, then I will come home and my bed will feel good." She did just that. She knew that getting really, really tired would help her to be able to sleep better once she got into bed than if she stayed home, knowing she would lie there and think hopeless, negative, depressing thoughts.

Once her chemotherapy regimen was finished, her strength started to return. She had continued many of her regularly scheduled activities during that time. She did have to cancel two speaking engagements, but one of the top priorities in her life was church attendance. She tried never to

"*Dear, need I remind you that God makes no mistakes, and all He does is right? He has no stereotyped way of doing what He does. He delivered Peter from prison but left John the Baptist in a dungeon to die. We are to accept whatever He does, however He does it. He sent this illness for a purpose.*"

— *Viola Walden*

[Excerpt from a letter written to Mrs. Evans]

miss church as she felt that was her biggest help and support during chemotherapy. She said about church attendance:

I PERSONALLY need to be in church every time it is at all possible. Sometimes I've crawled into church. Sometimes I've barely nodded or smiled at anyone and found myself better after hearing the preaching....hearing preaching sometimes helps me get my mind off my pain enough to relax. At times, the tenseness is lessened, and the pain is lessened in that way. Every day, ask the Holy Spirit to help you do what He wants you to do that day. Then tell yourself, "I'm doing the best I can." Toss the Devil out on his face and get rid of the guilt.

Mrs. Evans realized that she needed a bigger support group than ever to help her plan the Spectacular for the fall of 1994. Therefore, she formed a team of workers whom she called her "Dream Team." This committee included Gina Eyer, Belinda Gaona, Jane Grafton, Kris Grafton, June Ryland, Loretta Walker, and Brother Dan Wolfe. This group met each month and helped Mrs. Evans plan the Spectacular and also carried out the details that were planned in those meetings. She counted heavily on this group of people to make the Spectacular happen.

There was another group of people on whom Mrs. Evans heavily counted, and she organized a Tuesday meeting with them. This group included Bonny Beebe, Arlys Cooper, Jane Grafton, Kris Grafton, Vicki Mitchell, JoJo Moffitt, and Linda Stubblefield. Each of these people had different responsibilities, but sometimes input was needed on each others' duties, so Mrs. Evans felt it would simplify the work if they met once a week. Vicki was Mrs. Evans' secretary, and Bonny and Jane worked for Christian Womanhood, so much of their part in the Tuesday meeting had to do with those responsibilities. Kris Grafton was there to help with medical situations such as insurance billing, appointments, etc. Of course, JoJo cared for any business having to do with Mrs. Evans' classes.

Since Mrs. Evans wanted to keep her mind off of her own problems and her cancer, she started a "ministry" that few people (except those ministered to) knew about. She asked Arlys Cooper, who had worked for her in several capacities, to get the Wednesday evening prayer bulletin at church and purchase inexpensive get well cards to send to the people list-

Marlene Evans'
"Dream Team"

(back row l-r) Kris Grafton, June Ryland, Janice and Dan Wolfe, Jane Grafton (front) Loretta Walker, Belinda Gaona, Gina Eyer

Marlene Evans
A Biography

ed on the prayer sheet. Arlys would address envelopes with their name and address, and get those cards to Mrs. Evans who would then write a brief note of love and encouragement before mailing them.

Arlys had one other responsibility that was especially important to Mrs. Evans. Family was a priority to her, and she never wanted to miss a birthday or anniversary of a loved one. She was unable to go do the shopping herself, and so she explained the type of cards she wanted and then asked Arlys to purchase them for her. She didn't just want nice cards, she wanted beautiful cards with meaningful words. Arlys became expert at this, and Mrs. Evans once commented that Arlys seemed to purchase the cards she would have chosen herself had she been able to do the shopping. Arlys kept track of all the important dates, addressed and stamped the cards, and got them to Mrs. Evans in a timely manner for signing so they would not be late. She did this for everyone in her family (both those who lived in the local area and those out of town) for every special day including all holidays, birthdays, and anniversaries.

Linda Stubblefield was, by now, the assistant editor of *Christian Womanhood*. (Pat Hays had retired due to health problems, and Linda had been chosen to do the work Pat had done for so many years.) In addition to the tremendous duties of doing the layout for the paper, Linda also added the responsibility of doing Mrs. Evans' correspondence, which became especially massive after her second cancer diagnosis. So many people from First Baptist Church of Hammond and friends from all across the country did so much for her during this time that it was a monumental task to keep up with the thank-you letters. Mrs. Evans was careful to indicate on every card she received what she wanted in the thank-you response. Mrs. Evans then sent the cards and notes to Linda, who would type the thank you's for her. Linda also helped Mrs. Evans in her correspondence by keeping people informed of her health status.

In the years following, there were more chemotherapy treatments and recoveries, each one a little closer together than the last. Mrs. Evans continued to have much pain from her arthritis and degenerative disc disease, and by 1998 it seemed the only solution for her pain was a hip replacement. At the same time her dad, Alvin Zugmier, had suffered from a severe heart attack and had been hospitalized. She had gone home to see her dad and really believed he would soon be going to Heaven. She was

Kris Grafton, Mrs. Evans, Linda Stubblefield, and Mrs. Hyles took a two-day trip to Brown County, Indiana, in April 2001.

comforted by the fact that during one of her visits with Hazel and Alvin, she had been able to very carefully discuss salvation with both of them. She knew they were both very good people, but she had never been able to hear her dad give her a clear account of his salvation. She was thrilled when both Alvin and Hazel bowed their heads and trusted Christ as Saviour!

On November 30, 1998, Alvin Zugmier went to Heaven. This was the end of an era for Mrs. Evans. All of the people who had invested so much in her as a child and as a young person were gone. She had seen so much greatness in those people, and especially in her dad who had been her first hero. She remembered his work ethic and how he had worked several jobs at one time to support his family when he first purchased the Star View Motel. She remembered his justice, such as when he gave Kathryn, who had chosen not to attend college, a nice sum of money comparable to the amount he had put into Marlene's and Doris' college education.

She remembered and she was grateful…for her dad and for all of those who had invested in her. She always remembered that she was not a "self-made" person. She knew she was the product of all those great people who had invested in her, and she never forgot a one of them. She grieved terribly over the loss of her dad, but while she was grieving, she was also fighting her own struggles with cancer and other health issues. She seemed to realize that it would not be too long before she would be joining him. It would, in the end, only be about 31 months.

Exactly one month after her dad's Homegoing, Mrs. Evans had her hip replacement surgery at Mayo Clinic. She had realized that this surgery would require intense care and assistance once she got home. Carol Frye, who had so faithfully nursed Mrs. Evans through so many chemotherapy treatments, was no longer available in the way she had been. In the fall of 1997, Richard Tudor, whose wife Raynell had passed away, began showing interest in Carol. They fell in love, and at the Hyles-Anderson College Valentine Banquet in February 1998, they had gotten engaged. Everyone was excited for Carol, who was marrying for the first time at age 47.

Mrs. Evans showed the ultimate unselfishness for a woman in her

Dad Zugmier and his "girls" at the Star View Motel in Axtell, Nebraska

position. While she realized that most people don't have their own nurse, being able to depend on Carol's nursing care had enabled Mrs. Evans to continue teaching and speaking through all of her cancer and its subsequent treatments. When Mrs. Evans saw love growing between Carol and Richard, she very unselfishly encouraged the relationship. While jealousy and fear could have caused her to discourage Carol from dating, Mrs. Evans did what she believed was best for Carol and Richard. She actively supported their dating, engagement, and marriage in every way possible.

Richard and Carol were married on September 26, 1998, at First Baptist Church of Hammond. Since both of Carol's parents were already in Heaven, Mrs. Evans sat in place of the bride's mother, and Dr. Evans gave her away. It was a beautiful wedding, and Mrs. Evans delighted in every part of the planning and in the wedding itself. She was thrilled for Carol and Richard and seemed to be able to put her own needs on the back burner for a while.

Mr. and Mrs. Richard Tudor with Dr. and Mrs. Evans

When a hip replacement became inevitable, Mrs. Evans had asked God to show her the way and take care of her during her surgery and recovery. God heard and answered her prayer in a most beautiful way. Mary Purdum, who had worked for Mrs. Evans years earlier at Hyles-Anderson College, was making plans to leave the United States to be a missionary in Australia. When Mary heard of Mrs. Evans' impending surgery, she delayed her leaving and offered to stay with Mrs. Evans during her recovery. What an unbelievable blessing Mary was to Mrs. Evans as she helped her get from Mayo Clinic in Rochester, Minnesota, where she had her surgery, to her home in Schererville, Indiana. Mary assisted Mrs. Evans through nearly two months of recovery. Mrs. Evans was thrilled with the relief she got from the hip replacement, and she was even more thrilled with the way God had brought Mary Purdum in a time of need.

During their first tour in Papua New Guinea, Jeff and Joy Ryder had to return to the United States early due to health problems. Though Jeff had invested countless hours learning and translating the language, he was not the one who presented the Gospel to the tribe with which he had been working. Mrs. Evans did not want that to happen again, and so she prayed that God would keep her alive until Jeff had been able to present the Gospel to this second tribe with which they were working in Malaumanda. Once Jeff had learned the language and created a written dialect, it still took months for him to present the Gospel to this tribe. He had to begin with such simple truths as explaining that there is a world beyond their little village.

In May Jeff started holding daily meetings with the tribal people, and finally, in October of 1999, Jeff was able to present the plan of salvation. It was a very rewarding time for the Ryders when, after he presented the truth of the crucifixion, the widow of a man who had begged for a missionary to come to their village raised her hand and said, "It's the blood."

Mrs. Evans was thrilled to hear this news as her prayers had been answered. God had kept her alive, and Jeff had been allowed to present the Gospel. Before they left Papua New Guinea in December, 68 people had trusted Christ as Saviour. Jeff, Joy, Jordan, Grant, and Lindsey were rejoicing over these salvations as they returned to the United States in December of 1999. They would get to spend precious time with Mrs. Evans in the year 2000, and a few months into 2001, the last time they would be together with her this side of eternity.

"Counseling from the Pulpit"

February 6, 2001, brought devastating news to the First Baptist Church of Hammond, Indiana. Their beloved pastor of 41 years, Dr. Jack Hyles, went to Heaven. The people were in shock. They just believed they'd have their pastor for a long, long time. When she received the news, Mrs. Evans sat in her fireplace room and cried, realizing that the man who had "counseled her from the pulpit" through her cancer was gone. This was a time of tremendous grief as the hurting congregation wondered what would happen. Who would be their new pastor? Would the church continue to grow? Would the church keep the standards and convictions which had distinguished it for so many years?

It was a wonderful day when the pulpit committee of First Baptist Church nominated Dr. Jack Schaap, Dr. Hyles' son-in-law, to be the pastor. The church had only been without a pastor for 28 days when Dr.

New pastor and wife,
Dr. and Mrs. Jack Schaap

| *Marlene Evans*
A Biography

Schaap was voted in as pastor with a 96% majority by the great people of First Baptist Church. Mrs. Evans was clearly excited about the new pastor as she wrote in *Christian Womanhood*,

THOSE of us who know him best believe that Pastor Schaap has brought a godly passion to the work that will perpetuate Dr. Hyles' ministries for the next generation.

It was soon evident that Brother Schaap would not simply perpetuate the ministry his father-in-law had built; he would take it to a new level! Though Mrs. Evans was still very much grieving the loss of her pastor of nearly 30 years, she immediately viewed Brother Schaap as her pastor and looked to him as the man appointed by God to lead the First Baptist Church. Mrs. Evans had told her workers more than once, "Rebels come out when there is a change." She just always immediately placed herself on the side of godly leadership and supported her leaders in every way possible.

In the spring of 2001 Jeff and Joy made plans to return to New Guinea. Mrs. Evans realized that barring a miracle she would not see her grandchildren again. Though she was very weak and only a few months from death, she found ways to have fun with her granddaughter and teenage grandsons. She wanted them to remember her as a fun grandmother, not as "a sick, old lady." She was so adept at thinking through what would be fun for young people. She knew that driving would interest them, so she would take her grandsons, one at a time, to a parking lot or on the back roads, and let them drive her "red sleigh" as she referred to her ruby red Buick LeSabre. What great memories she created for that family!

On Tuesday, May 15, 2001, the Ryders said goodbye to Dr. and Mrs. Evans at O'Hare Airport as they left to return to the mission field. Joy wrote of that departure, "That last goodbye will forever be bronzed in my mind as I recall going up the stairs toward our gate. Dad kept inching Mom forward as far as possible in her wheelchair as we waved and blew kisses. We were all crying. We both wanted to keep our eyes on each other as long as possible. And then I bent down to catch one last glimpse of my mother's face—a moment I'll never forget. Somehow it seemed that we both knew it was the last time we would see each other on this side of

Mrs. Evans could never be misconstrued as a grandma who didn't have fun!
Above: with her husband and grandchildren—Tony and Amanda at Cracker Barrel
Below: with her grandsons, Jordan and Grant

Above: The Ryder family with Mrs. Evans before their departure to Papua New Guinea weeks shortly before her Homegoing
Below: Skip and Bev Buskol

| *Marlene Evans
A Biography*

Heaven. Dad told me later that after they returned from the airport, Mom went to her room, shut off the phones, closed the house to any visitors, and cried for two days. She loved me, and she loved my family. I know she was grieving because she knew that more than likely she would not see us again."

In June of 2001, Mrs. Evans and Jane Grafton were scheduled to fly to a ladies' meeting at Heritage Baptist Church in Great Falls, Montana, where Dr. Sheldon Schearer is the pastor. It was a difficult trip, to say the least. Shortly after the plane took off from O'Hare Airport, Jane called a steward because Mrs. Evans seemed as if she were going to pass out. Jane helped her get her feet elevated, and the kind steward put her on oxygen during the flight. They were to land in Minneapolis, so the steward called ahead to have paramedics ready when the plane landed. Mrs. Evans and Jane discussed the possibility of calling her good friend, Bev Buskol, to take her to Mayo Clinic. From the time their paths crossed, Bev and her husband Skip proved their friendship to Dr. and Mrs. Evans many times. Skip owns an auto repair shop in the Minneapolis area and used his talents and abilities to meet needs in the Evans family. Dr. Evans says, "Humanly speaking, I don't know how we would have gotten along as well as we did through Marlene's sicknesses without the help and friendship of the Buskols."

The tentative plan was for Jane to fly on to the meeting alone. However, the oxygen helped, and Mrs. Evans decided to go to the meeting as originally planned. Mrs. Evans' pulse and blood pressure had become very erratic, a complication of the cancer. The fluid building in her lungs prevented her from getting enough oxygen to her brain.

Mrs. Evans spent as much time as possible resting in her motel room but wanted to speak each time she was scheduled. Friday night she spoke nearly an hour and a half! When they were back at the motel, Mrs. Evans indicated that she didn't think she had spoken very well. She had; it had been a very powerful message on marriage. The next morning when the pastor's wife saw Mrs. Evans, she said, "I know why you came to this meeting." She went on to explain that a lady had come up to her after the meeting Friday night and said, "Mrs. Schearer, I was planning to file for divorce on Monday. Mrs. Evans' talk tonight helped me realize that I am the problem." Mrs. Evans was thrilled to hear that God had used her to save this woman's marriage.

At breakfast Mrs. Evans talked about her cancer and said to Jane, "I'm just tired of fighting." Jane, of course, didn't want to hear those words and brushed them off in her mind. "She'll rally like she has the other times," she thought. She had no idea that in three short weeks Mrs. Evans would be in Heaven!

"We Fought a Good Fight"

Mrs. Evans had a cancer checkup scheduled for June 27. Kris Grafton and Sara Rivera, a young married lady volunteer who had been helping Mrs. Evans, drove her to Minnesota. When the testing was finished, Mrs. Evans met with her oncologist. Her CA125 (cancer marker count) had risen from 1,600 to 5,500 in just one month. Dr. Hartman sweetly and compassionately said, "We have nothing to offer in our arsenal of cancer treatments that would be worth taking what little quality of life you have left."

Mrs. Evans kindly thanked Dr. Hartman for helping to give her extra years of life. Mrs. Evans had lived several years beyond the initial prognosis and said, "We fought a good fight, didn't we?" With tears freely flowing from their eyes, Kris and Sara watched Dr. Hartman and Mrs. Evans tearfully hug and say goodbye for the last time.

As Sara, Kris, and Mrs. Evans walked out of the Mayo Clinic building one final time, a flood of memories came over each of them. The moment seemed almost sacred as they realized they were leaving, never to return for the purpose of getting Mrs. Evans treatment for her cancer. The trip home was filled with tears and laughter. Sara drove while Mrs. Evans had Kris make some phone calls, letting loved ones and close friends know of the diagnosis.

Mrs. Evans' loved ones and workers were shaken. They all rallied around her and did all they could to help her and to do what she needed in those final days They all seemed to realize that this was the final chapter in Mrs. Evans' life, but none of them had any idea just how short that chapter would be. In nine brief days, Mrs. Evans would breathe her last breath. But until then, there was still a lot of living that woman had to do!

Above: A portion of Mrs. Evans' last appointment schedule at Mayo Clinic Below: Mrs. Evans and Sara Rivera, a caregiver who often drove Mrs. Evans to Mayo Clinic

(l-r) Joe, Loretta, Evangelist Kevin Walker, Jeannie Mae, and K.W.

She did not just "take to her bed and give up!"

Evangelist Kevin and Loretta Walker were in Ohio when they received the news of Mrs. Evans' report. They were on their way to Galesburg, Illinois, where Brother Kevin was to conduct a daily vacation Bible school on Monday. After their meeting ended in Ohio, they decided to drive through the night on Friday in order to be with Mrs. Evans. Their arrival at 5:00 a.m. on Saturday was a pleasant surprise. Loretta slipped a note under Mrs. Evans' door, letting her know that they were parked in her driveway (their usual custom when they were in town). About 6:00 a.m. Loretta's phone rang. It was Mrs. Evans. She asked Loretta to come inside.

When Loretta walked into her house, they both cried and hugged each other. They were saying goodbye after 24 years of working together. Mrs. Evans was a "planner" of her down times to protect her spirit, and she was happy to have Loretta there to help fill the hours the day after she had heard the prognosis from Dr. Hartman.

Dr. and Mrs. Evans and Brother Kevin and Loretta Walker left about 6:30 and went to breakfast. One more time (and the *final* time!) Mrs. Evans "re-planned" her funeral. She had done so with Loretta in April when she was speaking at the Mini-Spectacular at Liberty Baptist Church in Durham, North Carolina, but she wanted to be sure one more time that the details were cared for! She was especially concerned about the funeral meal. As the four ate together at Ginger's Garden in Merrillville, Mrs. Evans told the story about Jane Grafton's dad. He had realized he would soon go to Heaven, so one day he asked Jane to get a pen and a piece of paper. He then said, "I want to plan my funeral." He proceeded to tell that he wanted his son Melvin to preach the funeral, he wanted the grandchildren to sing, and so forth. Then he said, "Now, about the food...." Jane's mother had passed away about 18 months before this, and he had not been pleased with the food that had been served. He said, "I want you to take some money out of the bank right now and have it ready so we can have roast beef and ham. I don't want our Lutheran and Catholic neighbors coming to a Baptist funeral and being served a bunch of casseroles!" Mrs. Evans loved that story, and she wanted to be sure that the food at her "Baptist funeral dinner" was first class!

It was decided that Brother Kevin would go to Galesburg with the children, and Loretta would stay to help care for Mrs. Evans. Grandma Walker had been traveling with them for a few weeks, so it worked out well for her to be able to go to Galesburg and help care for the meals and the children.

The first call Mrs. Evans made when they returned from breakfast was to Carol Tudor who was working a summer job as a hospice nurse. Carol drove to Mrs. Evans' house immediately and signed her up for hospice. When that was finished, Mrs. Evans turned to Loretta and said, "Didn't I see your mother-in-law out there?" (meaning in the trailer). When Loretta answered in the affirmative, Mrs. Evans said, "Brother Schaap talked about sewing up slits in dresses last week. Can you take every skirt and dress out of my closet that has a slit and ask her to sew those up?" (Edna Walker is a professional seamstress.) Mrs. Evans had always tried to put into practice those principles, truths, and even suggestions that the man of God preached from the pulpit. In her last few days of life, she was still "going by the Preacher!"

Dr. and Mrs. Evans relaxing at the Wisconsin Dells

Mrs. Evans had Loretta help her make a list of guidelines for the duration of her journey. Mrs. Evans had so given herself to people her entire adult life, but it seemed she wanted some bit of privacy in her last days. While she did consent to seeing people who flew in from out of town, she did not feel she was able to entertain visitors from the local area. Neither did she want any pictures taken. Both of these requests were granted. Though it was not great numbers of people, in the next eight days people did come from Maine, from California, from North Carolina, from Florida, from Minnesota, from New York, and from other states around the country to say goodbye. None of these people stayed with her for more than a few minutes, but they represented a great host of people who wanted to give one more word of gratitude and express one more bit of love to this great lady.

Mrs. Evans also asked Loretta to place a special mailbox outside the back door so that people could place notes, cards, and any other expressions of love they desired into that box. This had a two-fold purpose. Mrs. Evans knew that the people would want to be able to express their love, and she also knew that she would be fighting to keep her mind in control. The letters and cards she received in that box would prove to be a tremendous blessing to her. On a daily basis Mrs. Evans had Loretta check

I owe anything God allows me to do through teaching, speaking, soul winning, counseling, or writing to you. No one knows more than I do how very impossible it would be for me to carry on any part of my work alone. When I go to a meeting, a team gets me ready. When I get off the plane, another team takes over in order to help me do my speaking. When I get ready for classes, a team member has prepared the way with clothes and medicine. Other team members have made my living space conducive to preparing to go to work. When I walk into class, another team member is there to meet me. When I sit down to eat, other team members have prepared special foods to keep me going.

I am often haunted by the question, "Is my work yielding eternal dividends to the point that top people of top abilities are investing themselves wisely in it?"

If the team were not in place, I would be staying home trying to care for myself and my needs. I think I would die emotionally and spiritually before I had to die physically.

I do owe you for my very life!
— Marlene Evans

[Excerpt from a letter by Mrs. Evans]

the box and read the cards and letters to her. Loretta saw just how much they meant to her when, on July 4, very few cards and letters were in the box. It was one of the more difficult days for Mrs. Evans. Mrs. Evans realized that she would need extra medical attention and had Loretta help her make a list of caregivers. These were people who had worked very closely with Mrs. Evans—her staff members.

On Sunday morning, just two days after her appointment with Dr. Hartman, Mrs. Evans wanted to go out to breakfast. Dr. Evans invited Loretta and Belinda Gaona to go with them. Belinda was leaving town to go to a wedding, and she was thrilled to get to spend this time with Mrs. Evans. From breakfast they went to church, where Mrs. Evans had a very difficult time sitting in her wheelchair. She kept falling forward as she would nearly pass out from a lack of oxygen. Loretta was relieved when the service was over as she had feared Mrs. Evans would fall out of her chair and be injured. Loretta had asked her if she wanted to go home, but she insisted on staying. She wanted to be there for Brother Schaap! This was Mrs. Evans' last church service.

Mrs. Evans had mentioned to Kris Grafton (a redhead) how sad it was that Loretta was no longer a redhead. Loretta was amazed that Mrs. Evans was still thinking of others when she was so sick. She felt she needed to do something about that remark if it was that important to Mrs. Evans. She left for a few hours to get her hair colored. There had been some problems in setting up the hospice equipment, and when Loretta returned to the house, Mrs. Evans was sitting alone at the kitchen table. Loretta could tell Mrs. Evans felt helpless and said, "This is pretty bad, isn't it?"

She answered calmly, "I'm just trying to keep quiet. Can you just fix everything?" Loretta closed the kitchen door to help keep Mrs. Evans out of the confusion and tried to get everything fixed as quickly as possible.

What Annoys You About Your Illness?

Once Mrs. Evans was signed up for hospice, the social worker was scheduled to come and question Mrs. Evans. Kris Grafton was with her during the interview. One of the questions the social worker asked was, "Mrs. Evans, what annoys you about your illness?"

Kris got so tickled by Mrs. Evans' response because, once again, she demonstrated that she was going to die the same way she lived. She cut her eyes toward Kris and answered deliberately, "It would annoy me if my caregivers did not get along." Even in death she was concerned that ladies love each other and get along!

Mrs. Evans was a person who liked things to be fixed and in working order, no matter how small or insignificant the problem seemed. When new carpet had been laid in the hallway and fireplace room, the installer was supposed to put matching carpet in the entrance area also, but instead, he put in white carpet with green designs. Needless to say, the carpet got dirty almost immediately and was nearly impossible to keep clean. When Mrs. Evans walked in after breakfast one day, she made a comment about that carpet. The company had promised to replace it but had failed to do so. Brother Larry Smith, a faculty member at Hyles-Anderson College had a remodeling business at the time. He got word that the carpet was bothering Mrs. Evans and, therefore, had one of his workers go to her house, tear out the carpet, and lay beautiful ceramic tile in its place. These types of thoughtful deeds were such a blessing to Mrs. Evans in her last days. She was thrilled to have the dirty carpet out and such beautiful tile installed.

Tom, Jane, and Carissa Grafton had been on vacation at Hilton Head Island when they received the news of Mrs. Evans' diagnosis. They cut their vacation short and arrived home Monday evening. On Tuesday morning, Jane went to see Mrs. Evans and after visiting for a few minutes asked, "What do you need from me?"

Mrs. Evans looked her in the eyes and said, "I want you to finish the books." Jane had been working on editing Mrs. Evans' last two books, *Sickness Without Despair* and *Teens Without Turmoil*. Jane agreed to go home and get busy on the books as Mrs. Evans wanted to read them one more time before her Homegoing. Jane worked on the books the rest of Tuesday and all day Wednesday.

On Wednesday the Stubblefields returned from vacation, and Mrs. Evans asked Linda to stop by when she went to church that evening. Mrs. Evans was lying on her bed and immediately put out her arms for a hug from Linda. She seemed incredibly healthier and stronger than the diagnosis suggested. The first thing Mrs. Evans wanted to know was all about the vacation. They talked and laughed for about 15 minutes, and then

Linda said they needed to get to church for David's singing group practice. Mrs. Evans asked, "Linda, is there anything between us?"

"Yes, Mrs. Evans, a whole lot of love," and they hugged.

On Thursday Loretta called to see if Jane would stay with Mrs. Evans so she could get some rest that night. Jane was thrilled to have the opportunity to care for this woman who had invested so much in her.

Jane marveled as she watched Mrs. Evans, who was up and down quite a bit that night. Each day that week it seemed she had a different complication which caused her treatment regimen to be somewhat complex. Loretta had warned Jane that Mrs. Evans had been sick to her stomach the day before, so when Mrs. Evans got up about 3:00 a.m., Jane said, "Mrs. Evans, are you nauseous?" to which Mrs. Evans quipped, "No, that was yesterday!"

Kris Grafton took Mrs. Evans' temperature one day and then told her, "You have a fever!" She replied with a smirk, "I have cancer, too!" Mrs. Evans kept her sense of humor to the end!

Friday seemed to be Mrs. Evans' last day that she was really able to "give" of herself. She wanted to go out to breakfast and used that time to brainstorm with Kris and Loretta about birthday parties. Kris's mother-in-law was about to celebrate her eightieth birthday, and Loretta's mom was going to be seventy in just a few days. The ladies wanted ideas, and Mrs. Evans, the "idea machine," gave them numbers of great ideas to make both of the celebrations memorable.

Mrs. Evans continued getting weaker and weaker, and the caregivers were afraid that if she walked all the way to the bathroom, she would trip on the oxygen line and fall. Therefore, they asked her to start using the portable chair that hospice had brought to her room. However, Mrs. Evans did not want to use that chair; she wanted to go to the bathroom!

When Loretta and Gina Eyer expressed their concern on Friday evening, Mrs. Evans said very deliberately, "I…will take… re…spons …i…bil…ity!" They let her walk to the bathroom!

"I Want to Keep My Christian Testimony!"

On Friday night Dr. Evans planned to spend a few hours with his wife. She had asked him not to cancel his speaking engagement that weekend, and he was to fly out Saturday morning. Mrs. Evans expressed concern to Kris and Loretta that her mind was not working well and that she was having difficulty putting sentences together. She asked them to stay in the room when her husband came so that they could help carry the conversation and get him to tell stories. She probably realized this was her last time with her husband, and she wanted it to be a fun, upbeat time! They did stay, and when Jane Grafton arrived about 9:00 for her "shift" to stay with Mrs. Evans, she wondered what all the ruckus was in the bedroom. The last she'd heard, she didn't think Mrs. Evans was doing so well, but she was hearing big laughter coming from her room. Mrs. Evans' desire had been granted. Her last time with her husband was fun and memorable for him.

After Dr. Evans went back upstairs, Loretta was helping Mrs. Evans get comfortable and she remarked, "Now, Mrs. Evans, tell me how you really feel."

Without missing a beat, Mrs. Evans responded, "I don't think I should. I want to keep my Christian testimony!"

Mrs. Evans was concerned about the "death rattle." She mentioned it several times to Loretta, and so the next time Kris Grafton came, Loretta asked her to discuss it with Mrs. Evans. Kris explained that what she was hearing was not the death rattle as she said, "Mrs. Evans, when you have the death rattle, you won't hear it." That explanation gave her peace, and she never asked about it again.

Doc and Mrs. Evans—always rejoicing—even in the hard times. This photo was taken on a trip to the wedding of their nephew, Jim Emery, in Texas.

She Died as She Had Lived

Those last nine days had to be very difficult, uncomfortable, and troublesome days for Mrs. Evans, and yet, she died the way she lived. She guarded her spirit and guarded what she said so that her spirit (that same positive and rejoicing spirit she had taught about for so many years) permeated her home.

Early Saturday morning with great trepidation, Dr. Evans did as Mrs. Evans had requested and left for his meeting in North Carolina. Throughout the weekend he kept very close contact with Mrs. Evans' caregivers. He also talked with Mrs. Evans several times on the phone until she was no longer able to do so Saturday evening. Sunday morning

Above: Beverly Hyles and Mrs. Evans
Below: Mrs. Cindy Schaap (r), and her
mother-in-law, Mrs. Marlene Schaap

before he went to preach, he called. This would be his last contact until he received word that his beloved wife of nearly 46 years had "graduated."

On Saturday Brother Dan and Janice Wolfe stopped by to see Mrs. Evans. They will forever remember the sweet time they had with her. As Brother Dan approached Mrs. Evans he said, "Mrs. Evans, I have my wife with me." Her eyes did not open, but she smiled. Mrs. Evans had been so thrilled when Dan and Janice married, and her smile was one last statement of her love for this couple.

Mrs. Evans did take another step down on Saturday and communicated very little. Mrs. Beverly Hyles came to visit her about noon. This was a very tender time as Mrs. Hyles was still in such deep grief over the Homegoing of her husband, and now she was also losing her good friend. She and Mrs. Evans hugged each other and cried together as Mrs. Hyles said, "It looks like you'll be seeing my husband before I will. Please give him my love."

"I will," Mrs. Evans said.

Jane Grafton and JoJo Moffitt were in the room and sat bawling as they observed the exchange of love between the two.

Mrs. Evans had continually shaken her head "No" when anyone suggested her lying in her bed. Up to that point she had slept in her recliner. But early Saturday evening it was evident that it was time for her to get into the hospital bed. Her hospice nurse, Carol Tudor, gently held her shoulders and laid her in bed for the last time. She asked, "Mrs. Evans, are you totally comfortable?" With a nod she answered, "Yes, totally."

Soon after Mrs. Evans was put into bed, Mrs. Cindy Schaap and her mother-in-law, Marlene Schaap, came to visit. Mrs. Evans was barely able to respond, but she showed she was pleased that her preacher's wife had come to visit. Mrs. Schaap mentioned that her husband would be visiting Mrs. Evans after the deacons' meeting that night.

The caregivers wanted to make it easy for Brother Schaap to get in and out of the house, so Brother Kevin Walker offered to watch for him. Gina Eyer was in Mrs. Evans' bedroom; Kris Grafton, Loretta Walker, and Jane Grafton were in the fireplace room. Jane and Loretta started hinting that they wanted to be in Mrs. Evans' room when Brother Schaap was there, but Kris never picked up on their hints.

Finally Loretta said, "Well, personally I want to be in that room when

| *Marlene Evans*
A Biography

the man of God goes in there!" Jane said, "So do I. Let's do it." Kris then conceded, "Well, I want to be there too, but I don't want to be presumptuous!"

They had just decided to go back to the bedroom when Brother Kevin knocked on the window and said, "He's here!" Simultaneously Loretta, Kris, and Jane ran back to the bedroom and gathered around Mrs. Evans' bed—as Gina wondered what in the world was going on! When Brother Schaap walked into the room seconds later, they all acted as if they'd been in the room a long time!

They were immediately glad that they had run to Mrs. Evans' room. When Brother Schaap walked in, Loretta announced, "Mrs. Evans, Brother Schaap is here."

Mrs. Evans had hardly communicated the entire day, especially in the afternoon or evening, but when she heard that her preacher was there, she lifted her head and shoulders off the pillow, opened her eyes, and said, "Where?!" Her head immediately dropped back down on the pillow and her eyes closed, but how precious it was to see her respond to her pastor!

Brother Schaap only spoke a few words, but they were poignant. "I'm going to come back tomorrow after church to see you and tell you about the sermon because I know you need it." She smiled faintly. Then he said, "I want you to stay here til I come back, okay?"

She shook her head ever so slightly. He prayed with her and then he was gone. How powerful those few moments with the man of God had been!

Sunday morning Loretta called Jane Grafton at home. Mrs. Evans' breathing had changed, and Loretta felt she was just hours from death. Jane was just about to leave for church, so she changed plans and drove to Mrs. Evans' house. They talked after Jane arrived and then decided to call Carol Tudor and Kris Grafton who, by now, were in their Sunday school classes. Loretta contacted security at the church and had them notify Kris Grafton and Brother Colsten. She also asked them to find Doris and Jerry Smith who, along with their daughter and son-in-law, immediately drove to Mrs. Evans' house. Mrs. Colsten informed Linda Stubblefield after Sunday school that Mrs. Evans was at an all-time low. Linda left immediately and drove to Mrs. Evans' house.

Jerry and Doris Smith, Chip and Dianne Dowdey and their two sons,

Above: The Jerry Smith family (l-r)
Mike, Dianne, Chip, Jerry, Chad,
Doris, and Benny
Below: Kathryn and Dick Emery

Chad and Benny, all arrived shortly after noon. Soon Carol Tudor and Kris Grafton arrived, followed by Brother Johnny Colsten, the hospital visitation pastor at First Baptist Church. JoJo Moffitt also came and was a tremendous blessing as she took the two Dowdey boys and played with them while the Smiths, the Dowdeys, Brother Colsten, and Carol Tudor gathered around Mrs. Evans' bed.

Mrs. Evans would have been so pleased that JoJo, whose own heart was breaking, took Mrs. Evans' precious great nephews and provided a fun time for them in order to give Chip and Dianne the opportunity to be with Dianne's parents at Mrs. Evans' side. The caregivers waited in the fireplace room. About 1:40 p.m. Pastor and Mrs. Schaap arrived.

As Brother Schaap approached Mrs. Evans' bed, he announced that he was there, and said, "Mrs. Evans, you can go Home now." He then led the small group of loved ones in singing for a brief time. At 1:55 p.m. her heart stopped beating, and she joined that great company of loved ones who were waiting for her.

When Pastor and Mrs. Schaap left the bedside, they walked to the fireplace room and told the caregivers that Mrs. Evans was in Heaven. He and Mrs. Schaap spoke individual words of comfort to each caregiver. Brother Schaap looked at Carol Tudor and said, "I'm so glad that you have Richard." He then went upstairs to call and break the news to Dr. Evans and to comfort him.

The days following Mrs. Evans' Homegoing were filled with planning the funeral as David and his family arrived from New Mexico and Joy flew in from Papua New Guinea. David and Joy were a special blessing and strength to their dad during this time of grief. Dick and Kathryn Emery, with their children, Jim and Sunny, and Beth arrived with Mike Smith, son of Jerry and Doris Smith, from Texas. Mrs. Evans had been so concerned for her "baby" sister. Kathryn had been diagnosed with breast cancer and was in the midst of chemotherapy at the time of Mrs. Evans' Homegoing.

On Friday July 13, 2001, Pastor Schaap honored Mrs. Evans and remembered her beautifully at the Memorial Service to a capacity crowd in the First Baptist Church auditorium. No doubt Mrs. Evans would have

been especially pleased with all the flowers! Hundreds of people showed their love and expressed their condolences to the family and loved ones of this great lady.

Following the Memorial Service, about 300 people attended a private funeral dinner at the Hyles-Anderson College dining hall. As Mrs. Evans had requested, a delicious dinner was served! The ladies of the First Baptist Church WMS provided much of the food which complemented the special meats that were prepared by Diane Robinson. Mrs. Evans would have been pleased.

The funeral dinner was a time of remembering. Family, friends, and loved ones waited in line to tell their stories and memories of this great woman. They reminisced…they laughed…they cried…and they stayed. No one wanted to leave, and so for more than three hours they continued to tell how Marlene Evans had touched their lives…and even after the dinner was officially ended, they stood in small groups throughout the dining hall continuing to reminisce…continuing to laugh…continuing to cry…and continuing to comfort each other in their grief…and they continue to remember that one woman, Marlene Evans, came into their lives…and made a difference!

"It mattered that Marlene Evans lived."
— Dr. Don Boyd

Clockwise: Dr. Evans, Jerry, and Mike looking at just a few of the many floral arrangements; Doris and Kathryn; Marlene, Doris, and Kathryn; Chip, Dianne, and Chad with Mike Smith at the funeral dinner at Hyles-Anderson College; Doris and Joy look at the floral arrangements that keep arriving.

A Final Tribute to Marlene Evans
by Jane Grafton

It seems that God gives to each generation a man—a prophet—upon whom He has given *"...the care of all the churches."* (II Corinthians 11:28) These are men such as Charles Haddon Spurgeon, Dr. John R. Rice, and Dr. Jack Hyles.

Could it be that God knew this generation also needed a woman—a prophetess, if you will—upon whom He could give "the care of all the homes"? If He did, God chose this woman knowing...

Mrs. Evans and the author, Jane Grafton

- the skeptic would need someone who was real.
- the intellectual would need someone who was learned.
- the down and out would need someone who was compassionate.
- the hurting would need someone whose spontaneous fun helped her laugh through her tears.
- the unsaved would need someone who was a soul winner.
- the lonely would need someone who was loving.
- the poor would need someone who was giving and generous.
- the afflicted would need someone whose mother had polio.
- the brusque would need someone who understood "Zugmierese."
- the beautiful would need someone who kept herself dressed attractively.
- the loose and sensual would need someone who was modest and appropriate.
- the rebellious would need someone who lived by her convictions.
- the defeated would need someone who picked herself up after a fall.
- the negative would need someone who rejoiced in the Lord.
- the critical gossip would need someone who found the good in everyone.
- the shy would need someone who was sensitive.

- the societal reject would need someone who was accepting.
- the strong would need someone who, tough and strong herself, submitted to leadership.
- the student would need someone who was teachable.
- the self-righteous would need someone who was truly spiritual.
- the proud would need someone who, though famous, remained humble.

God knew He needed a woman full of good works, a woman yielded to the Holy Spirit, a woman whose wisdom would portray the mind of Christ, and a woman whose influence would touch a generation of Christian ladies.

With all of this in mind, God fashioned Marlene June Zugmier Evans with a most unique personality, and she, in turn, humbly accepted the responsibility. As Mrs. Evans had the ear of fundamental women of America, she lovingly, wisely, and compassionately ministered to them in an attempt to help them salvage and build their homes for Christ. She graciously accepted the charge God gave her, the care of the homes of this generation, and what a difference she made!

It's easy to think, "Well, I'm no Marlene Evans!" You're right; I'm not either. But God has given each of us people who cross our paths, live in our homes, work in our places of business, and attend our churches who need us. God has a job for each of us. Let's do it as diligently and as purposefully as Marlene Evans did hers!

Appendix A

Dr. and Mrs. Evans are the parents of two children. They have six grandchildren.

Joy Lynn Evans . . . . .September 19, 1962
   Jordan Lee . . . . .May 31, 1986
   Grant Stephen . . . . .April 28, 1989
   Lindsay Dianne . . . . .April 24, 1991

David Lee Evans . . . . .April 1, 1965
   David Anthony . . . . .August 10, 1988
   Amanda Dawnn . . . . .March 19, 1991
   Jesse Lee . . . . .March 23, 2000

O Lord, Help Me to Be:

Firm but not harsh;
Realistic but not skeptical;
Scheduled but not rigid;
Pure but not proud;
Closed-mouthed but not unfriendly;
Appropriate but not stiff;
Funny but not frivolous;
Teachable but not gullible;
Flexible but not scatter-brained;
Humble but not pious;
Kind but not compromising;
Dependable but not dull;
Decisive but not stubborn;
Persistent but not needling;
Precise but not picky;
Simple but not foolish;
Demanding but not intolerant;
Thorough but not unkind;
Human but not worldly;
Spiritual but not impractical;
Generous but not irresponsible;
Enthusiastic but not "hyper";

Appendix B

THE memorial service for Marlene June Zugmier Evans was held, Friday, July 13, 2001, 10:00 a.m. at the First Baptist Church of Hammond, Indiana. A beautiful program with the following information was given to those who attended.

In Memory of
Marlene Evans
November 11, 1933-July 8, 2001
First Baptist Church of Hammond

Marlene June Zugmier Evans
November 11, 1933 - July 8, 2001

Memorial Service
Friday, July 13, 2001
10:00 a.m.
First Baptist Church of Hammond, Indiana

WHEN I fell in love with Miss Marlene Zugmier about 46½ years ago, I had no idea that she would become a prolific author. When I wrote these words, I wrote them for her sixth book. Yet the achievement of authorship is only one among her myriad of accomplishments. Marlene was a loving wife and mother, a college teacher, an editor, a counselor, and a tremendous speaker. She was a conference director and an unfailing confidante.

She has three earned degrees and an honorary doctorate. Yet, she is as down to earth as she was when I watched her serve meals in her father's restaurants over 45 years ago. She hated pretension, but she loved everyone. She was a modern "superwoman" and an old-fashioned Christian all wrapped up in one person. Marlene was so unselfish that it was almost impossible to keep anything extra in our house! I had to hide things, or they were given away!

At the age of 67, Marlene Zugmier Evans was almost a legend among thousands of Bible-believing women in America. There are very few women in this country who serve God and love the King James Bible but what have heard her speak or held one of her many books in their hands. Far more people—both men and women—have avidly perused the pages of *Christian Womanhood*, the premier monthly publication which is available for Christian women today.

Yet, Marlene is probably one of the most underestimated women in the world! I suppose I'm not really an unprejudiced observer since I happen to be in love with the gal, but you must admit that I should know her quite well after more than 46 years!

I have encountered a few captivating personalities in my time: Dr. Bob Jones, Sr.; Dr. Bob Jones, Jr.; Dr. Lee Roberson; Dr. J. R. Faulkner; and Dr. Jack Hyles. I have also seen politicians and entertainers such as Frank Sinatra, Jr.; Jesse Jackson; Harry Carey; Jack Kennedy; Richard Nixon; and a couple of Indiana governors. Now—let's be honest—Marlene did have a distinct advantage over those famous people. She's a lady! But **what** *a lady!* When I first met Marlene in November of 1954, her personality puzzled me and left me a bit confused. But within a few months, I was under her spell!

Years ago someone said that to brag on your mate is as vain as bragging on yourself. If so, I am incurably vain. She knows the halls of Mayo Clinic better than she knows the streets of our area.

Neither have I referred to her strong character, her positive Scriptural outlook, nor her tremendous sense of humor! She is quite a lady, but a one-page memorial could never capture the many facets and innumerable qualities which enabled Marlene Evans to touch the lives of so many people—especially mine.

                                                   – Dr. Wendell Evans

Honest but not brutal;
Fair but not unloving;
Proper but not unreal;
Confident but not snobbish;
Bold but not brazen;
Busy but not harried;
Efficient but not hurried;
Active but not shallow;
Deep but not dry;
Wise but not intimidating;
Intense but not forbidding;
Empathetic but not uncontrolled;
Forgiving but not naive;
Sympathetic but not pitying;
Helpful but not condescending;
Penitent but not paralyzed;
Organized but not bossy;
Spontaneous but not inconsistent;

Lord, I guess I'm asking to grow in favor with God and man. Am I asking You to help me become a balanced person? Amen.

                    – Marlene Evans

THE GRADUATION SERVICE OF MARLENE ZUGMIER EVANS

Special . . . . .Mrs. Marjorie Jones
"Hallelujah Square"
Scripture and prayer . . . . .Dr. Johnny Colsten

Marlene Evans
A Biography | 223

Special . . . . .Mrs. Beverly Hyles
"No One Ever Cared for Me Like Jesus"
Mrs. Evans' favorite song
Message . . . . .Dr. Jack Schaap
Special . . . . .Mr. Dan Daniel
"O What a Saviour"

W HEN God chose to define His love, He found no words in our vocabulary. He simply said that He **so** loved us. In Acts 14:1, the Holy Spirit tried to define to us in our vocabulary the power of the New Testament Christians. He said there were no words in our vocabulary that would adequately describe such power; He simply said they **so** spake. When the Apostle tried to tell us how great salvation is in Hebrews 2:3, he simply had to say it was **so** great salvation.

Such is the case when I try to express the courage of Marlene Evans. It is beyond description; I simply say she has **so** great courage.

I flounder when trying to find words to express her diligence in serving God during these days of cancer awareness. I can only say she has **so** served.

I likewise stumble over the vocabulary as I try to describe her loyalty, her devotion, her love, and her consecration. She is **so** loyal and **so** devoted. She **so** loves. She is **so** consecrated.

Those who know her best appreciate her most, love her most, and admire her the most. I am one of those.

She has looked cancer square in the eye and challenged it. She has faced death courageously and postponed it. She has been attacked by adversity and resisted it.

Thousands have been inspired not to quit and to persevere by the courage of this great lady. I am one of those.

– Dr. Jack Hyles
August, 1996
Introduction, *There's Life After Cancer*

Marlene Evans
A Biography

Honorary Attendants

Dwight Grafton	Roy Moffitt	Richard Tudor
Tom Grafton	David Stubblefield	Kevin Walker

Marlene (Zugmier) Evans
November 11, 1933 - July 8, 2001

AGE 67, passed away peacefully at her home in Schererville, Indiana, and went to be with her Lord after a courageous 19-year battle with cancer.

Marlene Evans was born November 11, 1933, in Wymore, Nebraska, to Alvin and Helen Zugmier. She is survived by her husband of 46½ years, Wendell Lee; stepmother, Hazel Zugmier of Kearney, Nebraska; two children, Joy (Jeff) Ryder of Papua New Guinea and David (Aileen) Evans of Smith Lake, New Mexico; six grandchildren, Jordan, Grant, and Lindsay Ryder; David Anthony, Amanda, and Jesse Evans; two sisters, Doris (Jerry) Smith of Schererville, Indiana, and Kathryn (Dick) Emery of Argyle, Texas; four nieces and nephews, Mike Smith of Dallas, Texas; Dianne (Chip) Dowdey of Merrillville, Indiana; Beth Emery of Uzbekistan; Jim (Sunny) Emery of Denton, Texas; two grandnephews, Chad and Ben Dowdey; and a host of caregivers and friends.

Mrs. Evans holds a Bachelor of Science degree in Secondary Education from Bob Jones University, a Master of Arts degree in Christian Education from Bob Jones University, a Master of Education degree in Educational Organization and Supervision from the University of Tennessee, and a Doctor of Humanities degree from Hyles-Anderson College. Mrs. Evans served as the Dean of Women at Hyles-Anderson College for over 20 years and as a faculty member for the entire history of the college since 1972. Mrs. Evans taught speech, psychology courses, education courses, and a unique class for ladies called Christian Womanhood.

In 1975 Mrs. Evans became the founder and editor of *Christian Womanhood*, America's first monthly newspaper designed to meet the needs of women and girls with the goal of inspiring and instructing them to be used of God in the home and in the local, fundamental, Bible-believing church. Through the 28+ year history of Christian Womanhood, Mrs. Evans authored 17 books and 1 pamphlet and traveled nationwide as an oft-requested conference speaker. For more than a quarter of a century, she conducted an annual convention for women, the Christian Womanhood Spectacular, which had as many as 8,000 women in attendance.

Mrs. Evans' down-to-earth teaching and homespun humor were used of God to help ladies in their marriages, in their child rearing, in their service to God, and in all other relationships of life. During her cancer battle, she had many "cancer buddies" who were inspired to continue on in spite of medical dilemmas. Her favorite Bible verse and the philosophy by which she lived was Philippians 4:4, "Rejoice in the Lord alway: and again I say, Rejoice."

Mrs. Evans "coined" many quotable expressions as she taught college girls, spoke to ladies at conferences, and led her team of coworkers. Among her statements that will be remembered are "Rejoice always"; "One step at a time"; "I see gold glittering"; "The five sins of Christian women"; "I'm going to live until I die"; "Give a gift of words"; "Make every day a Christmas day"; "Make the chimes ring!"; "Redbirds, rubies, and rainbows"; "You 'vill' bloom again!"; "Bronze every moment"; "Glory in not knowing"; "Circle of protection"; "My goal…a dirty Bible"; "My nest is best"; "Black dog! White dog! Which will it be?"; "Women used of God"; "Love is teamwork"; and "Different women are peculiar."

Appendix C

Marlene Evans taught seven courses at Hyles-Anderson College.
- Christian Womanhood
- Communication in Marriage
- Educational Concepts
- Educational Psychology
- General Psychology
- Speech
- Women Used of God

Mrs. Evans received many awards and honors at home and across America. Just a few of them include…
- The Marlene Evans Hospitality Room, Hopewell Baptist Church, Napa, California, Pastor Mike Ray
- The Marlene Evans Museum, Mt. Salem Revival Grounds, West Union, West Virginia, Dr. Randy Taylor
- Marlene Evans Building, Hyles-Anderson College campus
- The dedication of the 1983 Caber, the Hyles-Anderson College annual, to Mrs. Evans
- The Hylander Lion Award, Hyles-Anderson College
- Nominated and listed in Who's Who in American Educators
- In 1982 at a Christian Womanhood Mini-Spectacular, she was presented a key to the city of Princeton, West Virginia.
- A memorial bench was placed outside the Marlene Evans Building at Hyles-Anderson College. Paver bricks memorializing Mrs. Evans surround the bench.
- Featured on "The Medical Edge" Mayo Clinic program, 2001

Top: Memorial bench
Center: Marlene Evans Building
Lower: Marlene Evans Museum

Marlene Evans
A Biography | 227

Appendix D

Marlene Evans authored seventeen books and one pamphlet.

Pattern for Living
Pattern for Living Teacher's Manual
Cancer: My Enemy, My Friend
There's Life After Cancer
Help, Lord! They Call Me Mom
Comfort for Hurting Hearts
Christian Womanhood Cookbook and Homemaker's Guide
I'm Going to Live Until I Die
New Hope: Be the Parent You Were Meant to Be
Redbirds and Rubies and Rainbows
A Daily Chat Around the Bible with Marlene Evans
The Five Sins of Christian Women

THE LIFE SERIES
Marriage Without Divorce
Relationships Without Regrets
Kids Without Chaos
Sickness Without Despair
Teens Without Turmoil

Beginning in 1975 Mrs. Evans' works were featured in a column in *Christian Womanhood* called "Through a Woman's Eyes." In 1977, the first 18 articles were combined into a booklet called "Through a Woman's Eyes"-Volume I. In 1979, a second volume was produced with the next 18 articles from the "Through a Woman's Eyes" column.

In 1977 Mrs. Evans, Mrs. Beverly Hyles, and Mrs. JoJo Moffitt collaborated on a 72-page booklet entitled *Pattern for Living.* The booklet was an immediate success in the fundamental world. The book would eventually be revised and revamped into a full-length, 240-page book used in many classrooms around America.

The series of tapes, "The Five Sins of Christian Women" were transcribed for a booklet. This booklet was eventually reworked and revamped into a 256-page, full-length, hardback book, "The Five Sins of Christian Women," which was published in 2002.

Appendix E

Under the auspices of Christian Womanhood, Mrs. Evans recorded teaching tapes that have criss-crossed the nation and the world. The following list of titles are from tapes produced by the ministry of Christian Womanhood. At meetings around the country, Mrs. Evans also gave many speeches that were recorded and distributed by other ministries which have not been listed.

SETS OF TAPES:

The Five Sins of Christian Women (set of three tapes)
The Four Temperaments (set of two tapes)

Interviews

An Interview with Mrs. Olin Holbrook
An Interview with Mrs. Coystal Hyles
A Second Chat with Mrs. Coystal Hyles
An Interview with Mrs. Jack Hyles
An Interview with Mrs. John R. Rice

Women Used of God Series

Delilah
Lot's Wife
The Widow Who Fed Elijah & The Mother of James and John
Deborah & Job's Wife
Rebekah & Hagar
Esther & Naaman's Maid

A Creative Mind
A Lesson from the Redwoods
Apples of Gold ~ Your Greatest Gift

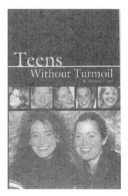

How to Date Well
How to Fall in Love with Your Husband Again and Again
How to Feel Loved
How to Fight Your Enemies
How to Get Close to Your Teens
How to Give Correction & How to Take Correction
How to Go Through Recession or Unemployment
How to Handle Constant Family Chaos
How to Handle Word of a Scandal
How to Help a Rebellious Teenager
How to Help Teens with Peer Pressure
How to Learn to Be Fun
How to Learn to Tolerate More People
How to Live with a Serious Illness
How to Make a Career out of Homemaking
How to Make and Keep Friends
How to Make Others Feel Loved
How to Overcome the Five Sins
How to Really Rejoice in the Lord Through the Problem Times
How to Stay Sane During Days of Temporary Insanity
How to Stop Leading Your Husband
I'm Not Compatible with Anyone
I Feel Like Such a Failure
If We Can't Do It Right, Let's Do It Wrong!
I Made a Difference to That One
Instant Peace
I See Gold Glittering
Is Your Life Changed?
It's a Worldly World
It's a World of Fun
Learning to Enjoy the Bible
Learning to Be Kind in the Home
Let's Hear It for the Teenagers
Let's Talk About PMS
Loving Those Who Are Different
Make Memories for Your Family

Marlene Evans
A Biography

Making Peace in the Home
Manage Your Priorities
Marriages Don't Work Out (How to Work Them Out)
Mend Those Broken Ties
Mind Control
Mind Control II
Mom, What Is Maturity?
My Goal, a Dirty Bible
One Step at a Time
Positive, Courageous Child Discipline
Questions Which Lead to Depression
Rebuilding Relationships with Alienated Family and Friends
Seven Common Time Wasters and What to Do About Them
Soul Winning—The YoYo Syndrome
So You're Having a Bridal Shower & So You're Having a Baby Shower
So You Want to Lead a Woman's Group
Surviving the Work Schedule
Telling Your Husband What You Need
Temperament Control
The 4 R's of Being Used
The High Cost of Insecurity
The Intimate Marital Relationship
There Is Hope for Healing
The Sixth Sin of Christian Women
The Strong-Willed Wife
Through Shades of Hell (But I'd Take Chemo Again)
Time-Released Teaching
Traps to Avoid in Older Years
Treating Your Children with Kindness
Turning Your 3-Ring Circus Into One
Turning the World Upside Down Through Spiritual Reproduction
25 Ways for Ladies to Make Money at Home
Utilizing Your Time Well
Ways to Thrive, Not Just Survive
What I Do When I Get Depressed
What to Do When the Doctor Says, "It's Cancer!"

Marlene Evans teaching a Sunday school class

Afterword

Mrs. Evans gave much of her life to building and nurturing relationships and helping to strengthen those in the relationships. She was also keenly aware of the fact that the most important relationship in life is our relationship with God. If you do not know for sure you are on your way to Heaven, Marlene Evans would not want you to put down this book until you have that doubt settled in your heart and mind. There are some simple facts you need to know in order to go to Heaven.

1. **Realize there is none good.** Romans 3:10 says, *"As it is written, There is none righteous, no, not one."*

2. **See yourself as a sinner.** Romans 3:23 says, *"For all have sinned, and come short of the glory of God."*

3. **Recognize where sin came from.** Romans 5:12 says, *"Wherefore, as by one man sin entered into the world, and death by sin; and so death passed upon all men, for that all have sinned."*

4. **Notice God's price on sin.** Romans 6:23 says, *"For the wages of sin is death; but the gift of God is eternal life through Jesus Christ our Lord."*

5. **Realize that Christ died for you.** Romans 5:8 says, *"But God commendeth his love toward us, in that, while we were yet sinners, Christ died for us."*

6. **Take God at His Word.** Romans 10:13 says, *"For whosoever shall call upon the name of the Lord shall be saved."*

7. **Claim God's promise for your salvation.** Romans 10:9-11 says, *"That if thou shalt confess with thy mouth the Lord Jesus, and shalt believe in thine heart that God hath raised him from the dead, thou shalt be saved. For with the heart man believeth unto righteousness; and with the mouth confession is made unto salvation. For the scripture saith, Whosoever believeth on him shall not be ashamed."*

Now pray. Confess that you are a sinner. Ask God to save you and receive Christ as your personal Saviour.

If you did pray and really meant it, God says you can be 100 percent sure you will go to Heaven. Please let us know if you made this decision so we can rejoice with you and let Marlene Evans' family know this good news. Please write to us at Christian Womanhood, 8400 Burr Street, Crown Point, Indiana 46307. Or you may call us at (219) 365-3202.

"*Say it with me again . . .*
'Rejoice in the Lord alway:
and again I say, Rejoice.'"